THE GREAT POWERS AND THE
DECLINE OF THE EUROPEAN STATES SYSTEM
1914–1945

The great powers and the decline of the European states system 1914–1945

Graham Ross

Longman
London and New York

Longman Group UK Limited,
Longman House, Burnt Mill, Harlow
Essex CM20 2JE, England
and Associated Companies throughout the world

*Published in the United States of America
by Longman Inc., New York*

© Longman Group Limited 1983

First published 1983
Fifth impression 1988

British Library Cataloguing in Publication Data

Ross, Graham
    The great powers and the decline of the European
    States system, 1914-1945.
    1. Europe - Foreign relations
    2. Europe - Politics and government
    1918-1945
    I. Title
    327'.0924   D727
    ISBN 0-582-49188-6

Library of Congress Cataloging in Publication Data

Ross, Graham, 1933-1985
    The great powers and the decline of the European
    states system, 1914-1945.

    Bibliography: p.
    Includes index.
    1. Europe - Foreign relations - 1871-1981.
    2. Europe - Foreign relations - 1918-1945.   3. Europe -
    Politics and government - 1871 - 1918.   4. Europe - Politics
    and government - 1918-1945.   I. Title.
    D424.R66   1983   327.4   83-686
    ISBN 0-582-49188-6

Produced by Longman Singapore Publishers (Pte) Ltd.
Printed in Singapore.

Contents

Preface

This book covers a much shorter timespan than its predecessor *The great powers and the European states system 1815–1914* by Roy Bridge and Roger Bullen. But the thirty-one years between the beginning of the First World War and the ending of the Second form a congested and complicated period. It is hoped that students of international history and international relations will find the present work a useful introductory guide.

I would like to thank David Dilks, Roy Bridge, Philip Taylor, Edward Spiers and Neale Vickery for reading sections of the book and commenting on it. Any errors or shortcomings are of course entirely the author's responsibility. I am most grateful to Mrs Lynne Riley for typing the manuscript.

GRAHAM ROSS

CHAPTER ONE

Introduction: Change and development in the European states system, 1914–1945

On the eve of the First World War the European states system was still dominated by a few great powers, who regarded themselves as the established arbiters of major international questions. Despite the rivalry between the Entente and the Triple Alliance it was possible for both groups to combine in an attempt to produce a settlement of the first Balkan war. From December 1912 until August 1913 a conference of ambassadors met in London for this purpose. The six participants – Britain, France, Russia, Germany, Austria-Hungary and Italy – were generally accepted as the great powers of the day, although there were some doubts about Italy's claim to equality with the others. This conference was the last expression before August 1914 of the principle that the European powers should act in concert to deal with crises and to keep conflicts localized. In the latter aim the powers were successful, but their inability to maintain joint action or to enforce a settlement on Turkey and the lesser Balkan states was clearly revealed. Nor did the limited success of the conference alter the basic division between the two rival camps. There was no unattached major power in Europe which could play the role of balancer between them.

What were the attributes which in early 1914 were thought to confer great power status? Still the most important was the ability to wage war quickly and successfully. A general European war was expected to be short and decisive; forces in being were therefore more important than reserves of manpower and underlying economic strength. Battleships were the main yardstick for measuring naval power and here Britain easily took first place, although Germany's growing fleet was now large enough to be a significant influence upon British naval strategy. Britain relied on a volunteer army, whereas the Continental powers all expected to be able to mobilize large numbers of men quickly. In terms of well trained manpower quickly available Germany held the lead. Tsarist Russia could outstrip her in sheer numbers but the inept performance of Russian forces against Japan in the war of 1904–06 raised doubts about their competence in a contest with Germany and Austria-Hungary. Britain could of course tap the manpower resources of her dominions and empire but the belief in a short war meant that her military, as distinct from her naval capacity tended to be discounted.

If one turns to economic measurements of power then Britain overshadowed the others in the volume of her exports and the size of her overseas investments. Germany, however, was catching up as an exporter and had become easily the leading European steel producer. Britain headed the table for coal production but here again Germany came a good second. The tangible measurements of power thus gave Germany a strong all-round position and although Britain was still ahead of her in some respects Germany's economy and overseas trade were growing faster. Even without a war Germany seemed well placed to attain predominance in Europe; this was a cause of concern for her allies as well as her enemies. France came some way below Britain and Germany by both military and economic measurements. Russia's manpower was not yet matched by comparable economic strength. Austria-Hungary and Italy could both lay claim to some naval and military capacity but economically they fell well behind Britain, France and Germany. Some of the smaller states showed evidence of economic strength; Belgian steel production, for example, was not far behind that of Austria-Hungary. None of the lesser European states, however, could expect to resist unaided an attack by one of the powers. The ability to coerce their weaker brethren was another of the characteristics which was assumed to distinguish the European great powers. The smaller states could seek the protection of one or more powers – thus Serbia looked to Russia for aid against Austria-Hungary – or they might seek safety in the proclamation of permanent neutrality. Such a policy served Sweden well, partly because Scandinavia had not been an area of interest to the powers since the congress of Vienna. Geographical obstacles to invasion had helped Switzerland to maintain a similar policy but Belgium was to find that neutrality could not be maintained in a Franco-German conflict as it had been in the war of 1870–71. Belgium was by now too obvious a route for outflanking French defences.

Less easy to measure than numbers of ships and men or tons of coal and steel were the morale and attitudes of individuals. Would the populations of the powers loyally support their governments in the event of war or would internal division prevent the effective mobilization of men and resources? States can rarely expect complete domestic harmony or a consensus on foreign policy for any lengthy period. In the first half of 1914 all the powers faced internal problems of one kind or another. Russia was open to the threat of another revolution such as had occurred in 1905. Austria-Hungary faced the challenge of Slav nationalism; in the north the Czechs sought equality with the Germans and in the south Serbia was a magnet to the Croats and Slovenes within the empire. She could form the nucleus for a South Slav state, and this was indeed a serious threat to the integrity of Austria-Hungary. Military defeat of Serbia, especially after her gains in the Balkan wars, was therefore an obvious temptation for Vienna, yet it was unlikely that Russia would again retreat from armed support of Serbia as she had done during the Bosnian crisis and the Balkan wars. For a power to repeatedly take no action in defence of a client state would be a serious blow to her reputation, and in August 1914 Russia was not prepared to suffer such damage to her prestige. Thus the fate of the two empires was linked: victory in war for Austria-Hungary could revive the danger of revolution for Russia; victory for the latter might threaten the unity of the Dual Monarchy. Could the two powers fight each other without serious domestic consequences? Italy and France seemed in less danger of internal collapse although both faced problems arising from the struggles between capital and labour and between anti-clericals and the Church. The class struggle was more obvious and bitter in Italy and was compounded by the gap in wealth between north and south. To demonstrate its standing as a power the Italian government had declared war on Turkey in 1911 and occupied Libya and the Dodecanese at the cost of adding greatly to the budgetary deficit. The parliamentary system appeared unable to cope with social and economic problems. This made Italy appear of doubtful value to the Triple Alliance. Her desire to liberate those Italians still under Austrian rule increased the doubt, and she was in fact to remain initially neutral when war broke out. France seemed by comparison more stable; the institutions of the Third Republic had survived a number of crises and scandals. An attempted general strike in 1910 was a failure. Internal divisions tended to be overshadowed by the growing and obvious disparity between French and German military and economic strength. In 1913 the term of military service for French conscripts was increased from two years to three in an effort to close the gap.

Imperial Germany and Britain were the most stable of the European powers but even they had their problems. William II and his advisers were concerned at the growing strength of the Social Democrats, who had become the largest single party in the Reichstag in 1912. In practice they were far from revolutionary and were to support the Imperial government when war was declared. The Reichstag could be vocal on occasion in its criticisms but it did not control either the Chancellor or his policies. But fears of revolution from within and of encirclement by the Entente gave to German policy-making an atmosphere of doubt and unpredictability despite her essentially strong material position. The erratic and impulsive interventions of the Kaiser in foreign policy added to the general mood of uncertainty. In December 1912 he could decide after discussion with his military and naval advisers that the time was not ripe for war with France and Russia. In the summer of 1914 he was to show much less caution. Since 1909 Britain had experienced a constitutional conflict over the powers of the House of Lords, industrial relations had worsened and by the summer of 1914 there was the possibility of civil war in Ireland over the question of Home Rule. This might have led observers to believe that Britain would avoid entry into a European war. Although there had been Anglo-French staff talks and there were plans to send an expeditionary force to the Continent if Germany invaded France, Britain had no formal alliance commitment to either France or Russia. The latter was in any case regarded with dislike and suspicion by many in the Liberal party. Nor had Britain any direct conflict of interest with Austria-Hungary. But fear of German predominance outweighed the ambiguities of Britain's diplomatic position and the dangers of domestic strife. The German invasion of Belgium gave an immediate and specific reason for joining the war that helped to convert those who were less concerned with the long-term balance of power. As with the other powers who went to war in August 1914, internal divisions were at least temporarily submerged in a wave of patriotic enthusiasm.

It was somewhat surprising that there was so little initial opposition to the war, The early years of the twentieth century had seen the steady growth in Europe of the 'peace movement'. Drawing its support mainly from liberals and social democrats, it criticized among other things increasing military expenditure, the undue influence of military establishments upon policy-making and the difficulty of controlling professional diplomats. The latter, it was alleged, were drawn from too narrow a social group, and acted too much in secret without having to justify or explain their policies in public. The peace movement was able to express itself most forcibly in those states where there was an active press and parliamentary system. Its practical achievements before 1914 were small, but it did at least have some influence upon the climate of opinion. The establishment of the Nobel peace prizes in 1896 (the first awards were not made until 1901) was one way of encouraging those who promoted harmony among states. Governments did begin to discuss disarmament and peaceful settlement of disputes, not so much because of pressure from the peace movement itself but as the result of a Russian initiative. Worried by the extent of their military expenditure and even more by the age of their equipment, some of the Russian ministers persuaded Nicholas II to issue invitations in August 1898 to a conference on arms limitation. The first Hague conference of 1899 produced no agreement on this topic but it did lead to the establishment of a Permanent Court of Arbitration to which states could submit disputes, although it was given no compulsory jurisdiction. Despite this limited result a precedent had been established and a second Hague conference was held in 1907. It produced some conventions on the rules of wars but made no progress on disarmament. The governments of the powers were openly unenthusiastic about the subject. Yet it was agreed to hold a third conference, which should have met in 1915. Thus the discussion of arbitration, arms limitation and disarmament was becoming respectable. Moreover, the Hague conferences were not restricted to the powers or only to European states. At the insistence of the United States, Latin America was represented at the second conference. This opened the way for a type of meeting very different from the more exclusive ambassadors' conference of 1912–13.

The European powers did not welcome the intrusion of outsiders at the Hague conference, yet they themselves did not restrict their activities to Europe itself. With the exception of Austria-Hungary all the powers had overseas territories and colonies, and this was also true of some of the lesser European states. The Netherlands controlled the East Indies, Belgium had the Congo; Spain and Portugal, now regarded as decaying states, still had colonies in Africa. Possession of an empire did not therefore guarantee great power status but it emphasized the dominance that Europe had obtained over other continents: Africa had been almost completely partitioned. Ethiopia had preserved her independence partly because she was able to play on the rival ambitions of Britain, France and Italy. The Balkan wars had eliminated most of Turkey in Europe, but the remains of the Ottoman Empire in Asia Minor and the Middle East were still objects of European ambition. In Persia, Britain and Russia had established spheres of influence in 1907, but stopped short of outright annexation. China had escaped partition and maintained formal independence despite the existence of spheres of influence and leased territories.

The appearance of European dominance in Africa and Asia was, however, misleading. European penetration provoked a reaction which developed from instinctive opposition to alien rule into more considered attempts to adopt European political and economic techniques as a means of maintaining or regaining independence. The rise to power of the Young Turks in 1908 and the Chinese revolution of 1911 were both examples of threatened empires attempting to save themselves through modernization. Their immediate results were to create more disorder rather than less, but they served as a warning that European control would increasingly be questioned. In India a National Congress met for the first time in 1886 and the Muslim League held its first conference in 1907. Outright independence for India might still be unthinkable in London but by 1914 considerable efforts had been made to give Indians a greater share in government and administration and it was acknowledged that it would be difficult to stop or reverse this process. Britain also found that the predominantly white dominions were demanding more consultation over matters that affected their interests.

Here, then, were potential challenges to European imperialism. More immediate threats were posed by the activities of the United States and Japan. The war of 1898 with Spain had given the United States an Asian colony in the shape of the Philippines and involved her more directly in Far Eastern rivalries. President Theodore Roosevelt began to play a more active diplomatic role in general. He mediated in the war between Russia and Japan, took part in the 1906 Algeciras conference on Morocco, and sent the American fleet on a round the world cruise between 1907 and 1909 to demonstrate the naval power of the United States. His successor, Taft, followed less dramatic policies, but the European powers now had to take the attitudes of the United States into account, especially over China. Neither the division of China into exclusive spheres of influence nor her dominance by one power would be in the interest of a United States concerned to maintain and increase overseas markets. There were fears that the home market would become satiated and unable to absorb America's growing production of manufactured goods, which explains why the United States tried to maintain China's territorial integrity and equal trading opportunities for all through the policy of the 'open door'. It would be wrong, however, to attribute this solely to economic motivations. While pursuing her own interests the United States regarded herself as set apart from the imperialism of the European powers; she could bring a less selfish and reactionary attitude to bear on international relations. After all, she had herself revolted against British rule and had avoided direct involvement in the affairs of the European continent. There was a particular combination of idealism and practicality in American policies which the Europeans were to experience more directly at the hands of Woodrow Wilson. In early 1914, however, they tended to underestimate her potential as a world power. She had a navy but only a small volunteer army which could have no influence on a short European war. In coal and steel production she was far ahead of the European powers and her exports were increasing at a faster rate; but her economic expansion owed much to European investment and she was still on balance a debtor to Europe. Only in a lengthy war would her latent strength come into play.

Japan had demonstrated that an Asian state could copy European techniques and use them to defeat a European power. Even before the war of 1904–06 with Russia she had been considered worthy of an alliance with Britain as a bulwark against Russian ambitions in China. It was in fact the alliance of 1902 which gave Japan the confidence to fight Russia two years later. Having gained a sphere of influence in Manchuria, Japan further strengthened her position by the annexation of Korea in 1910. Although a rival to the European powers in the competition for influence in China, she had little interest in developments in Europe itself. Nor had she the economic strength to play more than a local role – it was the financial burden of the war with Russia which had induced her to seek Theodore Roosevelt's mediation. Nevertheless, if China remained weak and the European powers became seriously divided, there would be favourable opportunities for Japanese expansion.

Such was the general position of the European powers and their two potential challengers when war began in 1914. Confronted with the Austrian ultimatum to Serbia, Russia stood by her client. Once Russia began to mobilize, Germany had to implement a plan which involved defeating France first and invading Belgium to do so. It was the breach of Belgian neutrality which helped to bring Britain into the hostilities. The assumption of a short decisive war made speed seem essential to the military planners. The European powers, however, were unable to resolve the conflict either by a clear-cut victory or through a negotiated settlement. Instead they succeeded in destroying the stability of the European state system and thus undermined European global predominance. Only with the help of the United States were Britain, France and Italy able to defeat the central powers. The importance of America's military contribution was to some extent concealed by the short period of her participation in hostilities. Had the war continued into 1919 the United States would have acquired a greater influence over strategy. In economic terms she was clearly in a strong position, being now a net creditor of the Allies as a result of their heavy borrowing. President Wilson had made it clear that the United States intended not only to defeat Germany but also to reshape international relations. It seemed likely that the United States would dominate the Paris peace conference.

In fact domestic support for Wilson was declining even before the conference opened. Nor did Clemenceau, Orlando and Lloyd George share his enthusiasm for radical innovation in the rules of inter-state behaviour. The peacemakers had in any case only an imperfect control over the situation in Europe. Since the revolution of 1917 it had become more and more difficult for the Allies to influence events in Russia. It was still unclear whether the Bolsheviks would survive and the confused position in Russia meant that it would be very difficult to secure a political and territorial settlement in eastern Europe. It would not be easy, for example, to fix the eastern frontiers of the Polish state which the Allies were committed to recreate. If the Bolshevik regime did survive for any length of time there was the danger of revolution spreading westward into Germany. In the wake of the Kaiser's abdication it was still not certain whether a stable republican system could be established. Austria-Hungary had collapsed but the boundaries of the successor states remainded to be settled. Even if the victors had been more united they would still have faced a complicated situation.

They had the added difficulty of trying to pursue contradictory objectives. Could a peace based on principle and intended to promote international stability be combined with a settlement which would effectively restrain Germany? How far would the implementation of the principle of self-determination assist either of these aims? Fears of a German economic and military revival made France feel insecure; if she could not obtain a punitive peace she would require assurances of help from Britain and America. French relations with Britain soon began to turn sour over their rival ambitions in the Middle East, and Britain did not want to replace a German preponderance in Europe by a French one. Italy was disgruntled at not obtaining all that had been promised to induce her to enter the war in 1915 on the side of the Allies. Japan had made good use of the war to extend her influence in China; she too was disgruntled at not obtaining the former German possessions in Shantung.

Given such differences the victorious coalition was likely to fall apart without firm leadership from the United States. The Senate's refusal to accept the Covenant of the League of Nations confirmed that America would not play the role of arbiter among the European powers. The peace settlement, not surprisingly, was a mixture of old and new. The creation of the League institutionalized the concert of the powers in a modified form and gave a formal standing to the smaller states. By providing machinery for the peaceful settlement of disputes and the promotion of disarmament it offered the hopes that the ideas discussed at the Hague conferences might produce practical results. The principle of self-determination was given partial expression, although plebiscites were used rather inconsistently to ascertain the popular will. It was in any case difficult to draw boundaries that would separate national groups and satisfy rival claims; the bitterness between Germany and Poland over Upper Silesia is a case in point. By obtaining a strategic frontier on the Brenner pass Italy obtained a German-speaking minority, thus transferring to Austria the sense of grievance which had been felt in Rome before 1914.

Czechoslovakia, Yugoslavia and Poland all contained substantial national minorities. (Yugoslavia did not formally replace the earlier name 'Kingdom of the Serbs, Croats and Slovenes' until 1929, but it is convenient to use it thoroughout.) The collapse of Austria-Hungary did not solve the nationality question. In Czechoslovakia there were significant German and Ruthenian minorities and some tensions existed between Czechs and Slovaks. Within Yugoslavia Serb predominance soon began to irritate the other nationalities; Belgrade tended to view the new state as a greater Serbia rather than a union of equals. Slovak and Croatian separatist movements (especially the latter) were to become problems for their respective governments. Not only did Poland acquire a German minority through the formalities of the peace settlement but she also obtained a Ukrainian minority as a result of fighting with Russia. In this instance the Allies had indeed little control over the course of events. Their most obvious rebuff, however, came in the case of Turkey, where they were unable to enforce their plans for virtual partition against a strong nationalist movement. Turkey lost her empire in the Middle East but retained her independence and finally regained effective control over the Straits by the Montreux Convention of 1936.

The central problem, however, was Germany and it was made no easier by the German refusal to accept that 1918 had been a year of defeat for them. They would have been likely to regard any settlement as harsh and, not surprisingly, they objected to the imputation of guilt for having started the war. To lose territory, to have to demilitarize the Rhineland, to be forced to disarm and to have to pay an as yet unspecified amount in reparations – here was an unjust settlement which did not correspond to the spirit of Wilson's Fourteen Points. They also made much of the fact that the peace was imposed. It is true that Germany was not allowed to participate in the peace negotiations; the Allies did not want German representatives to play the part of Talleyrand at the congress of Vienna and exploit differences among them. Some attention was paid to the representations of the German delegation after the treaty was first presented to them and some modifications were in fact made, but from the start the Germans felt they had been badly treated, and the criticism expressed by Keynes in his *Economic Consequences of the Peace* soon supplied them with further ammunition. Keynes also had a considerable influence on British opinion. Once one of the powers began to have doubts about the justice of the treaty with Germany, enforcement of its provisions would become more difficult.

This in fact proved to be the case. Germany was able in one way or another to evade the disarmament clauses of the treaty. France discovered that even military occupation of the Ruhr in 1923 could not secure the payment of reparations on anything like the scale envisaged. In the face of British non-cooperation, not to say hostility, France could not hope to suppress Germany. It required American intervention to resolve the crisis; the essence of the Dawes Plan was that an American loan would help to restore Germany's finances and enable her to pay much – reduced annual amounts of reparations. The United States continued to insist that the Allies must pay their war debts to her irrespective of what they obtained in reparations. This episode showed that America did not completely retreat into isolation after the rejection of the League. Through the Washington conference of 1921–22 she secured a general agreement to maintain the status quo in the Pacific, a limitation on the building of battle-ships and an end to the Japanese alliance with Britain. In Europe, however, she would take no direct responsibility for securing political stability.

If France could not coerce Germany she would have to come to terms with her. This was the logic that lay behind the Locarno agreements of 1925 and Germany's entry into the League in the following year. As foreign minister, Stresemann was prepared to use diplomatic means, but his aim was revision of Versailles, however discreetly expressed. Within Germany he enjoyed only a narrow base of support. Right-wing nationalists saw little need for such a cautious approach. There was the possibility that Germany could use friendship with Russia to frighten Britain and France. The signing of a treaty at Rapallo in 1922 gave warning that Germany could use her central position in Europe to play off Russia against the western powers. This danger receded because of the cautious policy of the Soviet Union, as it became in 1923. She was still suspected of encouraging subversion abroad but the pursuit of internal development diminished her challenge to the capitalist powers. This did not alter the fact that the states of eastern Europe were largely dependent for the maintenance of their independence upon German and Soviet inaction. If either or both tried to regain lost territories, much would depend on the western powers' willingness to intervene.

The attitude of all three was uncertain. Discontent over Italy's failures at the peace conference and fears of Bolshevism had helped to bring Mussolini and his Fascists to power in 1922. Here was a success for the new or radical right which opposed revolution from the left yet distrusted the established conservative groups which had dominated politics before the war. Fascism called for the regeneration of Italy and glorified violence and war as an end in itself. Mussolini's foreign policy in his early years was more restrained than Fascist doctrine suggested, with the exception of the attack on Corfu in 1923. Italy, however, had now to be seen as a revisionist and potentially more self-assertive power. In France there was a noticeable retreat into a cautious attitude bordering on defeatism. The losses of the war and postwar efforts to find security had failed to contain Germany. Another conflict on the same scale to prevent a German revival was too unpleasant to contemplate. This attitude was to find expression in the decision to build the Maginot line along the border with Germany. It was doubtful how active the French would be in defending the status quo in eastern Europe. Britain for her part sought to limit her commitments on the Continent; at Locarno she undertook no obligations in eastern Europe. In part this was the result of a disillusion with the results of the war, similar to, but weaker than that of the French. It was also in part the result of the restraining influence of her dominions. In 1914 Britain's declaration of war had applied automatically to them as well. Having appeared at the peace conference and obtained membership of the League they began to press for outright independence in foreign policy. This was conceded by the Statute of Westminster in 1931 but well before that the dominions were seeking to limit Britain's commitments in Europe. It could be said of Canada that she was far more isolationist than the United States.

By 1930 Germany had secured both a further modification of her reparations payments (the Young Plan) and an accelerated withdrawal of Allied troops from the west bank of the Rhine. The onset of economic depression, however, destroyed the fragile stability of the post-Locarno period. Inter-state cooperation declined as governments sought to protect their own economies. Thus reparations and war debts disappeared; the world economic conference of 1933 was a failure. Within states political extremism was encouraged, most noticeably in the case of Hitler's accession to power in 1933. In an atmosphere of economic dislocation it was to prove impossible to create a coalition to defend the Versailles, Washington or Locarno settlements. The beginning of the Japanese takeover of Manchuria in 1931 revealed that the European powers were not prepared to act in the name of the League Covenant and that the United States would not go beyond verbal condemnation of a forcible alteration of the status quo in the Far East. The Soviet Union had reason to be concerned at Japanese action, but she was still outside the League and would not intervene alone.

Inaction by the powers increased the self-confidence of the Japanese military and reduced the influence of the civilian politicians in Tokyo. A full-scale attack on China was delayed until 1937 but European power in Asia was now under threat. During the 1930s Britain had to face the danger of a war in the Far East while confronting a worsening situation in Europe. Like the Fascists, the Nazis were a party of the radical right but with a much more racialist and anti-semitic emphasis. As with the Fascists in Italy, there were public figures who mistakenly thought they could manipulate the new movement. The powers had found it possible to conduct relations with Mussolini; could they not do the same with Hitler? If Germany had legitimate grievances and if war in defence of an unjust peace settlement was unthinkable then it was logical to conciliate Hitler: but since he did not wish merely to restore Germany to the position of 1914 but to make another bid for predominance and since he had a strong ideological antipathy to the Soviet Union, the attempt to make Germany again part of a European concert was bound to fail.

Hitler was careful to avoid negotiated settlements which might imply any continuing inferiority on Germany's part. He chose his moment to leave the disarmament conference and the League; he unilaterally announced re-armament and reoccupied the demilitarized zone of the Rhineland. With each success and with the lack of reaction from Britain and France Hitler's confidence and prestige grew. Both countries seemed paralysed by the difficulties that confronted them. Little help was to be expected from the United States and Russia's entry into the League in 1934 did not make her in their eyes an attractive or reliable ally. The only possibility was Italy, who could be expected to oppose German designs on Austria. For a moment it seemed that the Stresa front of 1935 could serve as the basis for an effective coalition against Germany. Within a few months that hope was destroyed by Mussolini's invasion of Ethiopia. The cynical might argue that, since Germany was the main threat to their security, Britain and France should have abandoned Ethiopia to her fate. Neither power was prepared to ignore the League Covenant so blatantly, but the imposition of partial sanctions was a failure. The League was discredited and Mussolini moved closer to Hitler. Germany and Italy both gave aid to Franco in Spain and Mussolini was now prepared to abandon Austria.

In 1938, therefore, Hitler was able to annex Austria and take the Sudetenland from Czechoslovakia. In thus creating a greater Germany he could claim to be following the principle of self-determination. Although at one stage in the Czech crisis war seemed possible, neither Britain nor France was anxious to fight for the maintenance of Czechoslovakia's integrity; they were still not prepared to contemplate alliance with Russia. It required the German occupation of the rest of Czechoslovakia to push them into action. Hitler had now taken over non-German territory, and the states of eastern Europe were open to further economic and military pressure. The virtual collapse of the League and German expansion showed between them how illusory was the standing acquired by smaller states since 1919.

So in March 1939 Britain and France were prepared to give a guarantee to Poland, now an obvious target for German pressure. Without Soviet help they could not hope to defend her, yet they remained unwilling to commit themselves to a full-scale alliance. The Poles dangerously over-estimated their ability to meet a German attack and were unwilling to allow Russian troops on their soil. Stalin had little reason to trust British and French determination, whereas an agreement with Germany could give Russia immediate territorial gains. For Germany such an agreement offered the chance of localizing the conflict and breaking up a potential alliance against her. The Nazi-Soviet pact was therefore not as great an aberration as it might seem; it temporarily served the interests of both states. But despite the defeat and partition of Poland, Britain and France this time did not give in. It cannot be said, however, that they made any positive moves against Germany and they almost allowed themselves to be diverted by the Russian attack on Finland.

The rapid German victories of 1940 showed that the pattern of the Second World War would be very different from that of the first. Norway, Denmark and the Netherlands, who had all succeeded in remaining neutral in 1914–18, now found themselves occupied. France was defeated and British troops were forced off the Continent. At a stroke Nazi Germany had gained the victory in the west which eluded Ludendorff in 1918. Italy, having remained neutral in 1939, now entered the war in expectation of an early peace settlement. The Soviet Union moved to consolidate her position by absorbing the Baltic states and reclaiming the province of Bessarabia from Rumania. Stalin remained watchful and uneasy in the face of German predominance in eastern Europe.

In the first half of 1941 there appeared to be a stalemate. Britain remained undefeated but unable to challenge Germany's Continental supremacy, which seemed only to be confirmed by the rapid conquest of Greece and Yugoslavia. The United States was giving aid to Britain but Franklin Roosevelt was unwilling to risk accusations of dragging America into war. He had also to deal with the problem of how to restrain Japan from exploiting European weakness in the Pacific. Also worried by Japan's ambitions, the Soviet Union signed a neutrality pact with her in April. In the second half of the year the war was transformed from the European into a truly global struggle by the German attack on Russia and Japan's attack on the United States. Britain, the Soviet Union and America were thus pushed into a rather uneasy coalition. This time the full weight of American military and naval power was brought to bear in both Europe and the Pacific. The Russian collapse of 1917 was not repeated and as the Soviet war effort expanded Britain found herself more and more the junior partner in the triumvirate. Italy's military weakness led to the fall of Mussolini in 1943, followed by surrender to, and then co-belligerency with, the Allies.

By the summer of 1945 Germany and Japan had been decisively defeated. Britain was economically exhausted and would need American help for her recovery. France and Italy had been liberated by Anglo-American forces and they too faced the need for economic recovery. Despite the devastation she had suffered the Soviet Union now occupied most of eastern Europe and part of Germany. In the Far East she had regained the position held by Tsarist Russia in 1904. The reshaping of the European state system would depend on the attitudes of the two giants. The future development of American policy was still uncertain but there was unlikely to be a repetition of 1919–20 – the United States was now committed to the political and economic restructuring of the international order. How the Soviet Union would react to policies that might challenge her predominance in eastern Europe had still to be seen. It was not clear how far the ideological element in her policy had been replaced by a concern with security. Russia and the United States had still to agree on the treatment of Germany. Could they ensure that her defeat would be more constructively used than in 1919 to promote European stability? At least the United States and the Soviet Union agreed in disliking European imperialism. Japan's victories, however temporary, had undermined European prestige in Asia. It would be difficult for Britain, France and the Netherlands to regain full control over their colonial possessions given their economic exhaustion and dependence on the United States. The dwarfing of Europe seemed almost complete.

Such, in outline, were the main changes in relationships between the powers from 1914 to 1945. Later chapters will give a more detailed treatment of these developments. The nature of power itself changed during the period; scientific and economic capacity had become more important. Germany and Japan gained startling initial successes in the Second World War, but they could not in the long run offset American and Russian ability to produce more tanks, planes or aircraft carriers. War itself had become more destructive; strategic bombing campaigns made civilian populations direct targets for attack, although they proved less effective against morale and industrial capacity than had been expected. The harnessing of nuclear energy to produce the atomic bomb created the possibility of eliminating entire societies. The systematic extermination of Jews and Slavs on grounds of racial inferiority was yet another way in which the destructiveness of the Second World War exceeded that of the First; Imperial Germany had tried to dominate what it regarded as subject races, Nazi Germany tried to eliminate them. Brutality encouraged resistance, so that although military force was used more effectively than in the First World War, quick victories did not always mean the pacification of occupied territories. Resistance movements tied down large numbers of troops in guarding lines of communication, although they could not by themselves defeat an efficient occupying force.

How did the conduct of inter-state relations alter during this period? Professional diplomats found their influence restricted and their reputation diminished. Their critics in the peace movement were able to claim that the diplomats had helped to bring about the war of 1914 by committing their countries to alliances whose terms were not fully known. During the war they had compounded their folly, first by making secret treaties which cynically bartered territories and populations, and second by failing to produce a negotiated settlement. President Wilson was particularly critical of secret diplomacy because it failed to represent the true interests of the people. 'Open covenants of peace, openly arrived at' was the aim of the first of his Fourteen Points. In the liberal democracies, therefore, there were demands for greater scrutiny of, and control over, foreign policy. It cannot be said, however, that electorates showed more than an intermittent interest in foreign affairs. Some actions would meet with clear disapproval, as can be seen in the French and British reactions to the Hoare–Laval Plan. Politicians and diplomats assumed that certain policies were best avoided because they would not get public support. Roosevelt in the 1930s was unwilling to offend what was assumed to be strong American feeling against direct involvement in European affairs. But what public opinion was on particular issues was often uncertain; not until the second half of the 1930s did opinion polls begin to be taken on a regular and systematic basis.

More significant was the possibility that a strong-willed head of government would ignore or bypass his foreign minister and diplomats. This happened in Britain under Lloyd George and Neville Chamberlain. In the United States, where the State Department had never enjoyed the same standing as the British Foreign Office, it was possible for a president to rely on special advisers and to conduct his own foreign policy. Wilson made considerable use of Colonel House and largely ignored Secretary of State Lansing; Roosevelt relied on Harry Hopkins in the Second World War, and kept Cordell Hull in the background. In wartime, of course, departmental rivalries with the armed forces were likely to increase, as one can see from the arguments about war aims in Britain between the War Office and the Foreign Office during the First World War. That conflict encouraged efforts in various countries to make diplomatic and foreign services more efficient. Before this, changes had begun in France as early as 1907 but the war speeded them up. An attempt was made to reorganize the Foreign Ministry and to reduce the danger of purely political appointments. At the head of the bureaucracy in the Foreign Ministry there appeared in 1915 the post of Secretary-General. It was temporarily abolished in 1917 and again in 1922 but became firmly established in 1925. In Germany it required the shock of defeat and the creation of the Weimar Republic to produce a similar overhaul of the German Foreign Ministry. Here there was an attempt to ensure both greater efficiency and greater control by the Reichstag. A new post of foreign minister was created in 1919 so that the state secretary became clearly identified as the administrative head of the diplomatic bureaucracy. In Britain there were a number of reforms between 1919 and 1921 intended among other things to allow greater interchange between the Foreign Office and the diplomatic service. As for the United States, changes had begun before 1914 in an attempt to limit political appointment but it was the Rogers Act of 1924 which formally established a career foreign service. The reforms in the four countries mentioned seem to have produced some increases in efficiency. Officials were now better equipped to deal with the greater volume of business that confronted them, and the average level of competence increased. There continued, however, to be criticisms that diplomats were still recruited from too limited a social background. In that sense diplomacy was not democratized.

The diplomats in the democracies might find their authority challenged but at least they retained some independence. Under Mussolini and Hitler the situation was different. The radical right distrusted professional diplomats, partly because of their superior social background, partly because of doubts about their ideological reliability. Some Italian and German diplomats supported the Fascist and Nazi regimes, while others thought they could act as a restraining influence. In both countries the foreign ministries came under party influence or control. Mussolini put Grandi in charge, was for a time his own Foreign Minister, and then appointed his son-in-law Ciano. The more independently minded diplomats resigned or found themselves pushed out. Hitler was at first prepared to leave the career diplomat von Neurath in charge but Ribbentrop had established a personal office that dabbled in foreign affairs well before he replaced Neurath. German diplomats found the independence which they had enjoyed under Weimar steadily eroded. The multiplication of rival organizations within the Nazi bureaucracy and Hitler's personal style of decision-making combined to push the Foreign Ministry on to the sidelines. In the Soviet Union the effects of revolution, civil war and the purges of the 1930s meant that a diplomatic corps had to be reconstructed from scratch. Molotov, Maisky and Litvinov were not diplomats by training and in any case the People's Commissariat for Foreign Affairs was not an independent agency: the main decisions were taken in the Politburo.

Whatever the type of government they represented, diplomats were greatly affected by changes in means of communication. By 1914 the telegraph and the telephone had reduced the independence of ambassadors. The development of broadcasting and film between the wars made it possible to communicate directly with large audiences at home or abroad. Governments had used inspired articles in the press and interviews with chosen correspondents before 1914, and such techniques continued to be used thereafter, but the spoken word and the visual image had a greater immediacy and impact which did not require a high degree of literacy on the part of the audience. A single speech or public appearance could now have a more widespread effect. Woodrow Wilson destroyed his health through a speaking tour designed to win support for the League of Nations; Franklin Roosevelt could use his famous 'fireside chats' over the radio to influence opinion without leaving Washington. Diplomats became involved in public relations and propaganda, however reluctantly, and thus found themselves drawn into dealings with information departments, party propaganda organizations and broadcasting services. Foreign ministries had no monopoly over these developments and often found their authority challenged.

Negotiations did not become completely open but their character certainly changed. Before 1914 it was unusual for foreign ministers or heads of government to involve themselves directly in discussions or to attend conferences in person. The meetings at Algeciras and the Hague, and the London conference of ambassadors, were arranged on an *ad hoc* basis. During the First World War, however, both the Allies and the central powers found regular meetings necessary, and on the Allied side these became institutionalized in 1917 as the Supreme War Council. Heads of Government were directly involved in the Paris peace negotiations which were followed by a series of conferences under the auspices of the Supreme War Council. In addition there were the regular meetings of the conference of ambassadors in Paris, charged with supervising the execution of the peace treaties, and the meetings of the League of Nations. From 1924 it became normal practice for foreign ministers to appear in Geneva, especially at sessions of the League Council. In addition various conferences were arranged to deal with specific problems, such as the Washington Conference of 1921–22. The Supreme War Council ceased to meet after 1922 and the ambassadors conference after 1931, but the 1930s produced the disarmament conference, the world economic conference and, of course, the direct encounters between Chamberlain and Hitler at Godesberg and Munich. Multi-lateral diplomacy reached its zenith with the wartime meetings between Churchill, Roosevelt and Stalin. By now the aeroplane made it possible to travel long distances quickly and there was a greater temptation for heads of government to involve themselves directly in negotiations.

The results were mixed. Conferences accompanied by a good deal of publicity could raise expectations too high and create a corresponding sense of disappointment when little was achieved, as Lloyd George discovered when the Genoa conference of 1922 failed to produce results. It could be dangerous for a head of government or foreign minister to involve himself too closely with a particular policy, as Chamberlain found out once the Munich agreement became discredited. Busy men meeting for a few days during a crisis or in wartime could not adequately discuss every issue that came before them. The Teheran, Yalta and Potsdam conferences all left a residue of ambiguous or unsettled questions. On the other hand, where a conference was carefully prepared and dealt with specific topics a good deal could be achieved. At the Washington conference of 1921–22 Charles Evans Hughes had the advantage of a prepared plan on naval disarmament; by contrast, lack of preparation meant that the 1927 Geneva conference on naval disarmament was a failure. There was still a need for regular diplomatic contacts to provide a solid foundation for the more glamorous excursions into conferences and summits.

The style of diplomacy became more abrasive as the period progressed. The Soviet Union, for example, saw little reason to be polite to capitalist states who were assumed to be basically hostile, and even when the Russians were being cooperative there was a certain sharpness in their diplomatic communications. Mussolini specialized in bombast and striking phrases; Hitler could work himself into a calculated frenzy when he wanted to terrify people like Schushnigg and Hacha. The change in style reflected underlying changes in attitude: neither Communists nor Fascists found it easy to think in terms of a status quo in international relations, which for different reasons they saw as a form of continuing conflict. Treaties and agreements were therefore tactical devices in an unending contest. States have always been cynical about their treaty obligations; cynicism increased after 1918. There was little point in keeping agreements any longer than necessary. Locarno was never enforced and a general statement of intent like the Kellogg pact was unenforceable. The Nazi-Soviet pact of 1939 lasted for less than two years. When Russia attacked Japan in 1945 their neutrality pact still had a year to run. It can be argued that the general disillusion with the Versailles settlement helped to undermine confidence in the validity of other agreements. States certainly proved unwilling to shoulder the obligations contained in the League Covenant the effective working of which depended upon the assumption that agreements would be kept.

CHAPTER TWO
Secret treaties and war aims, 1914–1918

The belligerents of August 1914 expected the war to be short and decisive. By Christmas the fighting would be over and the victors could impose a settlement at their leisure. It would in any case be difficult if not impossible to find the resources for a lengthy conflict. Both sides over-estimated their ability to produce a decisive result and under-estimated their capacity to maintain a protracted and large-scale war. The fighting was not over by Christmas 1914 but the military situation as it stood then was to have a significant influence on the attitudes of the combatants during the later stages of the war.

In the west the Germans had failed to defeat the British and French armies completely, but they had occupied most of Belgium and an important part of north-east France. These were visible signs of success which the Germans were reluctant to abandon. Although the exact details varied from time to time, it was assumed in German thinking about war aims that Belgium would remain a client whether or not she regained a nominal independence and that for both strategic and economic reasons some territory would be taken from France. The German lack of flexibility over Belgium gave Britain and France little incentive to seek a compromise peace. It was the invasion of Belgium which had been the immediate cause of British entry into the war and so long as a hostile power controlled that country Britain could not feel secure. She sought to prevent German predominance in Europe and any retention of the occupied territories would be a visible sign that such a predominance existed. For France the situation was similar; until German troops were removed from her soil she would feel herself in an inferior position. There was in addition the hope of reversing the verdict of 1871 and regaining Alsace-Lorraine, something the Germans were unlikely to yield by negotiation. Thus the military stalemate which was beginning to settle on the Western Front by the end of 1914 was to be accompanied by diplomatic stalemate as well. The lack of diplomatic flexibility intensified the efforts of both sides to obtain an outright military victory in the west.

On the Eastern Front the situation was more fluid but still indecisive. The German victory at Tannenberg had removed the immediate threat of an invasion by the Russian steamroller. This success, however, was counterbalanced by the Austrian defeat in Galicia. German troops had to be sent to help the Austrians and there were already signs that the latter might become a military liability. They had not yet defeated the Serbians, the aim for which they had originally sought German diplomatic support in the July crisis. Austrian troops had entered Belgrade early in December but were soon driven out. Turkey had signed an alliance with Germany at the beginning of August, but because of divisions within the government did not join the hostilities until the end of October. This meant that supplies could not be sent to Russia by the Black Sea route and that Russia would have to divert troops to the Caucasus. Turkey needed money and supplies from Germany and here was another potential liability. However cumbersome and inefficient it might be, the Russian army had the advantage of large numbers and vast territory into which it might retreat. For the central powers the situation on the Eastern Front was still uncertain and a number of states had not yet declared their allegiance. Rumania, Bulgaria, Greece and Italy had all remained neutral at the beginning of the war so that in eastern Europe and the Mediterranean there seemed to be military and diplomatic possibilities for both sides. Overall the central powers had done well enough to hope they could still attain outright success. The Allies, having survived the opening offensives, had reason to hope that they could improve their position.

The situation at the end of 1914 thus encouraged both sides to continue searching for the knockout blow. By the end of 1916 they had still not found it. Britain and France had been unable to break through on the Western Front; Italian entry into the war had merely produced another stalemate on the border with Austria. At sea the anticipated decisive battle between the British and German fleets had not taken place – the encounter at Jutland had proved inconclusive. Here too attrition had become dominant; the blockade and the submarine had become more important than the battleship. The German attempt to wear down the French at Verdun had failed but in the east the central powers continued to score successes. Bulgaria entered the war in 1915 and helped to defeat Serbia. The Allies' attempt to capture the Dardanelles had been a failure and the force established in Salonika had achieved little while King Constantine's sympathy with the central powers helped to keep Greece neutral. Rumania came into the war on the Allied side in 1916 but was soon defeated. These developments meant that German communications with Turkey were much improved. The Russians had been forced out of Poland and the success of Brusilov's offensive in 1916 had proved only temporary, though it certainly gave the central powers a fright.

Two Christmases later, therefore, outright victory still seemed remote. But the search for it was steadily changing the character of the war. Both sides faced increasing demands for manpower, materials and money. Populations had to be mobilized not only on the battlefield but also in the factories. Increasingly governments had to intervene in economic activities to ensure that priority was given to the war effort. Shortages of food and raw materials led to experiments in rationing and price controls. The war had to be paid for and most governments relied heavily on borrowing rather than an increase in direct taxes. The central powers were driven back on their own financial resources; the Allies borrowed heavily from Britain, who in turn raised a good deal of money in the United States after the latter removed a ban on loans to the belligerents in September 1915. Thus governments broke new ground in mobilizing human and economic resources. The large armies they raised had to be persuaded that they were fighting in a just cause and that their opponents were not; the longer the war went on the more important it became to maintain morale. This increased the value of propaganda as both sides sought to present a favourable image of themselves and to undermine the reputation and confidence of their enemies. Britain paid particular attention to creating a favourable climate of opinion in the United States; the Germans devoted much effort to attempts to undermine morale in Russia.

The complexity of the war produced problems for both sides in civil/military relations and in alliance management. In August 1914 it had seemed reasonable to let the soldiers and sailors get on with producing the anticipated quick victory, but as the military proved consistently unable to produce victory tension grew between them and the civilian politicians. The latter usually lacked expertise in strategic matters and found it difficult to assert effective control or to choose from the conflicting advice offered to them. The situation varied from country to country. In Russia the civilian politicians in the Duma had little influence on policy and in any case Nicholas II took personal command of his armies in September 1915. In Austria-Hungary it was difficult for civilian politicians to challenge the authority of the Emperor Franz Joseph and the Chief of Staff Conrad. But the Hungarians with their separate government could put a brake on policies and did sometimes interfere in military matters. After Franz Joseph's death in November 1916 his successor Charles I took personal command of his armies and packed Conrad off to command the Italian front. It cannot be said that the Russian or the Austrian monarchs improved the performance of their armies but at least they avoided the bitter debates that took place in Germany, France and Britain.

The military held a special position in Germany from the outset and this was strengthened by wartime exigencies and the vacillating character of William II. Thus the influence of the Chancellor, Bethmann-Hollweg, was steadily eroded. While Falkenhayn was Chief of Staff Bethmann managed to maintain his position and keep some influence over policy; when Hindenburg became Chief of Staff at the end of August 1915, with Ludendorff as his assistant, the Chancellor's power declined rapidly. Hindenburg and Ludendorff established a virtual dictatorship over domestic and foreign policy. On war aims they took an inflexible position: Germany should seek the maximum gains possible, even at the expense of her own allies. Bethmann tried in vain to maintain a more flexible and subtle policy. He was forced to resign in 1917, as indeed was Foreign Minister Kühlmann in 1918. Neither man was opposed to German gains and annexations but both wanted to keep some freedom of action and to maintain at least the appearance of being conciliatory.

In France the civilian politicians had to fight hard to establish a grip on military matters. This process culminated in the dismissal of General Joffre as Commander-in-Chief at the beginning of December 1916 and the creation of a new government by Briand shortly afterwards. As for Britain, the real arguments came after the establishment of Lloyd George's coalition government at about the same time. Lloyd George succeeded in replacing Robertson as Chief of the Imperial General Staff at the beginning of 1918 but was unable to remove his arch-enemy Haig. One military commander could only be replaced by another and a change of face did not necessarily solve problems. Falkenhayn had argued for a decision in the west, Hindenburg and Ludendorff for concentrating on the defeat of Russia, but they too found difficulty in conducting a two-front war. In Britain and France there was continuing debate between those who wanted to seek a defeat of Germany in France and those who argued the case for trying to defeat Germany's allies and thus knock away the props. Despite the civil/military dispute it would be wrong to see politicians and soldiers as two monolithic groups with identical views. Moreover, these strategic arguments had diplomatic implications – military efforts could be supplemented by attempts to induce an enemy to make a separate peace. The Germans, for example, made unsuccessful overtures to Russia in 1915, and Britain and France in 1917 had some hopes of a separate peace with Austria-Hungary. But emphasis on opening a new front could give an exaggerated importance to the acquisition of allies. Britain and France overestimated the military value of Rumania and Italy.

These examples highlighted the fact that neither side had previous experience of the problems of managing coalitions over a lengthy period. The German experience of 1866 and 1870 had been of short wars against a single opponent. Britain and France had been allies in the Crimean war, but that had been a localized conflict as well as limited in the number of participants. Russia had fought wars against Turkey and Japan as individual opponents. The Balkan wars of 1912–13 had been of short duration. It was necessary to go back to the Napoleonic period for guidance in the techniques of coordinating strategy and maintaining unity of purpose. This was to prove difficult enough for the major powers on both sides: the Supreme Allied War Council to coordinate strategy was not created until November 1917 and the central powers never set up an equivalent body. The addition of lesser allies with specific claims to be met complicated matters still further, since an extra ally did not necessarily mean a net increase in military strength and usually produced adjustments in, and additions to, war aims. Not surprisingly, the lesser allies tried to extract as high a price as possible. The problem of how to win victory thus became entangled with the question of what the rival sides expected to obtain for themselves. Until the beginning of 1917 they thought largely in traditional terms of annexation, compensation and spheres of influence. Victory would permit the attainment of long-standing aspirations and therefore would have to be decisive enough to allow any peace settlement to be maintained over a long period. Yet there was a dangerous ambiguity about the concept of victory. If it was to be complete would the vanquished be reconciled to their fate? Could either side hope to attain such an overwhelming military predominance? If so, they would be moving away from the idea of negotiation and adjustment as a means of lubricating friction between states. 'Secret diplomacy' expressed itself in traditional terms yet carried with it the assumption that total victory was possible.

On the German side, Bethmann-Hollweg had drawn up a provisional list of war aims in September 1914 in anticipation of an early victory over France. He was therefore somewhat vague about the treatment of Russia and about colonial gains. As he saw it, German security entailed a considerable weakening of both France and Russia. France would have to be forced into economic dependence on Germany, partly through a heavy indemnity, partly through the loss of the ore-field at Briey. She might be forced to give up the coastal strip from Calais to Boulogne. Belgium should remain a client whatever her precise political status and Luxemburg would be absorbed into the German empire. Bethmann also envisaged a central European economic grouping under German domination. These ideas certainly implied the complete defeat of France and Russia, for they were unlikely to accept willingly such a degree of German dominance. It is true that Bethmann did not necessarily expect to get every item in his programme, but it represented the type of settlement that Germany was most likely to seek in the west. Her aims in eastern Europe were only to become clear later.

Bethmann's memorandum said little about Austria-Hungary save to include her as one of the subordinate units in the central European economic group. From the beginning of the war Germany tended to treat Austria-Hungary as very much the junior partner, in both military and economic terms. The interests of the two countries were far from identical. The Austrians were not seeking hegemony in Europe but rather the security of their empire. It would suit them to see ·Russia, as the patron of the Slavs, severely weakened, as they wished to dominate Serbia and have a strong influence over Rumania and Bulgaria. A punitive peace against France would have little benefit for the Austrians, who were always much more prepared than the Germans to contemplate the restoration of Belgian independence. But they faced a dilemma. Assuming that Germany relinquished Belgium she would probably seek further gains in eastern Europe as compensation. This was likely to bring German-Austrian rivalry into the open, as was indicated by the case of Poland. Having pushed the Russians out of Poland in 1915 the central powers now had the problem of what to do with it. Given their own Polish populations they had to be cautious about encouraging nationalist sentiments, but the hope of recruiting Poles to fight against Russia and the wish to appear more liberal than the Tsarist Empire led to a proclamation in November 1916 that Russian Poland would become an independent kingdom. Then came the question of who should rule it. The Germans contemplated annexations to strengthen the frontier and wanted economic predominance for themselves. The Austrians would have liked Poland to be ruled by a Habsburg and thus brought into their orbit. At one point in 1917 Austria was prepared to give up her interests in Poland in the hope of getting greater German flexibility in the west, but this position was soon abandoned. By the end of the war there was still no agreement on the future of Poland, for the Germans saw little need to make concessions to Austria. She had needed German military help to defeat Serbia and push back the Russians and was to need help again in 1917 to defeat the Italians.

Despite these strains and stresses the central powers succeeded in winning over Bulgaria as an ally. Smarting from her defeat in the Balkan wars, she wanted revenge on Serbia and control of Serbian Macedonia while on the other hand she distrusted Turkey. Both sides wooed her in 1914 and 1915 but the central powers had more to offer. Serbia would not give up territory to Bulgaria until sure of gaining compensation at the expense of Austria, whereas the Bulgarians wanted a more immediate reward. The Allies' bargaining position was weakened by the failure of the Dardanelles expedition. The central powers persuaded Turkey to make a frontier adjustment which gave Bulgaria complete control of the railway to the Aegean port of Dedeagatch. With that gained Bulgaria agreed in September 1915 to join the attack on Serbia and did so the following month.

The Rumanians also tried to bid up their price but with less immediate success. King Carol was sympathetic to the central powers but acted cautiously because of the strength of pro-Allied feeling in the country. After his death in October 1914 Rumania tried putting pressure on Austria-Hungary and asked for territorial concessions as the price of neutrality. The Austrians, and especially the Hungarians, were adamant against any concession, so Rumania signed a treaty with the Allies in August 1916 and declared war on Austria-Hungary in the same month. The Allies had reservations about her territorial ambitions but her rapid defeat rendered such doubts irrelevant. The success of the Brusilov offensive had led the Rumanians to overestimate Austrian weakness and they could do little when Bulgaria attacked from the south.

By the end of 1916 the Germans could be reasonably satisfied with the working of their alliance system, the Austrians rather less so. Neither country had encouraged public discussion of war aims, fearing disunity and the danger of being tied to fixed negotiating positions. The same considerations applied on the Allied side but here there was much more private diplomatic activity. Indeed, the bulk of wartime secret diplomacy was conducted among the Allies in the first two years of the conflict. France, Britain and Russia signed a treaty in London on 5 September 1914 in which they promised not to make a separate peace nor to offer peace terms without consultation. This did not, however, give any guidance as to their individual aims. The Russian Foreign Minister Sazonov was the first to produce a 'shopping list', which he discussed with the British and French ambassadors in Petrograd on 14 September. It makes an interesting comparison with the programme that Bethmann had compiled only five days earlier. Russia might annex territory from both Germany and Austria-Hungary; from the latter she would want to take at least part of Galicia. Serbia might take Bosnia, Hercegovina, Dalmatia and part of Albania. Austria should be induced or forced to create a Czech kingdom which would become a third element within the Habsburg Empire. In the west he talked of France taking part of the Rhineland and perhaps the Palatinate. Although these speculations would involve considerable territorial losses for Austria-Hungary, Sazonov was not thinking at this stage of dismemberment. He was much more interested in a weakening of Germany which would leave Russia with a strong position in Eastern Europe. British and French reactions were guarded. Neither felt any great hostility towards Austria nor a strong desire to commit themselves on the future treatment of Germany.

Turkish entry into the war created a new situation. All three Allies could now contemplate possible gains in the Ottoman Empire and in Turkey itself. After some preliminary soundings, Russia in March

1915 formally asked her partners for Constantinople, the Straits, part of southern Thrace and some islands in the Aegean. This would fulfil a long-standing Russian ambition to control access to the Black Sea. In the light of Anglo-Russian rivalry in Asia it might seem surprising that Britain should be prepared to concede such demands, yet both Britain and France did in fact reply favourably to the Russian request. Both had still to clarify their own expectations in the Ottoman Empire and made clear that they would seek equivalent gains. In addition, Britain specifically indicated that she would like to revise the 1907 agreement on Persia so as to bring the neutral zone into her sphere of influence. Even so, a significant change of attitude was indicated by the Anglo-French replies. Instead of being a buffer against Russian expansion, Turkey was now seen increasingly as an object for partition. Other countries were likely to be interested. Greece harboured ambitions of expansion in Asia Minor but the state most directly affected by the Allied agreement was Italy.

Italy had justified her neutrality in August 1914 on the grounds that the Triple Alliance did not apply, since it was Austria which had attacked Serbia and not the other way round. There now seemed an opportunity to gain from Austria the long-coveted Siuth Tyrol and the Trentino, if not more. Italy could ask for territorial concessions as the price of neutrality or she could offer to join the war on the Allied side. Neutrality might be cheaper but there was a risk that the war might be decided before Italy could exert much influence. The inconclusive nature of the fighting, however, increased her potential value to both sides. The Austrians, not surprisingly, were unwilling to buy off the Italians with any concession at all. The Germans pressed them to do so and sent the former chancellor von Bülow to Rome as ambassador in December 1914 in the belief that he could influence neutralist sentiment. In March 1915 the Austrians reluctantly agreed to make concessions, whereupon the Italians increased their price. The Germans continued to urge further concessions but by the time the Austrians were prepared to go further it was too late – Italy had begun negotiations with the Allies in February and the treaty of London was signed on 26 April 1915. The discussions had not been easy. Russia was far from happy about promises to Italy which would conflict with Serbian ambitions. Italy wanted to dominate the Adriatic and had designs on Albania. The Serbs themselves wanted access to the Adriatic.

In the event Italy was promised South Tyrol, the Trentino, Trieste, Gorizia, Dalmatia, most of Istria and various islands in the Adriatic. If an independent Albania was to be maintained Italy would direct its external relations. Her claim to the Dodecanese (occupied in the war of 1911–12) was confirmed and she was promised a share in the partition of Turkey. With these gains in hand Italy declared war on Austria-Hungary on 23 May. The decision was a close one, for the neutralist and interventionist groups were finely balanced, and Salandra's government had to use a good deal of pressure and intimidation to secure the required result. Italy had no immediate quarrel with Germany and did not in fact declare war on her until August 1916, in the wake of Rumanian entry into the conflict. The domestic division over the war and its subsequent lack of military success meant that any Italian government would have to cling hard to the promises made in the treaty of London. Italy wanted to make quite sure of her gains in Turkey as well and this was the primary reason for declaring war on Germany. The Allies would not confirm her claims until she did so, for by delaying the declaration against Germany Italy was technically in breach of article 2 of the treaty of London, which required her to fight all the enemies of her allies. Britain and France had begun negotiations between themselves in November 1915 and had reached an agreement by the following February, usually known as Sykes–Picot after the two principal negotiators. Both men went to Petrograd in March to try and win over the Russians. The latter then increased their own claims on Turkey. A revised agreement was embodied in an exchange of notes in May by which Britain and France defined their spheres of influence. France would be predominant in Syria and south-east Turkey, Britain in Mesopotamia with access to the Mediterranean at Haifa. Palestine would be placed under an international administration to be arranged later. Russia would acquire further territory in Armenia and Kurdistan. Britain and France would allow the creation of an Arab state or states. The promise of an independent Arab state had already been made in rather ambiguous terms in October 1915 by the British High Commissioner in Egypt, Sir Henry Macmahon, to the Sherif of Mecca. The aim was to induce him to revolt against the Turks, whereas the Sykes–Picot agreement was a compromise between rival imperial ambitions. The British regarded the internationalization proposal for Palestine as a success over the French, but it was to prove difficult to reconcile the long-term promises and agreements made with short-term considerations in mind, as the Allies were subsequently to discover.

The Italians were eventually accommodated in the agreement made at St Jean de Maurienne in April 1917 when Britain and France promised them an area of control and influence around Adalia and Smyrna, and in return they accepted the arrangements already made by Sykes and Picot. If implemented, these various agreements would have left independent Turkey as a small landlocked state, Russia would have acquired an even stronger position in Asia Minor and there would have been little room for Greek ambitions whether aimed against Albania or Turkey. There was an unspoken assumption that Turkey could be effectively defeated and held in subjection. Just as Germany over-estimated her capacity to defeat and hold down France and Russia, so the Allies too easily assumed that they had the military power to maintain the partition of the Ottoman Empire. Neither side had as yet fully understood the limitations inherent in military force.

There is one more item to be mentioned in the list of secret Allied agreements. The French were anxious to secure as free a hand as possible over the future of the Rhineland. Knowing that the British were not enthusiastic they made an approach to the Russians in February 1917. The proposal was that when Alsace-Lorraine was returned to France she should have discretion to extend its frontiers to include the Saar coalfield and in addition the left bank of the Rhine should become a separate state. The Russians were prepared to agree if the French would give them a free hand to decide their western frontiers and this Briand conceded in a note in March 1917. Thus the Russians obtained formal support for the ideas Sazonov had explored in September 1914. Ironically, the agreement came on the eve of the first Russian Revolution and the abdication of Nicholas II. Had Imperial Russia survived to join in the defeat of Germany she could have presented her allies with extensive claims.

While the European Allies thus bargained and intrigued another actor was performing on a different stage. Japan delivered an ultimatum to Germany and declared war on 23 August 1914, despite an attempt by the British to keep her out. Unlike her Allies Japan knew precisely what she wanted – the German possessions in the Far East and a predominant influence in China. She quickly occupied the German islands to the north of the equator and the German-leased territory in Shantung, but then concentrated on improving her position in China. In January 1915 she presented to the Chinese government the so-called 'Twenty-one Demands'. If accepted in their original form they would have secured Japan's control over Shantung, extended her economic influence in China, prevented further cession of Chinese coastal territory to other states and forced China to employ Japanese advisers. When the full details leaked out diplomatic pressure, especially from Britain, forced Japan to retreat. Nevertheless, a modified version of the demands was accepted by China in May, but without the requirement to employ Japanese advisers. Just over a year later, in July 1916, Japan signed a treaty with Russia which confirmed their respective interests in China and promised cooperation against any third power which might be hostile to those interests. By implication this meant the United States, the only challenger in the absence of the European powers. But the Lansing-Ishii agreement of November 1917 recognized that Japan had a special interest in China 'especially the part to which her possessions are contiguous'. To Japan this was virtual recognition of her pre-eminent role. In February 1917 she obtained formal British agreement that she should take over Shantung and the German islands north of the equator after the war, largely because the British wanted her to send a naval squadron to the Mediterranean. Thus Japan was playing the imperialist game just as cleverly as the Europeans and was building up a position which would threaten their interests in the Far East. During 1916 Japan made some contact with Germany through Stockholm; there was talk of an arrangement between the two involving Russian withdrawal from the war. Nothing came of this in the end but Japan was clearly prepared to follow an independent line.

At the end of 1916, however, it was the United States rather than Japan that was the main concern of the European rivals. Although her existing army was small, her naval and economic strength would make her a formidable opponent. It was as a mediator, however, that President Wilson saw his chief role. His emissary Colonel House had visited Europe in 1915 and 1916. On the latter occasion he appeared (in February) to have reached an agreement with the British Foreign Secretary Sir Edward Grey: at a suitable moment Britain and France would ask Wilson to call a peace conference. If Germany refused or the conference failed the United States would enter the war on the Allied side. Wilson qualified this by saying the United States would 'probably' enter the war, but even so his willingness to go so far is surprising in the light of his public statements about American neutrality. He was not in fact called upon to take action. The British Cabinet agreed in March not to follow up the agreement. House appears to have misunderstood the degree of enthusiasm which the British felt for a proposal that would have to be sold to France and Russia.

After Wilson's re-election in November it was highly likely that he would attempt to mediate or make some other peace proposal. The central powers were themselves contemplating a peace initiative but found it difficult to agree about timing and terms. The Austrians tried vainly in October and November to get the Germans to agree to concessions in the west, but Bethmann's hands were tied by the military. The latter wanted the proposal to originate from a position of strength and if it produced no result they were ready to contemplate the resumption of unrestricted submarine warfare against merchant shipping. An earlier campaign had been abandoned in the face of American protests in May 1916, but the German navy thought the submarine could starve Britain into submission and Hindenburg and Ludendorff agreed. The resumption of unrestricted warfare might well bring America into the war, but too late to save Britain. If German submarines could gain command of the Atlantic it would be difficult, if not impossible, to ferry American troops to Europe.

Bethmann gained a breathing space, however, and the defeat of Rumania seemed an opportune moment to make a peace proposal. The German note was transmitted to the United States embassy in

Berlin on 12 December 1916. It asked the Americans to convey to the Allies the willingness of the central powers to negotiate, but no specific terms were mentioned. The proposal was a damp squib; there was nothing in it to tempt the Allies and it was overtaken by Wilson's note to all the belligerents of 18 December inviting them to state their war aims. Both sides claimed to be fighting in a just cause; Wilson sought to clarify what divided them and to see if it was negotiable. In this he failed but his approach had two important consequences; the central powers were put at a tactical disadvantage and the Allies were pushed into some public but still rather general commitments. Unable to take a definite line in public, Bethmann tried to revive the idea of a direct meeting between the belligerents and an American attempt to get anything more specific out of him failed. The Allied reply of 10 January 1917, although carefully general in its commitments, appeared by comparison both more precise and more principled: Belgium and Serbia were to be restored with indemnities; the occupied territories of France, Russia and Rumania were to be evacuated and 'just reparation' paid. So far so good; the Allies could scarely say less. But they also called for the liberation of Italians, Slavs, Rumanians and Czechs from foreign domination. This was not intended to mean the break-up of Austria-Hungary, although that was how it was in fact interpreted in Vienna. The Allies assumed at this stage that liberation could be achieved by some form of autonomy. In the case of Turkey they were more specific, calling for her expulsion from Europe and for the liberation of her subject peoples. This neatly skated over the commitments made in the secret treaties. In deference to Russian susceptibilities they were cautious about the future of Poland and fell back on a recent proclamation by the Tsar that he would create a free Poland.

In an address to the Senate on 22 January Wilson showed more approval of the Allied response than of the evasion of the central powers. But he now made clear that he did not see any peace settlement as simply a matter of tinkering here and there to restore the status quo. There must be a new international order which did not rest on force or on the balance of power and such a new order would be dependent on American support. Wilson's willingness to rearrange the European system was not well received by either side, nor was his use of the phrase 'peace without victory'. There was a clear warning here that if America became involved in either fighting or peacemaking she would not be simply a cat's-paw of the European powers. But the full significance of Wilson's attitude was concealed at the time by the German decision, made on 9 January, to resume unrestricted submarine warfare from the end of the month. The effect on the United States was only to be expected. She broke off relations with Germany in February and declared war in April (though not on Austria until December). However, she joined the war as an associate, not as an ally. Wilson had his reservations about the Allies and was determined to keep his distance from them. He was not necessarily committed to their specific and individual aims.

American entry did not immediately improve Allied prospects. The submarine campaign failed in the end but for the first half of the year it seriously worried the British. Mutinies broke out in the French army in May, and October brought the Italian defeat at Caporetto. Most serious of all was the collapse of the Tsarist regime in March. The Provisional Government set up in its place sought to maintain some role in the war, but it was strongly challenged by the Petrograd Soviet which echoed the call for an early peace without victory. The Allies were now faced with the danger of the collapse of the Eastern Front and a transfer of German troops to the west. After Lenin was helped by the Germans to return to Russia from his Swiss exile in April the further threat loomed of a Bolshevik take-over. This would produce a government committed to revolution as well as to ending the war. The Provisional Government got the worst of both worlds: to appease the Petrograd Soviet it urged a negotiated peace on the Allies without effect. It then tried to demonstrate that it was still militarily effective by launching an offensive in June but this petered out after some initial success.

Not that all went entirely smoothly for the central powers in 1917. Under Allied pressure King Constantine of Greece abdicated in June and the country broke off relations with the central powers. There were strikes in Berlin and mutinies in the German fleet. The Reichstag peace resolution of 19 July called for 'a peace of understanding'. It had no immediate effect on German policy but it indicated a mood of doubt about whether the decisive blow could be struck. It was, however, the Austrians who were now most seriously worried. The longer the war dragged on the greater the risk of the empire disintegrating, especially if the Allies openly supported the various nationalities. Emperor Charles made contact with the Allies through his brother-in-law, Prince Sixtus, who was serving in the Belgian army. But Charles was acting without the full knowledge of his own officials and Sixtus proved an unreliable reporter of the Austrian position. The ideas of following up with an approach to Austria for a separate peace was rejected at the St Jean de Maurienne meeting in April 1917. The Italians were not given the full story of the Sixtus approach but were on principle opposed to any arrangement which might deprive them of their gains under the treaty of London. Charles was in no position to make a separate peace and his officials were not in favour of abandoning Germany, whatever their reservations about her. Britain and France continued to put out feelers in the hope of enticing the Austrians. In December Smuts, a prominent figure in South Africa and now in the Imperial War Cabinet, had conversations in Switzerland with the Austrian diplomat Count

Mensdorff, but these revealed the same difficulty. The Allies were looking for a separate peace; the Austrians saw themselves as possible brokers between Germany and the Allies in a more general settlement. Meanwhile the Allies were increasingly being pushed towards support of self-determination for the subject nationalities. By the end of 1917 this was most obvious in the case of the Poles and the Czechs. Arrangements were made to recruit Polish and Czech armies to serve under French command on the Western Front. The Allies had official dealings with the Polish and Czech National Committees (set up in August 1917 and January 1916 respectively) although not yet recognizing them as provisional governments. Some Croat and Slovene exiles had set up a Yugoslav Committee in London in 1915, but the Allies continued to deal mainly with the Serbian government over possible changes in the Balkans. In the Declaration of Corfu of July 1917 the Serbs and the Yugoslav Committee agreed on the creation of a Serb, Croat and Slovene kingdom under the Serbian royal family. Italy was not happy to see a potential rival on the other side of the Adriatic but the overall implications for Austria-Hungary tended to outweigh this problem.

Such aspirations were still in the future and it looked doubtful at the end of 1917 if they could be attained. In November the Bolsheviks had seized power in Russia and in the following month they signed an armistice with Germany. The Rumanians followed suit a few days later. The Allies were thus released from their treaty commitments to both but at the same time this seemed small consolation. Germany could impose a settlement in Eastern Europe and make one more attempt at a knockout blow against Britain and France before American troops arrived in large numbers in Europe.

The Bolsheviks had made no secret since March of their view that Russia should leave what they saw as an imperialist war. They were prepared to negotiate with Germany, since she seemed to be the more immediate threat, on the assumption that a rapid spread of revolution would soon undermine the German position. In this they were wrong, at least in the short term, and although Lenin soon realized there was no alternative to accepting a punitive peace, it took a renewed German offensive in February 1918 to convince most of his colleagues of the futility of resistance. By the treaty of Brest-Litovsk, signed on 3 March 1918, Russia lost Finland, the Baltic provinces, Poland and the Ukraine – the central powers intended to decide the ultimate fate of these areas themselves. It is important not to overlook two supplementary treaties signed in Berlin on 27 August. Russia now had to give up Georgia as well and agreed to pay an indemnity of 6,000 million marks. Here too the hard-pressed Bolsheviks had little choice. Not only was the internal situation in Russia extremely confused but Allied intervention had increased steadily since British marines had landed at Murmansk in March 1918, ironically at the request of the local Soviet. (The latter had feared an attack from German troops stationed in Finland.) The Bolsheviks needed aid against the Allies and the Germans did not wish to lose their newly-won dominance.

A settlement was reached with Rumania in the treaty of Bucharest of 7 May after some squabbling among the central powers. The lack of agreement over Poland made the Austrians anxious for compensation in Rumania. The Bulgarians wanted the whole of the Dobrudja; this led the Turks to demand compensation from Bulgaria in the shape of territory lost during the Balkan wars. A compromise was reached in the end. Bulgaria obtained the southern Dobrudja and the rest of the territory was to be jointly administered by the four allies, pending a final settlement. Rumania had to agree to pay the full cost of the occupation forces, to supply surplus agricultural production to the central powers, to cede territory to Austria-Hungary and to allow Germany a dominant position in her oil industry. The eastern settlement as a whole showed clearly the degree of dominance Germany expected to gain from victory and the extent to which Austria would have to play a minor role.

The two Russian revolutions and the Bolshevik publication of the secret treaties had a marked effect on public opinion in the Allied states. There was a call for a redefinition of war aims, and demands that the Allies show themselves to be fighting in a just cause. The gloomy military situation intensified these doubts, especially before the extent of German ambitions in eastern Europe became clear. It was against this background that the Balfour Declaration of 2 November 1917 announced British support for a Jewish national home in Palestine, thus adding another commitment to Britain's already complicated position in the Middle East. The Declaration was aimed partly at American Jewry and partly at encouraging Russian Jews to support the Provisional Government. Sponsorship of a Jewish state would give a respectable reason for British rather than international control over Palestine. Once again short-term considerations created long-term problems.

Allied opinion was in fact much more influenced by the speeches of Lloyd George and Wilson in January 1918, than by the implications of the Balfour Declaration. Addressing a trade union audience in London on 5 January the British Prime Minister denied that Allied policy aimed to destroy the central powers as states or to bring about political changes inside Germany. Instead he called for self-government for the nationalities within Austria-Hungary; for the non-Turkish nationalities within the Ottoman Empire he used an ambiguous formula which amounted to much the same thing. He was still trying to maintain the public position that the Allies were not committed to outright independence. On Italian and Rumanian claims he was equally cautious; it was over Poland that he called most specifically for independence. The Allies were anxious not to be left behind by German or Bolshevik promises to the Poles. In its aim of reassuring British trade unionists and the Labour Party the speech was on the whole a success. Internationally, however, it was eclipsed by Wilson's speech to Congress on 8 January, in which he enunciated the Fourteen Points.

Wilson was less concerned than Lloyd George with domestic political considerations. He particularly hoped to influence the Bolsheviks into renewed support of the Allies by showing that the United States stood for certain principles. She had not been a party to the secret treaties and had made no claim for annexations or spheres of influence. Some of Wilson's aims were unlikely to please the Allies. Freedom of the seas, for example, had been a sore point with the British prior to American entry into the war. But America's naval strength and the growth in her merchant marine during Wilson's period in office meant that there was bound to be some rivalry with Britain, even in peacetime. The call for an impartial adjustment of colonial claims was bound to annoy not only the European Allies but also Japan and the British dominions, who wanted their share of German colonies in Africa and the Pacific. The emphasis on open diplomacy was intended to answer Bolshevik criticisms of war aims and to rebuke the Allies for their secret treaties. Disarmament was not a theme which either side had particularly emphasized hitherto and the Bolsheviks had given it scant mention. Thus Wilson was anxious to enunciate general principles before making specific recommendations. He urged the evacuation of occupied Russian territory and sought to gain Bolshevik sympathy by saying that Russia should be allowed to choose her own institutions. In this he was more positive than Lloyd George, who had taken the line that the Russians would be left to their fate if they chose to make a separate peace. (In early January the negotiations at Brest-Litovsk had not made much progress, so there was still some hope of keeping Russia away from Germany.) But a good deal of what he proposed was similar to what Lloyd George had said: Belgium and Serbia must regain their independence; the French had a claim to Alsace-Lorraine; Austria-Hungary should continue to exist but its nationalities must gain autonomy. Over Italian claims he was equally cautious but went further than Lloyd George in his support for Polish independence, particularly in saying that any Polish state must have access to the sea. He made an implied criticism of the secret treaties when he said that Turkey proper must retain a secure sovereignty. There was therefore a good deal of common ground between the two speeches but also some very important differences of emphasis. It was noticeable that Wilson laid great stress on international guarantees for some of his proposals and in his fourteenth point he called specifically for an international organization to guarantee the independence and integrity of small as well as large states. (For the origins and development of the League of Nations see Chapter 7.) As in his speech of almost a year earlier, Wilson made clear that he saw any peace settlement as a means of restructuring the international system and of putting restraints on the major powers. The Allies had a clear warning that he was not tied to the arrangements they had made among themselves. Up to a point the British were prepared to go along with him; France and Italy would take some persuading. Neither saw a great need to enunciate principles. The French wanted to keep their options open, the Italians to obtain all that had been promised them. The Fourteen Points therefore implied future conflict between Wilson and his European colleagues.

Whatever Lloyd George and Wilson might say about not seeking to dismember Turkey and Austria-Hungary, the implication of their statements was that at best Turkey would be restricted to Asia Minor and the western side of the Dardanelles. It would be difficult to maintain the integrity of Austria-Hungary if the subject nationalities received a substantial degree of autonomy. The pact of Corfu had envisaged a South Slav state. A Polish state with boundaries still undefined would presumably include Galicia, and what was conceded to Poland (and Serbia) could hardly be denied to the Czechs. France in June 1918, the United States and Britain in September of that year, conceded a degree of recognition to the Czech National Committee which made it virtually a provisional government, though no specific boundaries were mentioned. This development was the result of events in Russia. There were large numbers of Czech prisoners-of-war and deserters in Russian hands and after the collapse of the Tsarist regime the National Committee hoped to bring them out through Vladivostock and move them to France. But the Czech troops found themselves caught up in the confused situation in Russia. Clashes with Bolshevik troops in May raised the possibility of using them to recreate an Eastern Front and to overthrow the Bolsheviks. At the very least the Czechs should be rescued. It was this situation which drew Wilson into intervention despite his earlier objections. During the summer Allied forces arrived at both Archangel and Vladivostock in addition to the forces already in Murmansk. Full-scale civil war was now raging in Russia and the anti-Bolshevik and anti-German aims of the Allies became considerably confused. That apart, open support for the Czech National Committee was a further threat to the integrity of Austria-Hungary.

The Allies failed to realize how soon they would be confronted by the problems of peacemaking. The German offensives in France were held and by August the Allies had launched a counter-offensive, but they did not fully grasp the weak position of the central powers.

An Austrian proposal in September for general negotiations in a neutral country was rejected. At the end of the month the first crack came when Bulgaria signed an armistice. On 3 October Germany asked America for an armistice on the basis of the Fourteen Points. The Germans had some hope that their forces would be allowed to stand their ground and thus gain a breathing space, but in this they were disappointed. Wilson made clear that the Allies would expect arrangements that would enable them to maintain a clear military superiority. Although he informed his European colleagues of the first German note he did not formally consult them about armistice terms until 23 October. The main difficulty was that the Allies had not in fact accepted the Fourteen Points as a basis for peace negotiations, and there was a good deal of argument at a meeting in Paris from 29 October until 4 November. House, representing Wilson, found it necessary to hint that the United States might pull out of the war. The chief sticking-point was the British objection to concessions on the freedom of the seas. It was finally agreed that this point could be discussed at the peace conference. The Allies also wanted to keep open possible reparations claims, since Wilson in the Fourteen Points had spoken only of restitution. The way was now clear for armistice terms to be offered to Germany, but Wilson's independent handling of the negotiations was another warning of possible trouble at the peace conference. A similar problem appeared over the armistice signed with Turkey on 30 October. The French bitterly resented the way in which the British had excluded them from the negotiations. Anglo-French distrust had never been far from the surface, especially over their rival ambitions in Turkey and the Middle East.

An armistice was signed with Austria-Hungary on 3 November but events had already overtaken it. A South Slav state had been proclaimed on 17 October (the triple kingdom of the Corfu Declaration did not appear until December). A Czechoslovak republic was proclaimed on 30 October and a Polish republic in Cracow on 6 November. The Hohenzollern and Habsburg dynasties disappeared with remarkable swiftness. Under some pressure from the Army, William II abdicated on 9 November. It was hoped that without him Germany would gain a more lenient peace. The Emperor Charles followed him on 12 November. The pace of events had run ahead of the Allies and decisions were being taken on the spot. They had assumed the war would continue into 1919, and had not yet prepared themselves mentally or physically for a full-scale peace settlement. Promises made in the secret treaties would have to be honoured in a situation more complex than anticipated when the agreements were signed. Traditional diplomacy would have to accommodate itself to the Wilsonian approach, and to the threat of a Bolshevik revolution.

CHAPTER THREE
The Paris Peace Conference and its aftermath, 1919–1923

The arrangements for a peace conference got under way at the end of 1918 against a background of economic dislocation and political uncertainty. It was at least clear that to the problems of settlement in Europe would be added an ideological contest with Bolshevik Russia. Despite the German surrender, Allied forces continued their operations in various parts of Russia in support of anti-Bolshevik groups. Lenin and his colleagues found the removal of the German threat only a partial relief. Equally, the peacemakers who assembled in Paris brought with them in varying degrees a fear of revolution in Central and Eastern Europe in addition to the many other problems that faced them.

Nor did they come to Paris with completely free hands or secure political positions at home. In the mid-term elections in the United States, Wilson's appeal to the electorate to support the Democrats had failed. On 5 November the Republicans gained control of both Houses of Congress and thus of the vital Senate Foreign Relations Committee. Not all Republicans were out-and-out isolationists, but personal antipathy to Wilson sharpened their doubts about his intention to commit the United States to a general reconstruction of the international system. Defeat did not lead Wilson, however, to seek a bi-partisan policy or to cultivate the Foreign Relations Committee. Instead he relied more and more on his own judgement and on those whom he personally trusted. He arrived in Europe in December with enormous prestige but increasingly lacking the domestic power to match it.

At first sight Lloyd George was in a stronger position. He used the opportunity of victory to call an election in December which gave an enormous majority to his coalition government. In the process, however, he had split the Liberal Party and left himself dangerously dependent on the Conservatives. The mood of the election campaign was not as vindictive as it has usually been depicted, but there was nevertheless general support for a harsh peace against Germany, which limited Lloyd George's freedom of action in negotiation. Despite differences of view within the coalition he and his colleagues shared certain assumptions. Britain must ensure the ending of the German colonial empire and the strengthening of her own position in the Middle East, not least because of pressures from her dominions and the government of India. The corollary of this was the limitation of commitments in Europe, especially in eastern Europe: Germany had not been defeated in order to create a French predominance. It was important to retain American goodwill and support; this made it necessary to show a degree of qualified approval for Wilsonian idealism. Britain must therefore seek to maintain good relations with both France and the United States without totally committing herself to either.

There was here some failure to grasp how far Britain herself had been weakened by the war and to understand the extent of French insecurity. For Clemenceau, victory had given France a short-term advantage which she must exploit before Germany's larger population and greater economic strength reasserted themselves. Russia could no longer be counted on as a potential ally; with Britain and Italy there were possible sources of friction; to Clemenceau's sceptical mind the Fourteen Points were no substitute for a predominance of power. Germany could not be destroyed, but she could be militarily and economically weakened. France in any case badly needed money for reconstruction, so heavy reparations could serve a dual purpose. Although he gained an impressive vote of confidence from the Chamber of Deputies at the end of December and kept his hands free of definite commitments, the French Prime Minister had to bear in mind strong pressures for a punitive peace and also the loss of morale which had shown itself in the 1917 mutinies, not to mention his many enemies in French politics. (They were to prevent his election to the presidency in 1920.)

Orlando, Prime Minister of Italy since October 1917, was in a weaker position than his colleagues. The war had increased his country's financial burdens and sharpened the political divisions which, even before 1915, had threatened the shaky parliamentary system. Defeat at Caporetto had further undermined the reputation of Italian politicians and had been only partly offset by the successful offensive of 1918. Any Italian prime minister would have to insist on the fulfilment of the treaty of London, especially with the appearance of a South Slav state as a rival in the Adriatic. Orlando was in any case strongly influenced by his Foreign Minister Sonnino in whom inflexibility and distrust of the Slavs were equally combined. Victory over Austria had produced near-hysteria among the Italian Right and Nationalist groups. Their attention focused on the port of Fiume, which had been specifically reserved in the treaty of London for a possible Croatian state, but whose acquisition now became a symbol of Italian prestige. Following the armistice with Austria-Hungary, Italian troops had occupied Fiume and in other places had moved well beyond the line agreed in the treaty of London. Other Allied troops appeared in Fiume but the Italians remained the dominant element. Military presence on the ground gave Orlando some advantage, yet he went to Paris unable to offer concessions and seeking more than Italy's original bargain.

Such was the background against which the first plenary session of the peace conference met on 18 January 1919. The timing and structure of the conference were the result of haphazard developments rather than any overall plan. Wilson decided to attend in person, thus becoming the first American president to go abroad on affairs of state while still in office. Doubts were expressed both in the United States and in Europe, but it is difficult to see how Wilson could have remained in Washington while others negotiated on his behalf. He did not feel confidence in Lansing, the Secretary of State, and House was somewhat too willing to compromise for the sake of smoothing things over. The President, however, could not leave until Congress had met in early December and the British election put Lloyd George out of action until the New Year. It would take the Japanese delegation some time to make the sea trip from Tokyo and there was also the problem of ensuring that the governments established in the former enemy states were capable of making and keeping treaty engagements.

The choice of Paris was largely the result of Clemenceau's advocacy, for the other leaders had some doubts about meeting in the excited and partisan atmosphere of the French capital; but suggestions of a neutral meeting place such as Geneva were soon dropped. Originally there was some thought of producing a preliminary settlement to be followed by a full-scale conference; the slow and piecemeal progress made at Paris forced the tacit abandonment of this idea. To begin with, the main organ of the conference was the Council of Ten, composed of two representatives each from America, Britain, France, Italy and Japan. This somewhat unwieldy body gave way in late March to a Council of Four to which Japan was admitted on matters that directly concerned her. (The Japanese delegation took little interest in European affairs.) The foreign ministers of the Five met as a separate body to deal with lesser and more routine matters. After the signature of the treaty with Germany on 28 June the major political personalities soon disappeared from the scene and a Council of Heads of Delegations became the principal decision-making body for most of the remainder of the conference. (It formally ended in January 1920.) Thus four or five powers dominated the discussions and the defeated states were excluded, only being summoned when the treaties applying to them had been completed. It was feared that their participation would allow them to play on divisions among the Allies. Neutral states, despite their protests, played only a limited role in matters which directly concerned them.

The most contentious period of the conference was that prior to the signing of the German treaty, with April the worst month for arguments among the Allies. Wilson launched discussion of the League of Nations as early as February. He wanted the constitution of the new organization to be an integral part of the treaties in order to demonstrate that the settlement would be based on rules and principles. The European Allies had their reservations about the effectiveness of the League but were not prepared to oppose the principle of its creation. After some argument and a few amendments the Covenant of the League was approved by a plenary session on 28 April. The fundamental arguments came over the treatment of Germany, the Italian claim to Fiume and the Japanese position in Shantung. On Germany Clemenceau showed a willingness to retreat from his maximum position and to compromise. He accepted a time limit for the occupation of the Rhineland instead of insisting on a permanent one and retreated from the idea of separate Rhineland states. He agreed to temporary control of the Saar coalfields instead of outright annexation by France. In return he gained the seemingly significant promise of help from Britain and the United States. On the same day as the German treaty was signed, Britain and America signed treaties of guarantee promising military help if Germany attacked France. There was, however, an important qualification: each treaty would only come into force when the other was ratified, so that if either the United States or Britain failed to ratify the other would be released from its obligation.

Nevertheless, in terms of military security Clemenceau could feel he had made some progress. On the economic side the situation was less satisfactory. The Americans made clear early on that they were unwilling to provide money for European reconstruction, which made it all the more important to reach agreement on reparations. This topic soon proved a source of difficulties and ambiguities. Did reparations cover only damage done directly in areas occupied by Germany? If so, France would be entitled to a much larger share than Britain. If reparations were to be calculated on a wider basis how much was to be included? The Allies agreed that pensions for the wounded and disabled should be included, thus greatly increasing the sums likely to be demanded. This in turn raised the question of how much to ask for: should the total be based on Germany's assumed liability or on her capacity to pay; however that might be calculated? The Americans and the French came close to agreeing on a specific sum to be quoted in the treaty, but Britain would not agree. Although prepared to be moderate on other matters, Lloyd George seemed to prefer a harsh reparations settlement and not just because of parliamentary pressure. The upshot was that no fixed figure was mentioned in the German treaty. Instead a Reparations Commission was to be set up to decide on an agreed sum by May 1921. Before then Germany was to pay something on account both in money and in kind. The Commission would not be required to take into account capacity to pay, though the principles on which it would operate were left rather vague. It has to be remembered that the United States was expected to remain on the Commission and to have a major influence over it, but even so the main difficulties were merely being postponed.

Wilson was prepared to concede the Italian claim to the Trentino and to the South Tyrol right up to the Brenner Pass, thus putting a large German-speaking minority under Italian rule. Here he seems to have allowed the argument for a strategic frontier to outweigh the ethnic argument. Over Fiume, however, he would not yield and went as far as to appeal to the Italian people over Orlando's head on 23 April. This attempt at open diplomacy backfired; Orlando left the conference next day and returned to Rome in triumph. Under some pressure from the Allies he came back to the conference on 6 May but this produced no compromise. Partly because of his failure to score a diplomatic success and partly because of domestic unrest, Orlando fell from power on 19 June. His successor Nitti had no greater success in Paris and the Italian government's increasing lack of control was demonstrated when D'Annunzio with a group of adventurers seized Fiume in September and defied the regular Italian garrison. Italy's attitude had largely lost her the support of the major powers and she found herself also increasingly under pressure to evacuate Albania, which she did in July 1920, formally recognizing that country's independence in the following month. By the treaty of Rapallo in November Italy gave up most of her claims in Dalmatia and agreed that Fiume should become a free city. D'Annunzio was driven out in December. It had proved easier, though not palatable, to negotiate directly with Yugoslavia. These defeats in foreign policy contributed to Mussolini's seizure of power at the end of October 1922. Although he annexed Fiume in March 1924 he had to accept, for the time being at least, that hopes of expansion in Dalmatia would have to be abandoned and that Yugoslavia would have to be tolerated, though not loved.

The Fiume episode soured the atmosphere of the peace conference and left the Italians with a sense of dissatisfaction and betrayal, however unjustified this might have been. It also had an important influence on the Shantung question. Foiled in an attempt to have a declaration on racial equality written into the League Covenant, the Japanese dug in their heels over Shantung and insisted on taking over the German concession. Had they too left the conference as had the Italians then the Allies would have been publicly revealed as in considerable disarray, and this was something Wilson could not risk. At the end of April it was agreed that Japan would succeed to German rights but would eventually restore Chinese sovereignty in the province. This was perhaps the best Wilson could do but it was not enough to satisfy the Chinese delegation. Having entered the war in 1917, China, they argued, had a right to regain the former German holdings. Nor did they place much faith in Japanese promises. As a result they refused to sign the treaty with Germany. There was considerable resentment in China at the attitude of America and the European powers; Japan had gained her point but was unhappy at failing to obtain a declaration on racial equality; in the United States there was considerable criticism of Wilson's handling of the Shantung question. Thus there was a compromise which in fact satisfied nobody.

The other European treaties caused fewer problems but were not entirely free from difficulty. The treaty of Neuilly was signed with Bulgaria on 27 November 1919; the treaty of St Germain was signed with Austria on 10 September 1919 and the treaty of Trianon with Hungary on 4 June 1920. Bulgaria lost territory to Yugoslavia and to Greece and as a result was deprived of direct access to the Aegean. She made a claim to retain the Southern Dobrudja but to concede that would have implied condoning the treaty of Bucharest, although on ethnic grounds Bulgaria had a case. The Austrian Republic claimed the right to be regarded as a new state and not as the successor of Austria-Hungary but the Allies rejected this argument. Furthermore they prohibited union with Germany. Austria was thus left in a financially weak position, cut off from her former empire, and aggrieved by the existence of German-speaking minorities in the South Tyrol and in Czechoslovakia. There was little she could do about it, however, and the same was true of Hungary. The latter complained bitterly about the loss of territory to Czechoslovakia, Rumania and Yugoslavia which also involved the loss of substantial Magyar minorities to all three. It was precisely their fear of Hungarian irredentism which brought the three states together by various agreements in 1920 and 1921, in what became known as the 'Little Entente'. Thus Hungary and to a lesser extent Bulgaria were contained and could do little without outside assistance. The French had shown some interest in an agreement with Hungary during 1920 and although nothing came of this it was an important factor in the timing of the Little Entente's creation.

The settlement with Turkey was quite a different matter. Here a major treaty was to be soon overturned by a nationalist movement which directly challenged the Allies. The treaty of Sèvres was signed with the Sultan's government on 10 August 1920. It confirmed that the Ottoman Empire would lose its Arab lands which, after some haggling, Britain and France had agreed to share between them. The mandate system which emerged from the discussions on the League of Nations enabled the two powers to give a spurious respectability to their ambitions. Instead of outright annexation they could claim to be advancing the inhabitants of the Middle East towards full independence. Britain was to have mandates for Iraq and Palestine, thus acquiring more than had been envisaged under the Sykes-Picot agreement, whereas the French were to be confirmed as mandatories for Syria and Lebanon. Despite Arab protests these arrangements went ahead.

In the case of Turkey itself imperialism was more blatant. Constantinople and the Straits would come under international control and a financial commission would exercise considerable control over the Turkish economy. By a separate agreement signed on the same day France and Italy delimited their spheres of influence in Turkey. These elements could be traced back to the wartime agreements, but a new factor in the situation was that part of the treaty of Sèvres gave Greece a zone of administration round Smyrna, for five years in the first instance. The Greek Prime Minister, Venizelos, had made a good impression at the peace conference and he was one of those who had long hoped to create a 'Greater Greece' in Asia Minor. His opportunity seemed to have come in May 1919. The Italians, already at odds with their allies over Fiume, seemed to be contemplating an occupation of Smyrna. The Greeks could be used to head them off and help in occupying a major port. Although the Allies had forces in the Straits they had little control over the interior and the Sultan's government itself was no better off, so Greek assistance was welcome.

The landing at Smyrna on 15 May stimulated an Italian landing in Adalia, but much more important was the nationalist reaction which it provoked. Kemal rapidly emerged as the leader of a movement pledged to maintain the integrity of Turkey proper, though accepting the loss of the Arab lands. By the end of 1919 the Nationalists effectively controlled most of the interior. As the details of the Sèvres treaty were worked out during 1920, it became clear that the Nationalists would have to be defeated if it were to be imposed. Here again the Greeks seemed to be the answer, and it was the success of their offensive in July which induced the Constantinople government to sign the treaty, albeit unwillingly. The Nationalists had not, however, been completely defeated and the Greeks maintained their attempt to control the area round Smyrna. Needless to say, the Nationalists would accept neither this nor the treaty of Sèvres. Greek intransigence was increased by the return of King Constantine in December 1920 and by the knowledge that they had the support of Lloyd George. As a result, attempts by the Allies to mediate at the London conference of February and March 1921 were a failure.

Italy and France began to disengage themselves from the Greeks and from Turkey. In October 1921 the French made an agreement which amounted to recognition of the Nationalist government. By then the Greeks had failed in an effort to defeat the Nationalists in a three-week battle on the Sakkaria river which exhausted both sides. But neither would accept another attempt at mediation by Britain, France and Italy in March 1922. By now the Greeks were politically almost isolated and lacking the military resources to maintain themselves indefinitely. In August the Turks launched an offensive which brought them to Smyrna in early September. This success marked the end of Greek ambitions and it brought the danger of a clash with Allied forces in the Straits. Lloyd George was prepared to fight but the French and the Italians were not. Nor were the dominions, with the exception of New Zealand, prepared to become involved in a possible war with Turkey. There was no choice but to invite the Nationalists to talk peace. The upshot was the Lausanne conference which produced a treaty and various other documents on 21 July 1923. Turkey regained her territorial integrity and again assumed control of Constantinople. Spheres of interest and special foreign concessions disappeared. By a separate agreement Turkey and Greece agreed to a compulsory exchange of minorities which did at least remove one source of friction.

The episode led to the fall of Lloyd George and the second abdication of King Constantine. It illustrated how easily the major powers could become involved in smaller powers' ambitions and how difficult it was to get a smaller state to reverse direction. But it also showed how a determined nationalist movement could resist the ambitions of the powers and play on differences between them. The discord and distrust between Britain, France and Italy were clearly revealed. The first two at least kept their mandated territories in the Middle East, whereas the Italians came away empty-handed except for another grievance to fuel their resentment.

At the time the Graeco-Turkish war seemed to be something of a sideshow while the central part of the Paris settlement was the treaty with Germany: would Germany accept it and could it be enforced? The German delegation to Versailles had signed only with extreme reluctance, objecting to the so-called 'war guilt' clause, the prospect of heavy reparations and the proposed territorial losses in the east. Whatever the merits of their complaints, the Germans would no doubt have objected to almost any treaty presented to them. Their country had escaped direct occupation and they did not see themselves as defeated. They claimed to have accepted an armistice on the basis of the Fourteen Points and then to have been badly treated. It was difficult for most German politicians to accept that Germany would have to work her passage back to respectability before the

Allies could be expected to accept her as an equal. This attitude of resentment made it likely that there would be considerable evasion of, and resistance to, the treaty provisions. Why should the Germans be bound by what they regarded as a dictated peace?

Moreover, enforcement of the Versailles treaty was going to fall largely on France and Britain. Japan was not interested, Italy was disgruntled, and the United States Senate refused to ratify it. This was the biggest blow of all to the maintenance of the Paris settlement. Opposition in the Senate concentrated on America's commitments under the Covenant and little was said about the substantive terms of the treaty with Germany, although there was opposition to the clauses concerning Shantung. Wilson exhausted himself on a speaking tour in September 1919 designed to rally support for the League and suffered a severe stroke. By November the issue in the Senate had become a straightforward choice between accepting the treaty as it stood or with reservations intended to preserve American freedom of action under the Covenant. The stricken Wilson made clear his opposition to the reservations; on 19 November the original treaty and the treaty with reservations both failed to get even an ordinary majority. By the time of the second vote on 19 March 1920 it was clear that an unmodified treaty was unlikely to pass through the Senate but Wilson remained adamant in his opposition to any reservation. Nevertheless, the treaty with reservations received a majority vote but not the necessary two-thirds. It was thus lost, with the result that the United States would have to make a separate peace with Germany. A treaty was signed on 25 August 1921, not very different in content from the original treaty minus the Covenant.

The decision of the Senate meant that the United States would cease to participate in the execution of the Versailles treaty or would remain only as an observer. In February 1921 the American representative was withdrawn from the Reparations Commission, thus giving the French greater scope on that body than had been originally anticipated. Most important of all, however, was the fact that the Senate was now unlikely to consider the proposed treaty of guarantee to France; in fact it never did discuss the treaty. Britain was therefore absolved from her commitment, and France now found herself in an uncomfortable position with all the more incentive to pursue tough policies over control of the Rhineland and over reparations. Here she could expect support from Belgium, but from Britain a much more ambiguous attitude verging on hostility. The French authorities continued to flirt with the idea of Rhineland separation, and the extraction of reparations became an increasingly important means of keeping Germany weak. Occupation of the Ruhr or other parts of the east bank of the Rhine seemed an attractive sanction for ensuring payment or merely for putting pressure on Germany. The French first employed it in April 1920 because German forces had entered the demilitarized zone on the east bank without Allied permission, in order to suppress a left-wing rising. This was only a preliminary skirmish, however, for it was the attempt to extract reparations that launched an undeclared war between France and Germany.

During 1920 there was a good deal of rather inconclusive discussion. Britain was still vainly trying to induce France to agree on a fixed sum. Weak German governments, unable to exert effective influence over their own industrialists, were unwilling to commit themselves or to make concessions. Yet this very weakness was an advantage, for if Germany carried out thorough fiscal and budgetary reforms she might leave herself open to heavy claims. The Spa conference in July did at least produce agreement on coal deliveries by Germany to the Allies and on the proportions in which the Allies would divide reparations as a whole among themselves. The French were less than happy about the Spa coal arrangement, feeling that the British had rather pushed them into it, and they did try direct talks with the Germans which, however, came to nothing. In 1921 the atmosphere worsened as the Germans seemed to be continuing their delays and evasion. Angered by what they considered inadequate German proposals at the London conference of March 1921, the Allies authorized French occupation of Düsseldorf, Ruhrort and Duisberg. The British preferred such a limited move to a full-scale occupation of the Ruhr. Technically Germany was not in default on her interim deliveries at that stage, though she did fall into default later in the month.

A new stage was reached with the publication of the Reparations Commission report on 27 April, though its figures owed as much to the political negotiations among the Allies as to the work of financial experts. In all, Germany was to pay a sum equivalent to a face value of some £6,650 million in gold marks. In May the Allies transmitted a schedule of payments to Germany together with a demand for £50 million at once. The newly formed Wirth government complied at the end of the month but by December was having to ask for a moratorium on the payments due in January and February 1922. The British were on the whole sympathetic to this request, whereas the French were not – they argued that the Germans had been largely responsible for their own problems by failing to balance the budget. Moreover, by encouraging a fall in the value of the mark to lower export prices the Germans had made themselves responsible for its virtual collapse in November. The British could agree up to a point but did not wish to become involved in direct control of German finances or to give the French an excuse for intervention by declaring Germany in default. At the Cannes conference in January 1922 Lloyd George tried to head off Briand by producing a package which involved agreement on reparations, a general economic conference on European reconstruction and a limited political guarantee to France which would not cover eastern Europe. Opposition in the French Cabinet brought Briand's resignation and the abrupt collapse of the British proposals.

To meet the immediate problem the Reparations Commission granted a partial moratorium which was renewed in the course of the year. This did not please Poincaré, Briand's successor, but he was not initially as rigid and inflexible as some accounts have made out. In the course of 1922 he continued to face the difficulty of getting what France could regard as satisfactory concessions from Germany or a good working arrangement with Britain. The latter opposed Poincaré's idea of assigning certain German revenues and resources for reparation payments. Meanwhile another problem increasingly complicated the situation – inter-Allied debts. The United States had made clear that she would expect to be repaid her wartime loans to the Allies irrespective of any reparations settlement. A commission was set up in February 1922 under the American Secretary of the Treasury to seek agreements with her debtors: for the French, payment of reparations must come before the settlement of her debts; for Britain, who had lent more to the other Allies than she had borrowed from the United States, the position was rather different. The Balfour Note of 1 August 1922 was an attempt at a compromise: Britain would expect to receive from her debtors, including Germany, enough to cover her payments to America. This merely succeeded in irritating the French. The Americans did in fact reach an agreement with Britain in 1923 on repayment and with the other European Allies during the next few years, but at the time their policies tended to intensify the difficulties of the reparations question. For most of 1922 the American government did not favour the idea of an international loan to help stabilize German finances.

Lloyd George fell from power in October but this did not immediately improve matters. The Wirth government asked for a further moratorium, to run for three or four years, shortly before it too fell in November. Yet another London conference in December produced no result and on the 26th the Reparations Commission declared Germany in default on timber deliveries. France now had the technical justification for an occupation of the Ruhr, which she proceeded to carry out with assistance from Belgium. Britain stood aside and the American occupation forces in Koblenz were withdrawn in protest.

Although Poincaré had several times threatened such action he had been by no means determined to carry it out right from the start of his ministry. In fact the French soon found that military occupation alone did not guarantee control of the Ruhr's resources. The German government organized a system of passive resistance which forced the French and the Belgians into tighter military control. They treated the Rhineland and the Ruhr as an economic unit and sealed it off from the rest of Germany. It proved possible to extract some resources for removal to France and Belgium and to maintain a minimum railway service, which allowed in particular the movement of coal stocks, but this was only achieved at considerable cost to both the French and Belgian currencies. The Belgians were the more vulnerable of the two, and by June were beginning to argue for negotiations with Germany. The British sought some compromise and in October proposed to the Americans the setting up of a committee of experts to examine the reparations problem. Coolidge had succeeded to the presidency on Harding's death, and the new administration was more willing to take an initiative. Rather surprisingly, Poincaré agreed as well. In fact France had been feeling the cost of a struggle which left her diplomatically isolated and there was little point in seeking the economic collapse of Germany: the cost of passive resistance had completely undermined the mark and hyperinflation was threatening to destroy the social stability of Germany. Stresemann became both Chancellor and Foreign Minister in August and called off passive resistance at the end of September. Poincaré did not immediately respond to this move; indeed, in October the French and the Belgians encouraged coups by separatist movements, which soon proved to be failures. Neither France nor Germany had won this final round in the struggle. Military force alone could only extract reparations with difficulty and passive resistance involved enormous economic costs. This economic war of attrition was perhaps even more destructive for Germany than the military occupation.

Two committees were nevertheless set up at the end of November by the Reparations Commission, the more important being that chaired by the American General Dawes. Meeting in Paris from January to April 1924, it produced a report which was accepted by the London conference of July and August. Poincaré had lost office in May and his successor Herriot was in a weaker bargaining position. The outcome was the so-called Dawes Plan by which Germany would receive an international loan to help stabilize her currency and enable her to pay a modified scale of reparations. Thus American intervention had been necessary to resolve a contest between two of the European powers; Britain had disapproved but had been unable to mediate effectively. Within Germany not all political groups were satisfied with the arrangement but with Stresemann remaining in control of the Foreign Ministry after losing the chancellorship in November 1923 there seemed to be possibilities of a more consistent German foreign policy. Certainly a new start was needed in Franco-German relations, now that it was clear how difficult the enforcement of Versailles would be for the divided Allies.

Over the ultimate settlement inside Russia and along its borders the peace conference had only a limited influence. There was no Bolshevik delegation at Paris, yet the future of Russia was clearly of great importance for the overall European balance of power. It was not only a question of which group would win the internal struggle but also of whether Russia would avoid major losses of territory. There was a fear of Bolshevism, however ill-defined, as a threat to the economic and social order, a fear which gained some support from developments within Germany and from the short-lived regime of Bela Kun in Hungary. The problem of how to deal with revolution outside Russia depended on how the Allies would deal with Russia itself. Their motives for intervention after November 1917 had been mixed and to some extent competitive. Wilson, for example, saw a limited intervention as a means of restraining Japanese ambitions as well as rescuing the Czechs. The removal of the German element of the problem still left Allied policy muddled and indecisive. Were they to mediate or to pursue a policy of large-scale intervention and, if so, which of the anti-Bolshevik groups should they support?

The Bolshevik military and economic position at the end of 1918 was not good and they gave several indications that they were prepared to consider negotiations. The Allies could not agree to let them be represented at Paris – Wilson and Lloyd George were in favour, Clemenceau and Orlando against – but in January 1919 they did propose a meeting of all the rival groups on the Prinkipo Islands in the Sea of Marmara, provided there was a ceasefire first. The Bolsheviks accepted but without mentioning the proviso for a ceasefire; the White Russian groups jointly refused. In March William Bullitt, a young State Department official, was sent on a mission to Moscow which did in fact produce an offer of Bolshevik peace terms. But the arrangements for the mission had been ambiguous; it is not clear how far it was generally realized that Bullitt was not just going on a fact-finding mission and in the event he found his efforts disowned. Thus the Allies may have missed a favourable opportunity for a settlement before the Bolshevik position improved.

On the other hand they rejected the idea of massive intervention so strongly supported by Marshal Foch. Once again, as in the case of Turkey, they did not have the forces to operate on such a scale and there was strong opposition to intervention in Britain and France. Instead, evacuation got under way during 1919. Odessa was abandoned in April; American forces left Archangel in June and the last British forces evacuated North Russia in October. This did not mean total abandonment of the Whites. Since the various White groups had agreed by the end of May to recognize Admiral Kolchak as their supreme authority, the Allies promised him support in an exchange of notes, though stopping short of recognition. The timing was bad, for Kolchak's initial successes were to be followed from June onwards by defeat. The main threat to the Bolsheviks now came from Denikin's offensive in South Russia, but that too collapsed after initial successes. By the end of the Paris peace conference the tide was clearly running against the Whites. One of the last decisions of the conference in January 1920 was to end the blockade of Russia and to re-open trade.

During 1920 the Russian Civil War sputtered out and the last Allied contigents left with the exception of the Japanese who did not evacuate Vladivostock until October 1922. The Americans withdrew from that port in April 1920 and the last British troops left Batum in the Caucasus in July. Admiral Kolchak had been executed in February but the threats to the Bolsheviks had not yet disappeared, for the Poles launched a full-scale attack on the Ukraine in April. The Poles had in general pursued a policy of seeking the maximum possible territorial gains. On the frontier with Germany they were bound, however unwillingly, by the decisions of the peace conference. Although they gained a corridor of territory that gave them access to the sea and acquired special rights in the free city of Danzig, they were unhappy with the partition of Upper Silesia agreed in 1921 and with the settlement of the Teschen dispute with Czechoslovakia in July 1920. On the eastern frontier, however, the unsettled situation in Russia and the fluid nature of the boundaries offered opportunities for expansion. Vilna was seized from Lithuania in October 1920 but the great prize was control of the Ukraine. Polish relations with the Bolsheviks had not been good since the end of the German war but the Polish attack was not strictly speaking part of the Russian Civil War and intervention. Like the other struggles in Russia it ebbed and flowed with great rapidity: in May the Poles captured Kiev only to be driven back nearly to Warsaw in August, before a counteroffensive forced the Russians to retreat. Anxious to finish off the White remnants in the Crimea, the Russians agreed to peace talks in September. The treaty of Riga of March 1921 gave Poland large Ukrainian and Byelorussian minorities. The Bolsheviks were not entirely happy but for the moment their frontier with Poland was defined. In the course of 1920 they had signed treaties which recognized the independence of the Baltic states and of Finland, but they refused to recognize the loss of Bessarabia, which had declared itself independent in January 1918 and had been later absorbed by Rumania. It was therefore by no means certain how long the settlement of Russia's western frontiers would last.

The Bolsheviks had survived with their worst suspicions of the capitalist powers confirmed. Distinctions between limited and all-out intervention might have been significant to the Allies; what mattered to Lenin and his colleagues was that intervention had taken place and might be renewed. Revolution had not spread through Europe and Russia was therefore isolated. She had to develop some kind of foreign policy to meet this unexpected situation. It made sense to accept capitalist overtures with some caution but to make the best use of them. (This helps to explain the trade agreement with Britain in March 1921: Lloyd Geroge had been particularly interested in the possibilities of trade with Russia and the latter gained some international standing thereby.) But equally it made sense to cooperate with those states at odds with the Allies. In December 1921 Russia signed an alliance with the Turkish Nationalists, although the effect of this was reduced by the Lausanne settlement which gave Kemal less need to seek Russian goodwill. More significant was the signing of a new peace treaty with Germany in March 1921 to be followed by the treaty of Rapallo in April 1922. The resumption of diplomatic and economic relations embodied in this agreement raised for Britain and France the danger of German–Russian collaboration at a time when the reparations question was still unsettled and the political stability of Germany still uncertain. Germany, however, did not intend to be used to further Russian ends; Rapallo gave her more freedom of manoeuvre in dealing with the Allies, for the threat of closer cooperation with Moscow was more valuable than its implementation. It was in fact the successor states of eastern Europe who would be most threatened by full-scale German–Russian reconciliation, Poland in particular. The territorial ambitions of the Poles had put them on bad or doubtful terms with all their neighbours except Rumania, but they saw themselves as a power of some significance, a view in which they were encouraged by the French. The loss of the alliance with Imperial Russia meant that France needed a substitute and Poland had good reason to resist any German attempt to upset the status quo. But France also saw Poland as a bulwark against Bolshevism, thus giving her a difficult dual role. Under a secret military convention of February 1921 France promised to come to the aid of Poland in the event of German and Russian pressure. This was a potentially dangerous commitment.

The Union of Soviet Socialist Republics formally came into existence in July 1923. It now had some diplomatic flexibility but was still weak and only half on the European stage. Its position makes an interesting contrast with that of the United States, far from weak, seeking to limit its international commitments yet forced to make sporadic incursions into European diplomacy. It was American backing which enabled the Dawes Plan to be launched and it was another American initiative which produced a settlement in the Far East as well as an agreement on arms limitation. The Harding administration was under some pressure from Congress to limit naval expenditure and to promote disarmament. Moreover, in 1921 the Anglo-Japanese alliance came up for renewal and the United States was anxious to see it ended. Britain in turn was anxious to keep on good terms with America and to avoid a race in naval building yet wanted to find some means of maintaining the Japanese alliance. These problems were discussed at the imperial conference in London during June and July 1921. There were differences of view both within the British government and between it and the dominions, which added to the difficulty of finding a clear-cut policy.

The American Secretary of State, Charles Evans Hughes, neatly stole a march on the British by sending out preliminary invitations in July to a conference in which both arms limitation and Far Eastern questions would be discussed. He also blocked British attempts to have a meeting in London before the main discussions. Hughes maintained the initiative when the Washington conference opened in November by producing specific proposals for naval disarmament. These were largely embodied in a five power treaty signed in February 1922 by which ratios for replacement tonnage of capital ships were fixed at 5–5–3–1.75–1.75 for the United States, Britain, Japan, France and Italy. The French had for a time resisted being put on the same level as the Italians and had tried to bring in questions of land disarmament in Europe, which Hughes refused to consider. A ban on new naval bases in an area west of Hawaii and north of Singapore on the whole benefited Japan, but she did less well in other respects. The four power treaty of December 1921, confirming the Pacific island possessions of the signatories, replaced the Anglo-Japanese alliance. Under a separate agreement Japan gave up her holdings in Shantung and also promised verbally to evacuate Siberia. A nine power treaty of 6 February 1922 upheld the principle of the 'open door' in China, though admittedly without any sanctions to support it. The United States had thus gained most of its objectives and Japan had been the main loser. British weakness relative to the United States had been revealed and Britain could not now use the alliance as a means of restraining Japan. At the time, however, the Washington treaties seemed to mark a step forward in arms limitation and in promoting stability in the Pacific.

By 1924, therefore, the general shape of the postwar settlement was becoming clearer, even if it was not always that envisaged at Paris. A number of techniques and instruments had been added to diplomatic practice. The peace treaties had made much wider use of plebiscites than had hitherto been the case, although not on a systematic basis. Nor did a plebiscite always guarantee a satisfactory border delimitation, as was shown in the case of Upper Silesia. The treaties made specific provision for the protection and rights of minorities, thus challenging the sovereignty of states. The immediate postwar years had seen a flurry of international conferences, some under the auspices of the Supreme Allied Council, some, like Washington, arranged independently. There were also various meetings of financial experts, particularly in connection with reparations and war debts. The record of these meetings was mixed; where they attracted much publicity there was likely to be a greater sense of disappointment if they did not bring quick results. The Genoa conference of April and May 1922, intended to discuss economic problems in Europe, was a failure, the treaty of Rapallo being only an unintended by-product.

A body of a more traditional type was the conference of ambassadors set up at the end of the Paris conference to oversee the execution of the treaties. Intended to have only a limited life, this conference survived until 1931, though it declined in importance after 1925. In its early years, however, it exercised a good deal of influence and tended to extend its competence. It was chaired by the French Prime Minister or his representative and included the British, Italian, Japanese, Belgian and American Ambassadors, the latter attending only as an observer. Meeting in Paris and in secret, it attracted some criticism as a relic of the old diplomacy. As a standing body, however, it was able to deal more quickly and consistently with problems than could the Supreme Council, which met at irregular intervals and for short periods. Over certain issues, such as the delimitation of Albanian frontiers and the supervision of German disarmament, the work of the conference was of considerable importance. In some ways it could be seen as a rival to the League of Nations, but that newly created body would have found it difficult to oversee effectively the execution of the treaties at a time when it had still to establish its own reputation. In view of the scope and complexity of the Paris settlement it is scarcely surprising that innovations and traditional methods had to seek an uneasy coexistence. In the last resort all forms of international cooperation and negotiation depend on the attitudes of the decision-makers who make use of them, and in the early 1920s, such men were mainly concerned with promoting the interests of their own state. There were few 'good Europeans'.

CHAPTER FOUR
A period of false stability, 1924–1929

The period from the London conference of August 1924 until the Wall Street crash of October 1929 was one of apparent economic recovery, underpinned by American loans, and of seeming continuity and stability in British, French and German foreign policy. Austen Chamberlain was British Foreign Secretary from November 1924 until the end of May 1929; Stresemann remained in charge of German foreign policy until his death in September 1929; Briand outlasted them both, holding the French foreign ministry with only brief interruptions from April 1925 until the beginning of 1932. Between July 1926 and July 1929 he held office under Poincaré, who reappeared in his last spell as prime minister as the saviour and stabilizer of the franc by contrast with his earlier manifestation as the stern upholder of the Versailles treaty.

There was, therefore, an element of continuity which enabled the three powers to adjust some of the differences between them. Such success as they enjoyed, however, was heavily dependent on the continuation of American financial support and on the maintenance of domestic stability in Germany. The latter was far from certain. There were signs of increasing support for right-wing nationalism and Stresemann's policies came increasingly under attack. The Müller cabinet set up in June 1928 was a very shaky coalition indeed. Outside Germany public opinion was too little aware of the dangers to European stability and tended to exaggerate the significance of treaties and agreements as an end in themselves. The Locarno agreements and the Kellogg–Briand pact did not eliminate conflicting national interests or change the nature of policy-makers. There was a dangerous gap between the reality of private negotiation and the widespread public belief that a new era of peace and reconciliation had dawned. In any case, Britain, France and Germany were only a part of the European system, however important their role. Mussolini's Italy was slow to develop clear-cut policies – it was only in 1925 that an outright Fascist dictatorship was established. Mussolini had made himself foreign minister when he first came to power in 1922 but it took him a few years to find his feet and to assert control over the professional diplomats. His early foreign policy was therefore tentative and somewhat inconsistent.

The Soviet Union began to obtain diplomatic recognition from 1924 onwards but remained in the main isolated, suspicious of and suspected by the capitalist powers. On the one hand Chicherin as People's Commissar for Foreign Affairs employed the techniques of traditional diplomacy, on the other hand the Comintern (established in 1920) used propaganda and subversion. Few capitalist governments believed in the fiction of its nominal independence from the Soviet government, and its activities were a mixed blessing as far as foreign policy was concerned. Lenin's death in January 1924 led to a struggle for the succession and to a sharp argument over policy. By 1928 Stalin had emerged predominant and the first Five Year Plan had been launched. It was not immediately clear how these developments would affect Soviet external relations. The Locarno era did not see the re-establishment of a full-scale concert of the European powers nor was there a general consensus among them about the aims of the European system. It would be wrong to blame policy-makers for failing to foresee exactly developments in the 1930s but there was ample evidence for those who cared to look for it of the fragility of the spirit of Locarno.

The Dawes Plan was not intended to be a final settlement of the reparations question. It would give Germany a breathing space to attain economic recovery and ensure in the meantime that her creditors received something, although her annual payments would not reach their maximum until the end of 1928. The attempt to obtain reparations from Germany's former allies was largely a failure: Austria had to be given a loan in 1922 to reorganize her finances under the supervision of the League and was allowed to abandon reparations altogether, while Hungary and Bulgaria obtained considerable reductions in their payments. These developments indicated the difficulty of extracting large amounts of money and goods from economically weak states but this did not affect the central issue. The Dawes Plan had not ended the French search for security nor removed the German intention to break free from the bonds of Versailles. To obtain German agreement to the Dawes Plan the French were forced to promise to evacuate the Ruhr, a process which was completed by the end of August 1925. The difficulties of the Ruhr occupation made it unlikely that France would resort to a similar operation again. Direct control of German heavy industry was no longer an option, and under the Versailles treaty Germany had been due to regain control over her own tariffs in January 1925. If she wanted she could then limit imports from the Saar and Alsace-Lorraine, which would seriously affect French iron and steel producers already facing surplus capacity. Talks between government officials and business groups began in 1924 and succeeded in producing an agreement on sharing out steel production in September 1926. More general Franco-German trade treaties were signed the following year. Quotas from the Saar and Alsace-Lorraine were allowed to enter Germany but the French steel producers remained the weaker partners. Despite the financial success of Poincaré's last ministry, French fears of German economic predominance were not removed. Uncertainty about the long-term future of reparations led in turn to a delay in ratifying the agreements made with Britain and the United States for the repayment of war debts. The French continued to insist on an assured income from reparations as a prerequisite for paying off debts to their allies.

If the French felt insecure in economic terms, the military position was not much better. Here too January 1925 was a significant month, since the Allies were supposed to evacuate the first of the three Rhineland zones of occupation (round Cologne). They had powers of delay which were in fact exercised when the Military Control Commission reported unfavourably on the progress of German disarmament at the end of 1924. The conference of ambassadors duly informed the German government that evacuation would not take place. From the French point of view this was only a temporary stay of execution, for once withdrawal began it could only be delayed, not reversed. Moreover, by the beginning of 1925 the British were clearly losing their enthusiasm for detailed supervision through the Control Commission. Their argument was that Germany was incapable of attacking France whatever infringements there might have been of the disarmament clauses of Versailles.

The French could try to offset the erosion of their position by seeking more allies among those states of eastern Europe who wished to maintain the status quo. After her brief flirtation with Hungary in 1920, France tried instead to improve relations with the Little Entente, in particular with Czechoslovakia. Marshal Foch visited Prague in May 1923 and specifically raised the question of an alliance, but the Czech Foreign Minister Beneš was cautious, and the treaty eventually signed in January 1924 was very general in its terms. Beneš was anxious to play down its anti-German implications, since for the Little Entente Hungarian revisionism was just as great a potential threat as that of Germany. There was the additional problem for the French that Czechoslovakia's relations with Poland remained bad despite some attempts at improvement. The two countries failed to reach any overall political agreement and this made wholehearted military cooperation in a crisis seem very unlikely.

Allies in the east were of limited value. Another line of approach was to seek more general arrangements to supplement and extend the system of collective security embodied in the League Covenant, but this too proved fruitless. Two documents emerged from discussions at Geneva – the draft treaty of mutual assistance in 1923 and the Geneva protocol of 1924. The draft treaty allowed for the creation of regional alliances and restricted the responsibility for military action to states on the Continent in which aggression took place. On the other hand it gave increased responsibility to the League Council and was intended to be a prelude to a scheme for general disarmament. A number of states had doubts about the draft treaty but what mattered most to the French was the British rejection in July 1924. Britain argued that her imperial connections made it impossible to limit her commitments to one continent; she could easily find herself engaged in military action in several different parts of the world. In reality the problem was somewhat different; the dominions objected strongly to any increase in their obligations under the Covenant. The aim of the Geneva protocol was to block a gap in the Covenant which allowed states to resort to war in certain circumstances. The intention was to insist on arbitration or peaceful settlement of disputes so that refusal to accept agreed procedures would clearly put a state in the wrong. The protocol got an enthusiastic reception from the League Assembly but that did not prevent Britain from rejecting it in March 1925. She was clearly determined not to undertake general and open-ended commitments.

Austen Chamberlain was anxious, however, to avoid a purely negative policy. He could see that France needed reassurance of some kind even though Britain could not commit herself to a straightforward alliance against Germany. By the beginning of 1925 he was contemplating a revival of the idea of a limited guarantee to France and Belgium but without any commitment in eastern Europe. The Cabinet was divided over the idea and it was the last thing Stresemann wanted. Franco-British cooperation would block his hopes of restoring Germany's position as a major European power. To do that he needed to remove the formal signs of her subjection to the Allies, such as the Control Commission and the occupation of the Rhineland. Beyond that he sought German admission to the League, as a symbol of her respectability, and the return of most of the territory lost in the peace settlement. Alsace-Lorraine he was prepared to abandon but he wanted to secure the return of the areas of Eupen and Malmedy which had been ceded to Belgium. There was to be a plebiscite in the Saar in 1935 but he hoped to regain it well before that date. It was against Poland, however, that Stresemann's main revisionist ambitions were directed. The Corridor, Danzig and Upper Silesia were all targets for eventual recapture. There was also the possibility of union with Austria and the continuing need to protect the interest of German minorities abroad. Over the Germans in

Czechoslovakia he was cautious, but more outspoken over the German-speakers in South Tyrol who found themselves subjected to a ruthless programme of Italianization.

Such aims and attitudes were widespread among Right-wing and nationalist politicians in the Weimar Republic but most of them lacked Stresemann's astuteness. He realized that a policy of bluster would achieve little; it was necessary to reassure Britain and France, not frighten them. Despite evasion of the disarmament clauses of the peace treaty and despite clandestine military cooperation with Russia since 1922, Germany lacked the military capacity to achieve her aims by force. To obtain a free hand in Eastern Europe would take time and would require at least the tolerance, if not the active support, of Britain and France. The shaky nature of Weimar coalitions, however, made it necessary for Stresemann to depict himself as a belligerent defender of German interests. This helped to make his ultimate intentions ambiguous; was there a point at which he would have regarded Germany as a satisfied power or would his ambition have grown with success? He was at least prepared to show restraint in his attempt to win back status and power for Germany, but it was for specifically German rather than European interests that he worked so hard.

A limited security pact with France was not a new idea; the Cuno government had tried it unsuccessfully at the end of 1922. But Stresemann was operating in more favourable circumstances. French options were limited and the British might be attracted by a proposal which did not threaten them with major new commitments. Equally, it was in Germany's interest to forestall a possible British initiative and to restore momentum to the evacuation of the Rhineland. Such were the considerations which led Stresemann to sound out Britain in January 1925 and to make a formal approach to France in February with a proposal for a security pact limited to western Europe. It was not until October, however, that the foreign ministers of France, Belgium, Britain, Germany and Italy gathered at Locarno. Britain, as expected, had been unwilling to commit herself to guarantees in eastern Europe, whereas France wanted to reassure Poland and Czechoslovakia by keeping some link between the western and eastern settlements. This led Briand to propose that France herself should guarantee whatever agreements Germany made with Poland and Czechoslovakia, an idea that Stresemann flatly rejected, and in the end Briand retreated.

Italy was less directly concerned but Mussolini saw the possibility of obtaining a guarantee of the frontier with Austria. Britain did not wish to become involved with this complication and Stresemann indicated that if the proposal were pursued he would raise the awkward question of a German–Austrian union. The best Mussolini could get was an offer from France of an individual guarantee outside the main settlement. He had no wish to appear dependent on France alone for the protection of Italy's frontiers and so the idea of a guarantee for the Brenner Pass lapsed. Stresemann for his part found himself having to reassure the Russians. At the end of 1924 they had suggested a general political agreement with Germany and showed some alarm when the proposed western pact became known. It seemed likely to undermine Rapallo and to move Germany into an anti-Soviet group. Stresemann did not wish to commit himself too closely to Russia yet did not wish to abandon her. She was a useful bargaining counter in dealing with Britain and France, both of whom tended to take fright at signs of German–Russian friendship. He therefore tried to give reassurance that Germany would not undertake any obligations which might force her to act against Russia. Here he was thinking of the League Covenant and specifically of article 16, which provided for economic sanctions and possible military action by member states.

These various problems, therefore, delayed the decisive meeting until October. Although formal ratification took place in London in December it was upon the Locarno discussions that public attention fastened and the name became for a time a synonym for reconciliation and goodwill. Certainly Locarno saw a partial reappearance of a European concert of powers. Her geographical situation and her share in the Rhineland occupation gave Belgium a place at the table of the great, but it was noticeable that Poland and Czechoslovakia were only admitted towards the end of the conference to be informed of what had already been decided. The western settlement was embodied in a treaty of mutual guarantee accompanied by arbitration treaties between Germany and France and Germany and Belgium. The treaty confirmed the frontiers as established at Versailles and also the continued demilitarization of the Rhineland. Alleged breaches of the treaty would be brought before the League; 'flagrant' violations would require Britain and Italy, as guaranteeing powers, to intervene without waiting for a decision from the League. In theory they could find themselves fighting either France or Germany, but the French assumption was that the treaty in practice was a protection against Germany. Much would depend on how Britain and Italy chose to define a 'flagrant' violation, for the treaty itself gave no guidance on this point. On the whole this left the British with the kind of limited commitment they wanted, able to act as a restraining influence on both France and Germany. It was made clear that her signature did not commit the dominions and thus an important obstacle to Britain's undertaking a guarantee was removed. Italy could claim to have received recognition of her position as a European power, if not much else.

The western arbitration treaties were specifically linked to the main treaty, which had no counterpart in the eastern settlement. Germany signed identical arbitration treaties with Poland and Czechoslovakia but these stood on their own. No outside power was obliged to intervene and the territorial status quo was therefore not guaranteed; Germany's expressed willingness to settle disputes peacefully need not prevent her seeking revision of frontiers. In an attempt to offset this weakness France signed new treaties with Poland and Czechoslovakia at the end of the Locarno conference, but these were not formally linked to the main settlement. It would in any case be difficult for France to help her allies by attacking Germany without risking charges of being in breach of the treaty of mutual guarantee. Stresemann had gained a good deal and, as he had indicated to the Russians, he made clear that when Germany entered the League she would not regard herself as bound by article 16 to take action against the Soviet Union. Membership of the League was part of Stresemann's price for accepting Locarno. A dispute over the allocation of permanent seats on the Council delayed German entry until September 1926, but it was now clear that she had regained respectability and was no longer an ex-enemy state but once again part of the European system. On other fronts also there was progress. The Cologne zone was evacuated by the end of January 1926 and the Control Commission was wound up a year later. Supervision of German disarmament then became the responsibility of the League, which showed little interest in exercising it.

These successes were not enough to satisfy Stresemann's domestic critics, so he was driven to ask for more. At the same time he was careful to keep up contacts with the Russians as a reminder to the western powers of Germany's freedom of manoeuvre. A trade agreement was signed while the Locarno conference was still in progress and Stresemann now made a delayed response to the earlier Russian suggestion of a new political agreement. The upshot was the treaty of Berlin signed in April 1926 which, as expected, created some excitement in eastern Europe. But each country merely promised the other neutrality should either be attacked by one or more states. Perhaps more important was an accompanying exchange of notes in which Germany confirmed that she would not be bound by article 16 to take action against Russia. The Soviet Union was only partly reassured by the treaty and notes, but her relations with Germany in the late 1920s were on the whole calm. It is doubtful if she gained much more than a confirmation of German goodwill, for Stresemann was careful to point out in public that the treaty did not in any way weaken Locarno. What he really meant was that the Russians might be useful but they could not give him accelerated evacuation of the Rhineland or a new reparations agreement.

Stresemann tried for a direct agreement with Briand. The two men met in the French village of Thoiry in September 1926 and talked for several hours. Stresemann in effect offered an overall settlement in which France and Belgium would give up territory for cash. Germany would buy back Eupen, Malmedy and the Saar and make some reparation bonds available for sale to private investors. The attraction of this last idea for France lay in obtaining cash in hand from the sale of bonds in advance of the normal annual payments. In return, of course, Germany wanted an early end to occupation of the Rhineland. Briand was prepared to explore these ideas, although he seems to have given Stresemann a greater sense of commitment than was in fact the case. There were strong criticisms within the French Cabinet and Stresemann's colleagues also had their doubts. It would certainly be difficult to sell large numbers of reparation bonds on the open market without running the risk of a fall in their face value. The French in effect would get a cash advance but possibly would have to pay a considerable discount. From the German point of view it would be dangerous to put the country's commercial credit at risk; any default on interest payments would endanger the flow of loans from the United States. The latter was unlikely to allow bond sales in New York unless France ratified the war debts agreement. How could Germany in addition raise the money needed to redeem Eupen, Malmedy and the Saar? The idea of a comprehensive Franco-German settlement soon died.

Still Stresemann kept pressing. He obtained one further gain in September 1927, when the Allies made a cut in the number of troops stationed in the Rhineland. They had promised to do this, though without setting a firm date, nearly two years earlier, and it was not in Stresemann's character to let them forget such a definite commitment. But he failed in attempts to speed up evacuation, whether through private approaches or public speeches. His tactics of persistently asking for new concessions were producing diminishing returns as Briand and Chamberlain became steadily more resistant. Both had to consider their own political positions and Briand was particularly vulnerable to accusations of surrendering French interests too easily. Chamberlain tended to sympathize with the French position and he found Briand personally much more agreeable than Stresemann. It would be wrong, however, to give the impression of an Anglo-French entente in the years immediately after Locarno. The Foreign Office developed the practice of referring to the French as 'former' allies and was quick to resist their attempts to give the conference of ambassadors a new or extended role. In the spring and summer of 1927 the British made clear that they wanted the conference to pass away quietly as its duties steadily disappeared. Nevertheless, as long as Chamberlain remained in office Germany could not drive a wedge between Britain and France.

Nor could Germany make any progress over rectification of the frontiers with Poland. Locarno might have given her a freer hand in eastern Europe but she was unable to do much with it. Britain wished to avoid commitments in eastern Europe but that was not the same as giving Germany permission to do anything she wanted. The German army did not have the capacity to wage an offensive war against Poland and Stresemann did not go as far as contemplating joint action with Russia to extract territorial concessions. He therefore faced a stalemate and German–Polish relations remained generally poor. In particular the anomalous position of Danzig as a free city under Polish supervision gave rise to continuing friction. The German majority in Danzig was quick to accuse the Poles of encroaching on the port facilities and of interfering with the affairs of the city in general. Financial support for Danzig was a continuing drain on Germany, especially after the Poles constructed their own port at Gdynia. On the other hand, entry into the League gave Germany greater opportunity to criticize Polish policies and in 1928 she was able to secure the appointment of a new High Commissioner who was regarded as sympathetic to the Danzig case. But by the end of the 1920s Germany was no nearer regaining the frontiers of 1914 or anything approaching them and it was difficult to see how she could put effective pressure on Poland. Yet it was unthinkable to abandon hopes of frontier revision altogether. This impasse increased nationalist frustration inside Germany and suspicion within Poland.

Over reparations, however, the breakthrough that Germany wanted was secured during private discussions at the meeting of the League Assembly in September 1928. Ironically, Stresemann himself was too ill to attend. It was agreed that a new committee of experts should be set up to work out a final reparations settlement and that there would be negotiations on an accelerated withdrawal from the Rhineland. The idea of a new reparations settlement was very much in the air. The Agent-General responsible for supervising the Dawes Plan had indicated at the end of 1927 that he thought the time was now ripe for a new scheme in which bonds could be sold direct to the public. Germany's creditors could thus gain money in advance and with a completely fresh start it should be possible to overcome the difficulties that had blocked the Thoiry proposals. For Germany herself there was the hope of paying lower annuities than those now becoming due under the Dawes Plan. In 1930 evacuation of the Koblenz zone would take place in any case; thereafter the value of maintaining occupation of the Mainz zone as a bargaining counter would diminish rapidly the nearer one came to the terminal date of 1935. An agreement was therefore in France's interest. The British position was somewhat mixed. On the one hand the government was willing to end the evacuation, on the other the Treasury feared that Britain might be the loser from a new reparations agreement. The committee of experts began work in Paris in February 1929 under Owen D.

Young, who had also served on the Dawes Committee. Its report, in June, proposed a scheme which would benefit Germany in that she would make lower payments in the first ten years than under the Dawes Plan. She would, however, continue to pay reparations for fifty-nine years and there was explicit recognition that a proportion of the payments would be used to cover war debt payments to the United States. (The term of fifty-nine years was chosen to coincide with the standard repayment period in America's war debt agreements.) As the Treasury had feared, the distribution among Germany's creditors had been changed to Britain's disadvantage.

Stresemann and his colleagues were not entirely happy but decided to make the best of a bad job. To reject the Young Plan would mean continuing with the higher Dawes payments and acceptance left the possibility of seeking modifications in a few years' time. When the interested parties met at the Hague in August the main difficulties came from Britain. The second Labour government had been formed in June and Snowden, the new Chancellor of the Exchequer, made clear his displeasure at Britain's reduced share. In the end he settled for less than his full demands but it was noticeable that neither he nor Henderson, the Foreign Secretary, showed much sympathy for the French. Henderson decided to go ahead unilaterally with evacuation of the Rhineland regardless of the final date of 30 June 1930 agreed between France and Germany. All British troops had left by the end of 1929; the French evacuated the Koblenz zone by November and remained in the Mainz zone until the agreed date.

Thus Stresemann attained his objective, even though he did not live to see it. But his relations with Briand at the Hague conference were far from good. There was a good deal of haggling before the final date for evacuation was agreed; Briand failed in an attempt to create a civilian inspection agency that would ensure demilitarization of the Rhineland was maintained; for his part Stresemann gained nothing from yet another attempt to secure an early return of the Saar. The French remained fearful of a possible German attack although the German army had not as yet the capacity to launch one. It had been decided in 1927 to build a chain of fortifications along the border with Germany but work did not begin until 1930. The Maginot line (named after the then Minister of War) would give France the protection she had now lost in the Rhineland, or so it was hoped. Such a defensive attitude put in doubt the alliances with Poland and Czechoslovakia. Were they now liabilities to France rather than assets? The increasing French reliance on passive defence would in turn further reduce her value to her allies. Yet France had good cause to be concerned about the future shape of German policy. Although the Young Plan was approved by the Reichstag and duly came into force in May 1930 there had been strong opposition from the Right-wing parties, who insisted on a referendum. They failed to prevent ratification but obtained nearly 6 million votes against the Young Plan when the referendum was held in December 1929, and the campaign gave a good deal of publicity to Hitler and the Nazis. It was clear at the beginning of 1930 that a violently nationalist government could well appear in Germany. If it were to repudiate both the reparations settlement and Locarno then France and Britain would face a direct challenge.

If Franco-German relations were uneasy, the position of Italy among the European powers was ambiguous. Mussolini had come to power partly because of dissatisfaction with Italy's alleged ill-treatment at the peace conference. In one sense, therefore, he represented the long-standing nationalist demand that Italy be recognized as a great power and consulted on major issues. Her greatness might manifest itself in various ways but most Italian nationalists wanted a dominant position in the Adriatic and south-east Europe and the right to frontier colonies: she must stand on an equal footing with France and Britain in the Mediterranean and Africa. Of the two, France was in the main a rival and Britain a friend. To these beliefs Mussolini added a specifically Fascist approach with its emphasis on force and bold action and its disdain for compromise. Not for Mussolini the quiet negotiation or the hidden diplomatic victory; Italy had to make herself feared and respected, though in practice this often meant bluster rather than action. In the 1920s, however, Mussolini had not yet become the victim of his own rhetoric. He had to establish his position inside Italy and initially had to rely on the professional diplomats until he himself obtained a grasp of foreign policy. On the other hand he was under considerable pressure from sections of the Fascist party to continue with the revolution inside Italy. Matters came to a head with the murder of the Socialist politician Matteoti in June 1924, which for a time seemed to threaten Mussolini's position. Instead the crisis pushed him into consolidating his power during 1925 over both the opposition parties and the Fascists. This had serious implications for the Italian diplomatic service. In May 1925 Dino Grandi, who had made his name as a Fascist strong-arm man, was introduced into the foreign ministry and by 1929 Mussolini felt confident enough to promote him to Foreign Minister.

As a result of these developments Italian policy moved by fits and starts. At Lausanne and the London reparations conference of 1922 Mussolini was an uncomfortable newcomer. Multilateral gatherings of this kind gave little opportunity for individual coups, yet for the sake of prestige he could not afford to ignore international conferences completely. Despite his doubts about the intrinsic value of the Locarno agreements he chose to make a dramatic last-minute appearance for the initialling of the treaties. The more adventurous side of his policies was seen in the bombardment and occupation of Corfu in August 1923. The occasion arose when an Italian general and his staff were murdered on Greek territory while helping to demarcate the Albanian frontier. Italy succeeded in having the matter handled by the conference of ambassadors instead of the League Council. Needing support for the Ruhr occupation, the French were sympathetic to Italian demands for an indemnity but were not prepared to condone outright acquisition of the island. With the British also opposed to Italy's remaining on Corfu, Mussolini somewhat unwillingly accepted the cash and withdrew.

As he saw it, the episode demonstrated Italian firmness; to others it showed a dangerous unpredictability and a willingness to ignore normal diplomatic practices. Mussolini did subsequently seek to improve relations with Greece and soothed the ruffled feathers of the League Council by inviting it to meet in Rome at the end of 1924. Yet he did not lose his taste for similar adventures. Having apparently learned nothing from the Greek defeat in 1922 he toyed from time to time with the idea of expansion at the expense of Turkey. It was in Albania, however, that Italy next made a forward move. After some hesitation Mussolini decided to intervene in the complicated politics of that country and support Ahmed Zogu against his rivals. Apart from financial help Italy signed two treaties with Zogu, in November 1926 and November 1927 respectively.

This attempt to establish predominance in Albania ruined any hopes of improving relations with Yugoslavia. Mussolini had taken over Fiume in 1924 but had not otherwise sought to upset the Rapallo treaty of 1920. Relations with Yugoslavia had not been entirely bad and the latter had shown some interest in a tripartite pact with France and Italy to maintain the status quo in the Adriatic. Not surprisingly Mussolini resisted the proposal, even though the Yugoslavs delayed final signature of a treaty which they had initialled with France in March 1926 in the vain hope of getting a tripartite agreement. Italy's policy in Albania and her claims that Yugoslavia was planning an invasion of that country helped to bring about signature of the Franco-Yugoslav treaty in November 1927. In spite of France's help over the Corfu incident she seemed increasingly to stand in Italy's way. Until 1928 France had blocked Italy's participation in the supervision of the international port of Tangier; there was an unresolved conflict over the status of Italian settlers in Tunisia; as the patron of the Little Entente from 1924 onwards, France was an obstacle to Italian influence in the Danube basin and the Balkans.

In 1927 Mussolini made an unsuccessful attempt to detach Rumania from the Little Entente. Thereafter he increasingly showed sympathy for Hungary and Bulgaria, the two revisionist states in the area. A friendship treaty in April 1927 brought Hungary out of her diplomatic isolation. No further benefits accrued for either party but it showed in which direction Mussolini's mind was working. From

1928 he began to speak of the need to revise the peace settlement and Grandi echoed this line on becoming Foreign Minister. At this stage, however, Mussolini was careful not to be too specific. His main challenge was to France and the Little Entente, whereas his relations with Britain were still good. In 1924 the latter had ceded Jubaland in East Africa and in 1925 induced Egypt to hand over the Jarabub oasis to Libya. These arrangements were a delayed implementation of promises in the treaty of London to give Italy colonial compensation in Africa. An exchange of notes at the end of 1925 confirmed British and Italian spheres of economic interest in Ethiopia. The two countries and France had made a similar agreement in 1906 but it suited Mussolini to indicate his independence of the French. Ethiopia had long been regarded as a suitable object for Italian penetration and colonization, and there was the defeat of Adowa in 1896 to avenge. Mussolini was not yet prepared to push his claims, however, and the wish to keep on good terms with Britain seems to have been a restraining influence on his East African ambitions.

Italian policy towards Germany was ambivalent. The existence of the German-speaking minority in the South Tyrol was bound to cause friction with any government in Berlin. Mussolini gave some aid to Right-wing and nationalist groups in Germany, including the Nazis. He had a low opinion of Stresemann and of Weimar politicians in general, yet it would not be in his interest to see a revisionist German government which would actively support German minorities abroad or promote union with Austria. The Nazis had made clear from the early years of Mussolini's rule that they wanted his support and were prepared to ignore the South Tyrol question, but they were the exception among German nationalist groups and by no means certain to obtain power. At the beginning of 1930, therefore, there was still a considerable obstacle to Germany and Italy combining against France, particularly if it meant for Italy the loss of British goodwill. Yet Mussolini was unpredictable and his appetite for diplomatic success still strong.

The Soviet Union was also something of an unknown quantity. It had looked in 1924 as if she might be moving back into the European system. In February Britain conceded *de jure* recognition, to be followed by Italy in the same month and France in October. But recognition did not produce the trade agreements and loans for which the Russians hoped, nor did continued friendship with Germany do very much to improve Russia's position – she was more useful to Berlin that Berlin was to her. Moreover, the Soviet Union interpreted the Dawes Plan and Locarno as moves to draw Germany into an anti-Russian group. These fears seemed to be confirmed by German entry into the League, an institution which the Soviet Union regarded with great suspicion. Her fears of a possible capitalist attack were increased by the coup in Poland in May 1926 which brought Pilsudski back to power. No attack materialized but the murder of the Soviet envoy in Warsaw in May 1927 severely worsened Russo-Polish relations. Ill-founded though Soviet fears of a general capitalist offensive might be, they created a mood of uncertainty which Stalin played upon during 1927 to strengthen his domestic political position.

Most capitalist governments remained suspicious of the Soviet Union, not least because of the work of the Comintern. Chicherin and his colleagues might disclaim all responsibility for its activities but capitalist fears of conspiracy and subversion were as easily aroused as Soviet fears of imminent attack. Which was the real voice of Soviet policy, the People's Commissariat for Foreign Affairs or the Comintern? It was not always easy to be sure and western governments tended to assume the worst. In the case of Britain, for example, fears of Communist conspiracies were easily wakened. The Zinoviev letter urging British communists to promote sedition in the armed forces and revolt in the colonies was almost certainly a forgery, but it was precisely the type of instruction that Comintern officials were thought to be producing regularly. Publication of extracts from the alleged letter seems to have helped the Conservatives win the election of October 1924 and it was noticeable that Austen Chamberlain kept contacts with the Soviet government to a minimum. Diplomatic relations were in fact broken off in May 1927, following a police raid on the offices of the Soviet trade mission in London, but were restored when Labour came into office again in 1929. The underlying doubts of the British Right were matched elsewhere in western Europe, yet so too were persistent hopes of increased trade to be gained from helping to develop the Soviet economy.

The Comintern was probably, therefore, more of a hindrance than a help to the improvement of Russia's international standing. Certainly it failed to produce revolution in Europe, and suffered a disastrous setback in China in 1927 at the hands of Chiang Kai-Shek. This led in the following year to a change of line; cooperation with progressive elements in the capitalist countries was to be abandoned in favour of an offensive against Social Democratic parties. Revolutionary opportunities were now said to be improving in Europe, especially in Germany. In spite of a number of setbacks the Comintern had never quite abandoned hope of success in Germany; the effect of its policy was to add to the forces opposed to the Weimar parliamentary system. Yet from 1927 Soviet delegates began to appear at economic and disarmament discussions sponsored by the League of Nations, indicating some change of attitude to that body. Stalin advanced as one of the main reasons for the Five Year Plan the need to build up Soviet strength in the face of capitalist hostility; yet in February 1929 Russia signed an agreement with Poland, Rumania,

Estonia and Latvia renouncing the use of force. The 'Litvinov protocol', as this was generally called, indicated that the Soviet Union was not to be outdone in declarations of good intention, but her policies as the end of the 1920s showed some inconsistency.

The United States was prepared to supply loans to Europe and to support the activities of individual Americans such as Dawes and Young. Financial stability and rectitude was what the United States asked of the Europeans. French ratification of her war debts agreements with America and Britain in 1929 appeared to dispose of that troublesome issue. Beyond this the United States showed no systematic or sustained policies in Europe. She participated in the League's discussions on economic problems and disarmament but was careful to avoid either any direct political cooperation and/or any action which might suggest a willingness to join. For this reason the United States did not join the Permanent Court of International Justice. The right of the League Council to seek advisory opinions from the Court might involve it in issues of direct interest to the United States, especially in Latin America. This sensitivity is perhaps surprising, for since Woodrow Wilson's death in 1924 there had been no public figures who were prepared to support actively American entry into the League.

In this period there were two ways in which the diplomacy of the United States impinged upon Europe – the signing of the pact of Paris in August 1928 and the pursuit of further naval disarmament. April 1927 brought the tenth anniversary of the United States' entry into the war and Briand took the opportunity to publish a message to the American people proposing a treaty in which the two countries would renounce the use of force against each other. They had shown no sign of going to war; what Briand wanted was a general indication of American friendship which would strengthen France's position in relation to Germany. In June he followed up the message with a formal proposal for a treaty to Secretary of State Frank Kellogg. The latter saw plainly what Briand's purpose was but was not willing to undertake a direct commitment to a European state in this way. Outright rejection would be difficult, however, since the April message had roused a good deal of interest among American liberals and pacifists. In December Kellogg replied with a counter-proposal for a general treaty by which all signatories would renounce war and during 1928 he proceeded to sound out other European states. Such a general agreement would be of little use to France but now it was Briand's turn to find outright rejection impossible. Initially fifteen states signed the pact, which in the end attracted sixty-five signatures. It was simply a promise that states would renounce war as an instrument of policy and would settle disputes peacefully. Most states, America included, reserved the right to fight in self-defence. It seems surprising now that a mere promise of good behaviour, to which no sanctions were attached, should have attracted such widespread public enthusiasm. As with Locarno, there was a tendency to exaggerate the significance of agreements and to ignore their substance.

Underlying differences of interest could not be so easily conjured away when it came to the attempt to extend the Washington treaty to other types of naval vessel, in particular cruisers. President Coolidge called a conference for this purpose which met in Geneva from June to August 1927, without result. At Washington, limitation on battleships had been discussed along with political issues. At Geneva, cruiser limitation was approached in isolation as a purely technical problem. But the European powers could not be expected to separate disarmament from their other security concerns and for this reason France and Italy refused to attend. France in particular did not wish to be forced into granting parity in cruisers to Italy. The conference turned into a battle between America and Britain over the total tonnage to be allowed for cruisers and how it should be divided between heavy and light cruisers. America wanted more of the former and Britain more of the latter. The Japanese were able to sit back and say little and the conference ended with a good deal of ill-feeling.

It proved possible to make some progress once Hoover replaced Coolidge as President and MacDonald replaced Baldwin as Prime Minister. The London naval conference of January to April 1930 produced among other things agreement on limiting cruiser tonnages and on numbers of light and heavy cruisers. Neither France nor Italy would accept this part of the agreement. France would not concede parity and Italy would not accept less. The Japanese delegation was sharply criticized on its return home for failing to obtain a cruiser strength equivalent to 70 per cent of the American figure. All in all, further progress in naval disarmament seemed unlikely.

The Fourteen Points, the League Covenant and the Versailles treaty all called for general disarmament. There was an assumption, rather taken for granted, that armaments in themselves were a cause of war and that their removal would reduce tensions between states. On the other hand it is fair to say that, in discussions at the League, disarmament was seen as only part of an attempt to promote peace. It would have to be accompanied by procedures for arbitration and peaceful settlement of disputes so that the need for states to resort to force would be removed. Ideas like these lay behind the draft treaty and the Geneva protocol. Progress, however, was slow. The Allies were unwilling to let the League proceed until they had made satisfactory progress in disarming Germany. As a result, it was not until the end of 1925 that the League Council charged the preparatory commission to prepare for a general disarmament conference. The commission did not begin its work until May 1926 and did not produce a draft convention until 1930. There were, of course, technical problems in abundance; should trained reserves be counted as part of a country's armed forces; should limitations be made by numbers or by ceilings on defence budgets; what was to be done about equipment such as civil aircraft which could be put to military uses? Above all there was the difficulty of establishing an effective means of inspection. But behind the technical arguments lay the conflicting interests of states anxious to maintain their security, as they saw it. France remained afraid of a German revival and did not accept that she was obliged to disarm to satisfy wounded German pride. Germany argued that since she had been disarmed under the Versailles treaty other states had an obligation to disarm as well. Whatever was agreed, Germany must be treated as an equal. The implication was clear. If other states did not disarm, Germany would rearm. With the production of the draft convention it was agreed to summon a full-scale conference for 1932, but the prospects of its success looked poor even before the onset of economic depression worsened the international atmosphere.

The payment of reparations and war debts was a circular process. American investment enabled Germany to pay reparations to her creditors who in turn paid war debts to the United States. The process depended on the continued willingness and ability of the United States to sustain large-scale foreign lending. Germany did not use the borrowed money wisely; there was a dangerous tendency to borrow short-term funds and tie them up in long-term or unproductive ventures. Heavy borrowing eventually increased the problem of debt servicing, so that fresh loans were needed to pay off old ones. Germany was not the only culprit but her central role in the reparations process made her particularly vulnerable. Signs of trouble began to appear in 1928. The fall in prices of agricultural products reduced the export earnings of countries in eastern Europe, thus making it more difficult for them to service loans. Moreover, the United States Federal Reserve Board raised interest rates in an effort to stem stock market speculation. This diverted investment funds into the domestic market, so that even before the Young Plan was launched loans to Germany were beginning to fall away. Speculation continued until the Wall Street crash of October 1929 struck a blow at American business confidence and further limited foreign lending. Much of the speculation had been done on credit so that financial institutions and investors now began to call in short-term foreign loans. As overall business activity declined so did American imports. The outflow of dollars to Europe was thus checked and then reversed. During 1930 the American recession worsened and the full effects of the crisis began to be felt in Europe. The precarious economic and political stability of the post-Locarno period collapsed.

CHAPTER FIVE

The breakdown of the European system: from Wall Street to Ethiopia, 1929–1935

Hitler became Chancellor of Germany at the end of January 1933. It is tempting but misleading to see the previous three years as simply a prelude to this ominous event. The spread of economic depression certainly contributed to the rise of the Nazis to power and one can see other states adjusting to the possibility of a virulently nationalist government in Germany even before January 1933. On the other hand, the impact of the Depression on the attitudes and morale of European governments was quite severe enough even without taking developments in Germany into account. There was a general loss of confidence and a breakdown in international cooperation which made it difficult to obtain concerted action in defence of the status quo. This can be seen in European reactions to the Manchurian crisis, which had almost run its course by the time of Hitler's appointment. Here the challenge was to the Washington settlement, rather than the remnants of Versailles, but the caution and uncertainty demonstrated in dealing with Japan foreshadowed the fumbling and doubt which other European powers would display when faced with a resurgent Germany. Moreover, the disarmament conference was already in serious difficulties by the beginning of 1933 and pressure for open rearmament was building up steadily within the German army. Any chancellor of Germany would have faced the problem of whether to leave the conference and if so at what moment.

The full effects of the Wall Street crash took some time to make themselves felt and the worst point of the Depression varied from country to country. In the United States the nadir was reached at the time of Roosevelt's inauguration as president in March 1933. France began to experience serious economic difficulty somewhat later than Britain and Germany, whereas the Soviet Union was confronted by the very different problems arising from rapid industrialization and collectivization of agriculture. She did not suffer the symptoms which afflicted the capitalist states – a sharp decline in output, prices and external trade accompanied by heavy unemployment. What most

71

directly affected inter-governmental relations was the liquidity crisis which attacked central banks and private institutions alike. One or two French banks failed towards the end of 1930, but the European financial situation really became serious in May 1931 when it became known that the Austrian Credit-Anstalt was in serious difficulties. Despite foreign loans, from Britain among others, there was a flight of funds from Austria which by June was beginning to affect confidence in German banks as well. The failure of the Danatbank led to the temporary closure of all German banks and a freeze on the repayments of foreign credits. Then sterling came under pressure, leading to the resignation of the second Labour government in August. The National government which succeeded it was forced to abandon the gold standard on 21 September and a number of countries followed suit. This amounted to a devaluation of sterling, especially against the dollar, which might be expected to stimulate exports. In practice it caused a good deal of confusion in exchange rates and an immediate run on gold holdings in the United States, on the assumption that she too would abandon the gold standard.

Faced with instability and volatile movements of funds, central banks and private institutions were unwilling to lend such resources as they could still command, fearing that governments under financial pressure would impose exchange controls or refuse to repay foreign debts. To obtain loans governments had to demonstrate their soundness by balancing their budgets, which was in any case the orthodox reaction to a financial crisis. The Labour government in Britain fell over this very issue; the report of the May Committee published at the end of July forecast a budget deficit and recommended cuts in unemployment benefit. Not surprisingly the government was divided, but found that American loans would only be obtained if the budget was balanced. American institutions did not insist that unemployment benefits must be cut, but without some reduction the budget would not balance. Britain was not, of course, the only country to find that the rise in unemployment tended to push government spending into deficit. Memories of the inflation of the early 1920s made the idea of deficit spending to produce reflation look both unattractive and dangerous. Conscious attempts to stimulate the economy by counter-cyclical spending were as yet little understood. The reduction in unemployment in Germany in the later 1930s was largely the result of Hitler's interest in rearmament, and Roosevelt's haphazard experiments with spending on public works owed little to Keynesian theory. Japan did pursue a deliberately reflationary policy but this too was linked to increases in defence spending. Sweden is the main European example of government intervention to reflate the economy. At the other extreme France remained on the gold standard until 1936, having to maintain deflationary policies to do so. This limited her capacity and willingness to increase military expenditure at the very time that German rearmament was getting under way.

The economic crisis brought an end to reparations, more or less by agreement, and an end to war debt payments, with considerable disagreement – the Depression did not make the United States more benevolent towards its European debtors. Indeed, the protectionist Hawley-Smoot tariff of 1930 made it even more difficult for Europeans to earn dollars at a time when world trade was falling in any case. Although more flexible in his views, President Hoover was unwilling to pursue policies that were likely to provoke congressional opposition. His proposal for a one-year moratorium on reparation and war debt payments was made in June 1931 after considerable hesitation. He wanted to prevent a unilateral German freeze on foreign debt payments and a possible outright repudiation of German obligations. International confidence would be further shaken and American banks stood to lose such funds as they still had in Germany. From this point of view his proposal was not successful. As already mentioned, the Germans did freeze foreign repayments and American bank failures continued, and indeed increased, during 1932. On the other hand he did give the Europeans a breathing space to decide what to do before war debt payments to the United States were due to resume at the end of 1932. Agreement on the moratorium was delayed by the French. As they saw it, once reparations stopped they were unlikely to be resumed, whereas Congress would probably insist on the continuation of war debt payments. This was an accurate assessment, but French doubts created ill-feeling in Washington and helped to intensify the banking crisis in Germany.

Then Germany postponed a proposed conference of the European participants in the Young Plan, calculating that this would improve her bargaining position. Eventually the meeting took place at Lausanne in June and July of 1932. It was agreed that there would be a three-year moratorium on reparations after which Germany would make a final reduced payment, with the important qualification that she should be in a financial position to do so. Britain, France and Italy agreed that formal ratification of Lausanne would be delayed until war debt obligations to the United States had been reduced. In practice, however, reparations were now dead, whatever the attitude of the United States. No German government was likely to resume payment. Hoover had hinted to Laval in October 1931 that a European conference on reparations might lead to a reconsideration of war debts but Congress made its opposition clear in December and the admistration therefore did not pursue the idea. The presidential election of 1932 further complicated the situation; there was then a four-month interregnum between the election and the inauguration of a new President. Roosevelt and Hoover disliked each other and the former wished to keep his hand free. He therefore refused to join in any attempt to deal with war debts or the economic crisis in general.

Both Britain and France asked for postponement of the war debt payments due in December 1932. When Hoover refused the British paid up but the French defaulted. The Herriot government was in fact defeated over an attempt to gain approval for the payment; it had been earlier criticized for yielding to British and Italian pressure at Lausanne. This was the beginning of the end for war debts. Britain made two token payments in 1933 but after the failure of talks with the Americans she too defaulted. Other European debtors, with the exception of Finland, did likewise. Once in office Roosevelt made clear his unwillingness to modify or cancel war debts or to seek powers from Congress to do so. His economic policy was to seek domestic recovery without too much regard for the international implications. In April 1933 he took the dollar off the gold standard, and in July he abruptly announced his refusal to cooperate with a scheme for exchange rate stability then being discussed at the world economic conference in London. This meeting had been agreed on at Lausanne but Hoover had insisted that tariffs and war debts should not be discussed, which left little over for consideration. Roosevelt's 'bombshell' effectively ruined the conference and left in Britain and France considerable doubts about American reliability. The atmosphere was not improved by the refusal of the United States to accept formally that war debts had been abandoned. In her eyes the Europeans had reneged on their debts. This mutual ill-will was to have important consequences later in the decade.

Reparations and war debts thus ended appropriately amidst recriminations. The attempt by France to extract reparations and by Germany to avoid or eliminate them had given particular bitterness to European inter-state relations in the 1920s. The insistence of the United States on the repayment of war debts irrespective of reparation arrangements had poisoned relations with her former allies and the arrangements she had helped to make through the Dawes and Young plans proved in the end economically fragile and incapable of resolving Franco-German differences. Up to a point the Dawes Plan was a success but the Young Plan was overtaken by the economic crisis and never had a chance to prove its merits. Even if the Allies had asked for smaller reparations, Germany would still have resented paying and she had other complaints against the Versailles settlement. Any economic gain to France was more than outweighed by the general ill-will which reparations created. They also made a convenient scapegoat for Germany's economic problems between 1930 and 1932, and Hitler made good use of this.

Economic depression and the breakdown of international financial cooperation affected the attitudes of governments to wider political problems. Preoccupied with their individual economic salvation,

74

states found it difficult to collaborate over disarmament or to face the new and unwelcome problem of the Manchurian crisis. The lack of initiative and imagination that was revealed in economic matters extended also to foreign policy. The National government in Britain was as unwilling as its predecessors to undertake new commitments and remained on balance suspicious of France. A reappraisal of British foreign policy was developing before January 1933 but this was largely a reaction to developments in the Far East. The United States participated in the disarmament conference but would undertake nothing that implied direct political involvement in European affairs. France began the decade in a strong financial position but moved into increasing political instability as well as economic depression. The passing of Briand symbolized the change of atmosphere; in 1929 he had addressed the League in characteristically high-flown but vague terms on the need for a united Europe; two years later he failed in an attempt to be elected president and he died in March 1932. Among the new generation of politicians Pierre Laval was beginning to exert an important influence on foreign policy. Opportunistic and devious, he was prepared to seek an accommodation with Italy and even with Germany, but was compelled to bear in mind the danger that would confront France after 1935. The low French birthrate of the First World War would increase the imbalance between the number of Frenchmen and Germans available for military service. Would Germany in a few years time still be bound by any limitations on her armaments?

The Comintern continued to denounce social democrats as the main enemy but there were signs of change in Soviet foreign policy. Litvinov's appointment as Commissar for Foreign Affairs in July 1930 hinted at a move away from the previous emphasis on good relations with Germany. This trend seemed to be confirmed by the signature in the course of 1932 of a series of non-aggression pacts. Those with Finland, Latvia, Estonia and Poland could be regarded as simply confirming the Litvinov protocol of 1929 but the pact with Poland of July 1932 has more significance than appeared on the surface. Poland was moving away from her previous reliance on France towards a policy of balancing between Germany and Russia, a trend which was strengthened when Josef Beck became Foreign Minister in November 1932. Such a policy had obvious dangers and Poland was not seeking a complete break with France. The latter's value as an ally was, however, cast into doubt by the defensive strategy implicit in the building of the Maginot line. The pact with Russia was reassuring at a time when the political situation in Germany was uncertain. The Russians continued to assert that any Right-wing dictatorship in Germany would be of short duration and would pave the way for a Communist takeover but in the face of capitalist economic instability it was nevertheless wise to insure against trouble with Russia's neighbours. The Manchurian crisis was an added reason for avoiding problems in Europe. Japan might be tempted to revive pressure against the Soviet Far East provinces or to attempt the conquest of Outer Mongolia, a Russian client since the early 1920s.

Italian foreign policy was less obviously affected by the Depression. Despite his background in the Fascist party, Grandi proved to be a cautious foreign minister and Mussolini on the whole left him alone until he resumed direct control of foreign policy in July 1932. Mussolini seemed to feel the need for a bold stroke to maintain Italy's reputation and his attention was beginning to turn again to the conquest of Ethiopia. A desire to avenge the defeat at Adowa in 1896 was combined with the belief that Ethiopia could provide an area of settlement for Italy's surplus population. Diplomatic contacts with the French in 1931 and 1932 suggested that they might be willing to sacrifice their interests in Ethiopia in return for Italian support against Germany. Mussolini could not be expected to welcome a revisionist government in Berlin that might seek union with Austria and challenge Italian policies in the South Tyrol. In a speech at Turin in October 1932 he broached the idea of a four power pact to promote revision of the Versailles settlement. He hoped to play the honest broker and divert German attention away from Austria towards Poland. Italy did not produce detailed proposals, however, until after Hitler's accession to power. Meanwhile relations with France remained uncertain. There was a continuing dispute over naval parity between the two and France resented Italian help to Croatian separatists in Yugoslavia.

One can thus see during 1931 and 1932 signs of policy changes in the light of developments in the Far East and the political crisis inside Germany. The Manchurian crisis ended such stability as the Washington agreements had produced in relations between the major powers over China, and Japan could no longer be regarded as an upholder of the status quo. The seizure of Manchuria was in part a response to the effect of the Depression upon Japan's exports, especially silk, in part a reaction to Chiang Kai-Shek's establishment of a relatively effective central Chinese government by the summer of 1928. His avowed aim of removing foreign concessions and extra-territorial rights presented a challenge to European as well as Japanese interests and a number of clashes and incidents took place. British reinforcements were sent to Shanghai in 1927, Japanese forces appeared in Shantung in 1927 and 1928, and in 1929 Soviet troops intervened in Manchuria to protect the Russian-owned Chinese Eastern Railway. The European powers on balance seemed willing to come to terms with China and this intensified Japanese fears of losing their special position in Manchuria where Chiang's influence was in any case largely nominal.

By 1931 power was beginning to slip away from the civilian politicians in Tokyo into the hands of the army and navy. There was resentment at the humiliations which it was felt Japan had suffered since 1919. She had failed at Versailles to secure acceptance of the principle of racial equality; she had been forced to abandon Shantung; she had made concessions at the Washington and London conferences which had left her without naval parity. Yet she had gained little in return. Why not secure her position in Manchuria? So reasoned the group of army officers who staged an incident on the South Manchurian railway in September 1931. This became the pretext for the conquest of all Manchuria and its conversion into the republic of Manchukuo at the beginning of 1932. Formal Japanese recognition was given in September; in practice the new state was a Japanese satellite. This departure from Japan's previously cautious behaviour took the major powers by surprise. They had been slow to recognize the growth of nationalist feeling and military influence inside Japan and reactions to the initial incident at Mukden were mixed. Japan could claim special rights in Manchuria going back to 1906. If she chose to assert them without harming European interests in China proper this would be a useful limit on Chiang Kai-Shek's freedom of action.

The incident came at the height of the financial crisis in Europe, which made Britain in particular even more reluctant to intervene. The existence of the League, however, meant that the problem could not be completely ignored. China brought the issue before the Council and thus confronted the powers with the possibility of having to impose economic or even military sanctions against Japan. The Soviet Union and the United States were both outside the League. The former refused to become involved in any way, so there was no means of directly resisting Japanese troops in Manchuria except through the efforts of the Chinese themselves. An American observer did attend the Council meeting of 13 October but thereafter the United States retreated to a more cautious policy. Stimson, the Secretary of State, proclaimed America's non-recognition of the creation of Manchukuo on 7 January 1932 but it was clear that the Hoover administration would not go beyond disapproval of Japan and America would not act as an ally of the League. A procedural point allowed the Council to delay the need for action by its members. China's initial appeal was made under article 11 of the Covenant, which did not specifically debar a party to a dispute from voting; since the Council normally required unanimity, Japan was thus able to veto the resolution of 24 October which called upon her to withdraw her forces to the railway zone within three weeks.

Having scored a tactical success, the Japanese seized the initiative by proposing a commission of inquiry, which was eventually agreed upon in a Council resolution of 10 December. This meant further delay while the commission, headed by Lord Lytton, travelled out to the Far East, and the Japanese were thus given time to consolidate their hold over Manchuria. In an effort to strengthen her position China transferred her case to the Assembly which met in special session in March 1932. Although more sympathetic than the Council to the Chinese case, the Assembly was not in practice prepared to take action in advance of the Commission's report. This was eventually considered by the Council in November 1932 and passed on the Assembly, which in February 1933 produced a report of its own but based largely on the findings of the Lytton Commission. The Assembly tried to produce a compromise by suggesting that Manchuria should revert to Chinese sovereignty but remain autonomous and that Japanese rights should be recognized. But Japan had by now no reason to accept half a loaf when she could keep the whole of it. She opposed the proposal and on 27 March 1933 gave notice of her intention to leave the League, thus setting a useful precedent for Hitler. Having secured control of Manchuria and absorbed into it the neighbouring province of Jehol, the Japanese were now willing to stop. But when would expansion at China's expense be resumed, now that outside powers had shown themselves unwilling and unable to intervene?

For the European powers there was some glimmer of hope in the slightly more restrained Japanese behaviour in Shanghai. Here fighting had started in January 1932 as the result of a decision by the local Japanese naval commander. Chinese troops put up stiff resistance and the Japanese had to send in reinforcements to save face and secure a clear-cut victory. The Japanese withdrawal in May was interpreted by the European powers as a sign that Japan could be induced to compromise, but this was a dangerous misreading of the situation. Shanghai was a somewhat awkward sideshow for the Japanese which was not intended to interfere with the conquest of Manchuria. It also showed how easily incidents between Japanese and Chinese forces could be provoked. Moreover, the affair had a bad effect on Anglo-American relations. Stimson had wanted to make a joint complaint to the Japanese but the British prevaricated. Hoping to secure a cease-fire on the spot, they were unwilling to provoke Japan by outright criticism. Unfortunately it took some time for them to make this clear to Stimson, who felt that he had been let down by British weakness and ambiguity. They in turn felt that little more than words could be expected from the Americans. The mistrust thus created was further intensified by Roosevelt's early attempts at economic diplomacy described above.

One must bear in mind, therefore, that the combination of the economic and Manchurian crises prevented the European powers from giving their undivided attention to developments in Germany. The shaky Müller cabinet, much weakened by the death of Stresemann, fell in March 1930. Its successor, the Brüning cabinet, relied heavily on the use of emergency decrees, which made it dependent on the continued goodwill and support of President Hindenburg. When he refused, at the end of May 1932, to sign any more decrees for Brüning the latter had no choice but to resign. The arguments over the Young Plan had shown clearly the depths of German resentment against the Versailles settlement, and this was not reduced by the evacuation of the Rhineland. The Saar and the territories lost to Poland had still to be regained and, above all, the restrictions imposed on German rearmament by part five of the Versailles treaty had to be removed. During 1931 the first German pocket battleship was launched and the Reichstag voted funds for another. This was an ominous warning of how near Germany was to abandoning any pretence of restraint. The problem facing the army was becoming more acute, for the limitation to a small long-service force meant that the veterans of the 1914–18 war would increasingly become too old for active service and Germany would lose a pool of trained reservists who could be called up in an emergency. If France and Poland launched a joint attack the German army would find it difficult to resist. It is true that the French were by now unlikely to undertake a major offensive and to that extent German fears were unreal. Nevertheless German politicians and soldiers were conscious of their country's vulnerable position. There was little disagreement about the need for rearmament; the question was how best to achieve it without alarming the other powers.

The need for caution, however, did not mean a continuation of the policy of propitiating France. Stresemann's policy died with him, as was shown by the tone of the 1930 election campaign. There were few votes to be gained from the maintenance of conciliatory attitudes; on the contrary, Brüning and his Foreign Minister Curtius had to outbid the right by demonstrating that they were standing up for German interests. Up to a point pressure from the right suited them, since they could argue that it was impossible for Germany to make concessions without gaining something in return. In particular, Brüning wanted modification or abandonment of the Young Plan. His personal inclination towards deflation and a balanced budget (at the expense of unemployment benefits) was strengthened by the hope that he could demonstrate Germany's incapacity to pay. Understandable though the reasoning behind his policies may be, he only succeeded in worsening the domestic economic situation without obtaining compensatory successes in foreign policy. The suspicions of the French were increased by Germany's hardening of attitude, and during the 1931 crisis they were unwilling to lend Germany money except in return for promises to maintain the status quo in Europe. Brüning would not give these and the French would not concede an end to reparations, one of the few things that might have strengthened his domestic position. It was ironic that the Lausanne conference did not meet until after Brüning's fall.

His main attempt at a diplomatic initiative – the proposal for a customs union with Austria in March 1931 – was a failure. Launched without preliminary soundings, it provoked opposition in varying degrees from Britain, France, Italy and Czechoslovakia who all objected on two main grounds. The proposal could be seen not only as a breach of the terms of the 1922 loan agreement for Austria but also as a prelude to political union, specifically forbidden in the treaties of Versailles and St Germain. Under the 1922 agreement Austria had promised not to make agreements that would affect her independence and not to concede special economic advantages to any state. The Austrians retreated under a combination of political pressure and the effects of the financial crisis, although it was not until September that they abandoned the project. The Germans had to accept this decision in practice, although they refused to make any formal renunciation. The Permanent Court of International Justice gave a ruling in September that the customs union was a breach of the 1922 agreement, but only by the narrow margin of eight votes to seven. This tended to increase German disgruntlement at what was clearly a diplomatic defeat and Curtius had to resign in October. For the remainder of his time in office Brüning himself took over the Foreign Ministry. He seems to have underestimated the amount of opposition there would be and the timing of the proposal was bad. It intensified French unwillingness to bail out Austrian and German banks during the crisis of the spring and summer. Economic and political failures meant that Brüning and his successors were unable to block the rise in electoral support for both the Nazis and the Communists. In September 1930 the Nazis increased their seats from 12 to 107 and then to 230 in July 1932, falling back to 196 in November of that year. The Communist figures were more modest, given their higher starting point; in September 1930 they went from 54 to 77 seats, then to 89 in July 1932 and to 100 in November 1932. The parliamentary system was under assault from right and left and it could hardly hope to survive by permanent reliance on emergency decrees.

The general international scene and developments inside Germany combined to provide an inauspicious background for the opening of the disarmament conference in February 1932 at Geneva. Only on the surface were the participants concerned with the technical details of a general disarmament convention. Although little use was made of the work of the preparatory commission the underlying argument which had prolonged its proceedings now continued in sharper and more urgent form. The real debate was about the balance of armaments between France and Germany. France sought to maintain a degree of military superiority linked to guarantees of support under the auspices of the League. The plans put forward in the course of 1932, first by Tardieu then by Paul-Boncour, envisaged at least the earmarking of units for service under the League if not the creation of a full-scale international force. When Daladier became Prime Minister (one day after Hitler became Chancellor) he added an emphasis on effective supervision and inspection. Disarmament would have to proceed by stages; procedures for supervision and inspection would have to be thoroughly tested before reductions in arms and manpower could take place. In short, the French wanted security before disarmament.

This was difficult to combine with Germany's demand for formal equality of treatment. The restrictions imposed by part five of the Versailles treaty must go; in any agreement reached, Germany should have the right to weapons not specifically forbidden to all powers. The argument that other states should disarm down to her level was by 1932 little more than a debating point; in practice she was claiming the right to rearm. In July 1932 the von Papen cabinet, under heavy pressure from the army, accepted the principle of early rearmament. It faced a dilemma; any convention agreed at Geneva was unlikely to suit German interests, and might make future expansion of the armed forces difficult; on the other hand Germany did not wish to be accused of breaking up the conference or causing unnecessary difficulties. Until rearmament was well under way she could not afford to antagonize other powers. The French problem was the difficulty of getting more than limited support from Britain and the United States.

Britain still tended to see the French insistence on security as the main obstacle to a disarmament agreement. She was not prepared to give France the kind of guarantees that the latter desired and she did not want to accept further commitments in the name of the League. To deal with genuine grievances, it was argued, would lessen the pressure from Germany. This amounted to saying that France should disarm to some extent and allow a degree of German rearmament, though the British were certainly not contemplating the scale of rearmament which the Germans had in mind. The British attitude was based on the rather dubious proposition that concessions could be found which would satisfy Germany. Even at the time there were signs that this was unlikely. The British also assumed that some agreement was better than none at all. They too wished to avoid accusations of causing the failure of the conference, fearing the electoral repercussions at home.

The United States tended to share the British view of France as the main obstacle and to believe that a compromise could be reached. But she took a less active part in discussions as the presidential election drew nearer. Nevertheless Hoover did obtain a good deal of publicity for the proposals which he released to the press in June 1932. He divided land forces into two types, those needed for internal security and those needed for defence against external attack, and proposed cuts of one-third in the latter. In an effort to meet French concerns he proposed the abolition of tanks and bombers but the retention of fixed fortifications. To some extent he clouded the issue by his continued insistence on naval disarmament according to fixed ratios. Hoover, in other words, was unwilling to admit that after the London conference of 1930 there was unlikely to be much further progress in that direction.

In any case his proposals were largely irrelevant to the central issue of the conference during 1932 – the German demand for equality of rights. After the conference adjourned in July the German delegation made clear that it would not return unless this principle was openly conceded. They were able to play on the British desire to avoid a breakdown. Once the Lausanne conference was out of the way it was easier for Britain to put pressure on France to compromise. During the autumn British policy was aimed at getting a five power conference to discuss the issue and the French somewhat reluctantly agreed to a meeting in Geneva. So, on 11 December, Britain, France, Germany Italy and the United States were able to agree on the formula that Germany should have 'equality of rights in a system which would provide security for all nations'. Agreement came none too soon, for Herriot's government fell only a week later over the question of war debt repayments. This anodyne formula was enough to bring Germany back to the main disarmament conference but as yet it did not give her any specific concessions. She had still to exploit the opening thus gained when Hitler was appointed Chancellor, presenting other European states with a challenge whose full extent was not immediately clear.

That Hitler would attempt to remove the remnants of Versailles was obvious enough. There was a minimum programme which might be expected of him – an end to restrictions on German armaments, an end to the demilitarization of the Rhineland, a return to the frontiers of 1914 and the absorption of the Germans of Austria and Czechoslovakia within a greater Germany. This would involve the overthrow of existing treaties and agreements and would face the signatories with the question of how to react. In early 1933 it hardly seemed likely that Hitler could hope to achieve his territorial aims without resort to force. Removal of restrictions on armaments might be negotiated, but union with Austria would provoke Italian hostility and attempts to gain territory from Poland or Czechoslovakia would presumably mean war and French intervention to help her allies. Would Hitler take the risks involved or would he abandon some at least of his aims in the course of time? If so, it might be possible to draw Germany into a European concert by meeting her more reasonable complaints. Appeasement in the sense of meeting genuine grievances might blunt the ambitions of German nationalism.

Such reasoning presupposed that Hitler had limited aims and was willing to be contained as one of several roughly equal powers within the European system. If, however, one read *Mein Kampf* and studied Hitler's utterances since its completion in 1925, a more disturbing picture emerged. Here was to be found a strident racialism, directed principally but not entirely against Jews, which justified German expansion at the expense of inferior groups. The concept of 'living space' was not very clearly articulated but its implications were obvious enough: Germany could only find living space for her population by expansion eastward at the expense of Russia, not merely to establish satellite or client states but to bring about massive colonization of the conquered areas. Expulsion was the best that the defeated races could expect. Thus Germany could establish a European domination which would allow her at some later stage to make a bid for world power. Control of Europe would certainly entail the destruction of the arch-enemy France; towards Britain Hitler's attitude was more ambiguous. Though he talked of the need to regain German colonies, he seems to have put them well down his list of priorities and was willing to accept Britain as a junior partner.

Such aims went well beyond the restoration of the status quo and could not be achieved without war. Were they to be taken seriously or would Hitler once in power abandon such wild ideas? The European powers were worried about his intentions but found it difficult to believe that he intended to carry out his maximum programme quite as literally as he had proposed. Just as both supporters and opponents within Germany under-estimated Hitler so too states threatened by his ambitions failed to grasp the seriousness of his intent.

Whereas few European leaders contemplated the prospect of another war with enthusiasm, Hitler was quite prepared to use force if necessary. This is not to say that he intended from the start the war which finally broke out in September 1939, but he was ready to fight if the conditions were favourable and the potential enemy isolated. Nor did he have an exact timetable for his various objectives. Considerable tactical skill and opportunism were combined with a rigid and ruthless view of the world. It is perhaps understand-

able that policy-makers in other European capitals found it difficult
to recognize this. Hitler's skill in putting out contradictory signals
helped to confuse them further. He could combine unilateral action
with promises of negotiation and agreement in a way that bewildered
his adversaries and kept them uncertain of the best way to react.

To begin with it was necessary to proceed cautiously. Externally he
must avoid provoking an attack and for a time in the spring of 1933
he seems to have feared that France and Poland might launch a preventive war. Until he had taken the measure of his opponents and
got rearmament well under way, Hitler on the whole preferred to
be conciliatory. Internally he had to consolidate his position; 1933
saw the disappearance of parliamentary opposition, 1934 brought the
elimination of rivals within the Nazi party. For the time being, however, he interfered little with senior posts in the armed forces and the
foreign ministry. Outsiders could try to convince themselves that he
was bringing stability to Germany and that the regime would be
easier to deal with in its external relations, provided they could
overlook the blatant persecution of German Jews.

Two specific issues soon confronted Hitler. Anxious to keep the
disarmament conference alive, the British in March put up a new
plan and Mussolini made specific proposals for a four power pact.
MacDonald himself came to Geneva to present the British plan,
though he had little to do with the preparation of it. France, Germany, Italy and Poland would move towards roughly equal armies
of short-service conscripts over a five-year period. This would allow
Germany rearmament in the sense of increased numbers but would
not give her complete access to all types of weapon. France, moreover, would be allowed to retain troops in her overseas possessions
outside the European numerical limits. She could hope in an emergency to move troops from North Africa to mainland France.
Although the plan was adopted by the conference as a basis for discussion it was not quite what the German delegation wanted. The
French were unhappy that it did not go far enough over inspection
and supervision, and discussions again became bogged down. A conciliatory speech by Hitler in May allowed the conference to adjourn
in June with the hope of avoiding a breakdown, though with little
prospect of making progress. A four-power pact was initialled in
Rome between Britain, France, Italy and Germany on 7 June but
never in fact came into effect. It consisted mainly of a promise to
consult and collaborate within the framework of the League, and to
work for the success of the disarmament conference. Mussolini's
original draft was considerably modified. France objected to the idea
that the four should act outside the League to consider the revision
of treaties, which was precisely what Germany would have liked.
Britain pressed for the commitment to the disarmament conference

but opposed any reference to a common policy on colonies. Mussolini put the best face he could on what thus turned out to be a diplomatic damp squib. Even if the pact had been ratified it would have given him little influence over the policies of the other three powers, but it was in any case soon overtaken by events.

The disarmament conference adjourned because of the meeting of the world economic conference in London and also to allow private discussions to continue during the summer. These showed that Britain was ready to go some way to meet France over the the need for adequate inspection and for disarmament by stages. On the other hand, Britain was less enthusiastic about the French desire to denounce publicly the secret German rearmament which had already taken place. When the conference reconvened in October, Germany was faced first with Anglo-French proposals which would offer little scope for major rearmament and second with the risk of outright condemnation. Hitler decided that the time had come for a break and on 14 October Germany announced her withdrawal from both the conference and the League. The conference adjourned in confusion and, although it met again briefly in May 1934, it was now effectively dead. Hitler had pulled off a diplomatic coup and increased his freedom of action. Now he could offer bilateral agreements and play off one country against another; while hinting at a willingness to return to the League and to accept disarmament agreements he could ensure that German rearmament went ahead as quickly as possible. To this he added another success in the shape of a non-aggression pact with Poland. A new Polish ambassador, Lipski, arrived in Berlin in November and soon indicated that Beck and Pilsudski were prepared to seek an improvement in relations as part of the policy of balance. Hitler seized on the hint, despite the doubts of the Foreign Ministry, and a ten-year non-aggression pact was signed in January 1934. Hitler was quite prepared to put the Polish question on ice until a more suitable moment. The agreement would show Germany's peaceful intentions, and in any case Hitler did not wish to become entangled in detailed arguments about frontier revision which might tie him down to restoration of the 1914 frontier. Beck can be accused of putting too much faith in German goodwill, but he was careful not to commit himself too far. He rejected German hints in 1935 at an alliance aimed against Russia; the policy of balance was intended to avoid so explicit an alignment.

These successes were to some extent offset by Hitler's clumsiness over Austria. During 1933 and early 1934 Germany gave open support to the Austrian Nazis, assuming that they could fairly easily seize power without direct help. Once in power they would no doubt seek union with Germany. Hitler, however, underestimated the extent to which Mussolini was prepared to support Austrian independence and give backing to Dollfuss, who had become chancellor in May 1932. Mussolini forced Dollfuss to dismiss the more liberal members of his government and encouraged the crushing of the Social Democrats. The first meeting between Hitler and Mussolini in Venice in June 1934 failed to clarify their differences over Austria. In the following month Dollfuss himself was due to visit Mussolini and the Austrian Nazis decided to launch a coup before the meeting could take place. Although Dollfuss was killed, the attempted seizure of power on 25 July was a failure. Italian troops were moved up to the border with the Austrian province of Carinthia and for a few days the situation was tense – Yugoslavia threatened to intervene if Italian troops crossed the border. Hitler, however, disclaimed responsibility for the activities of the Austrian Nazis and thereafter showed himself more cautious over the question of an ultimate union between Germany and Austria. Irritated by the episode, Mussolini was inclined towards better relations with France, whose goodwill he would need in any event for an attack on Ethiopia.

For France, Italy would be a useful counterweight to Germany. After Hitler's withdrawal from the League it was logical for France to seek to maintain her existing alliances and to find new friends. Barthou became Foreign Minister in February 1934 and, until his assassination in October, energetically pursued a policy of improved relations with Italy and the Soviet Union. The latter was prepared to go beyond the non-aggression pact of 1932, once it was clear that Hitler was not merely a temporary prelude to Communist rule in Germany. The Russians ended the clandestine military cooperation of the Weimar period after Hitler came to power but were careful not to break completely with Germany. Perhaps the most notable Russian move in 1933 was the establishment of diplomatic relations with the United States in November. The initiative came from Roosevelt but the Russians took it up willingly, seeing in the United States a means of limiting Japanese influence. In this, like the British, they were to be disappointed and American recognition contributed little to Soviet security. The general trend of Soviet policy, however, was clearly towards cooperation with other states who felt themselves threatened by Germany. One possible source of conflict with Japan was removed by the sale of the Chinese Eastern Railway to the latter in March 1935 after much haggling. In September 1934 the Soviet Union at last joined the League and in May 1935 she signed treaties with France and Czechoslovakia, being careful in both cases to relate her obligations to specific articles of the Covenant. During 1935 the Comintern changed its line from criticism of the social democratic parties to one of advocating cooperation in popular fronts against Fascism.

   The Soviet Union was thus coming back into the European concert in a way advantageous to France. In addition to a straighforward alliance, Barthou explored the idea of an agreement in eastern Europe, on the lines of Locarno, which would tie down Germany as well as securing Russian support for the status quo. But here he had to consider the attitude of Britain. The latter would undertake no commitments in eastern Europe; she had doubts about Russian intentions and military capacity and was still anxious to pursue a disarmament agreement which might commit Hitler to specific obligations. The discussions went through various stages; in early 1934 Britain tried to find a compromise on disarmament that would satisfy both France and Germany. This phase ended in April when the French made clear that they would reject any proposals which allowed German rearmament; no agreement was better than dangerous concessions to Germany. By the time of Barthou's death it was equally clear that Germany was unlikely to enter an eastern Locarno. Instead, in November she indicated to Britain her interest in a bilateral naval pact. The intention was to divide Britain from France and to anticipate the naval conference which was expected to take place when the London agreements expired at the end of 1935.

Britain did not respond immediately to this overture; instead the government decided to make an attempt at a more general settlement with Germany. Laval had succeeded Barthou and was prepared to explore the possibility of agreement with Germany, although continuing his predecessor's policy of friendship with Italy and the Soviet Union. Whereas Britain was interested mainly in an air agreement, Laval revived the idea of an eastern Locarno and also proposed a Danubian agreement. Multilateral pacts of this kind had no interest for Hitler, although he kept discussions going during 1935 by suggesting that Germany might make a series of non-aggression pacts in eastern Europe. Meanwhile his position had been strengthened by the plebiscite in the Saar in January 1935: the overwhelming vote for a return to Germany had removed one bargaining counter from the French. Britain seemed the best candidate for a bilateral arrangement but there was the danger that she might try to make German rearmament part of an overall bargain. Sir John Simon, the Foreign Secretary, was due to visit Berlin in early March. Hitler postponed the visit and on the 16 March announced the reintroduction of conscription. Rather surprisingly the British government decided to let Simon's visit go ahead.

While in Berlin (on 25 and 26 March) he found Hitler far from conciliatory and boasting that he had already attained air parity with Britain. He showed some interest in a naval agreement and this time the British rose to the bait. Later discussions produced an agreement on the 18 June which gave Germany up to 35 per cent of British surface tonnage and virtual parity in submarine building. Britain did not inform France and Italy until the discussions were well under way and she proceeded to conclude the agreement despite their objections. The timing seemed inept, for the three powers had met at Stresa in April to discuss the German announcement of the reintroduction of conscription. The Stresa front was in no sense an alliance nor did the three powers propose specific action against Germany. They contented themselves with criticisms of her unilateral action but it could be regarded as significant that they were prepared jointly to reaffirm their commitments under the League and Locarno. The Franco-Soviet treaty, signed the following month, seemed to increase the chances of creating an effective coalition against Germany. That Britain should break ranks so soon afterwards caused much irritation in Paris.

British policy was going through an uncertain phase. The Manchurian crisis had made it clear that it would be difficult for Britain to defend her interests in the Far East against strong Japanese pressure. From 1933 onwards there was growing uncertainty about Hitler's intentions. Germany and Japan were not yet allies but there was the dangerous possibility that Britain would have to confront simultaneous crises in Europe and the Far East. In 1932 the ten-year rule (that the armed forces should assume that Britain would not be involved in a major war for ten years) was effectively dropped, but this did not immediately produce rearmament. The electorate was thought to be hostile and there were doubts about how much Britain could afford to spend. It made sense, therefore, to seek accommodations with Japan and Germany. At the very least this would gain time, at best it might remove some genuine sources of conflict. During 1934 Neville Chamberlain, then Chancellor of the Exchequer, argued for a non-aggression pact with Japan. Such a move, however, would antagonize the United States, and although she was a doubtful ally in the Pacific there was no point in provoking her into outright hostility. Moreover, the Japanese proved difficult to pin down. In July 1934 and again in March 1935 they showed interest in a possible political agreement but did not follow it up with specific proposals. Their attention was concentrated on gaining naval parity with America and Britain and when the second London naval conference met in December 1935 it soon became clear that the United States would not concede this. Japan gave notice of her intention to end the Washington agreements and left the conference in January, thus ending any hopes of further naval disarmament.

Britain had not succeeded in improving her position in the Far East, but the earlier hope of an arrangement with Japan encouraged the British to make the German agreement. Thus she could hope to limit the risks of simultaneous naval competion in both Europe and Asia. Hitler's unpredictable behaviour made Germany look more and more like a potential enemy, yet there was no point in provoking a quarrel until Britain was militarily stronger. However reluctantly, the government was driven to accept the need for rearmament. This was publicly admitted with the publication of the first Defence White Paper in March 1935. At this stage the main fear was of heavy bombing of London and southern England, which was expected to cause rapid demoralization among the civilian population. The need, therefore, was to build up a bomber force as a deterrent, not to plan for a large expeditionary force to be sent to the Continent. One can see the rationale behind the British position but there was a good deal of tactical clumsiness in the handling of both France and Germany from 1933 to 1935. This came in part from the uncertainties of the international situation, in part from the impact of individual personalities. MacDonald's powers were failing well before he resigned as Prime Minister in June 1935; Baldwin's interest in foreign affairs was intermittent and Simon lacked the initiative to match his analytical abilities.

The real problem was that Hitler would not enter into the kind of multi-lateral agreements in which Britain hoped to enmesh him. By the end of 1935 it was clear that there was little hope of securing agreement on an air pact, a Danubian pact or an eastern Locarno. Failure to obtain an agreement with Japan was thus matched by Britain's inability to pin Germany down save for the naval agreement. It suited Hitler for the moment to avoid naval competition. For both Britain and France there was also the added complication of Italy's attack on Ethiopia. In the course of 1935 the dilemma which confronted them became yet more obvious; could they retain Italian friendship while upholding their professed commitment to the League?

CHAPTER SIX
The breakdown of the European system: from Ethiopia to the Second World War, 1935–1939

In December 1934 Mussolini finally committed himself to an invasion of Ethiopia when the rainy season ended in the following October. There was the general consideration that it seemed wise to attain his East African ambitions before German strength in Europe increased, but the timing of his decision was largely the result of a clash between Ethiopian and Italian forces at Wal Wal early in December. The Ethiopians refused either to take responsibility or to pay an indemnity; instead they proposed conciliation and arbitration under a 1928 treaty with Italy, and they also raised the matter before the League. Angered by this defiance, Mussolini decided on military action. Nevertheless it suited him to keep the Wal Wal incident alive while he concentrated troops in East Africa. After some delay he agreed to arbitration but then postponed the appointment of Italian representatives. The report of the arbitration committee finally appeared in September 1935 and was rather inconclusive, but Mussolini was not particularly interested in its findings.

In view of their interests in Ethiopia, French and British goodwill would be needed for Italy's plans. But for his assassination in October 1934, Barthou would have paid a formal visit to Rome and in view of his wish to build up a coalition against Germany he might well have made substantial concessions. Certainly his successor Laval seemed only too willing to conciliate Italy when he arrived in Rome in January 1935. He agreed that Italy could have a free hand in Ethiopia and that France would seek only to maintain her existing economic interests there. Perhaps he did not anticipate that Mussolini was aiming at outright annexation and in any case he gained something in return. Mussolini was now prepared to compromise over the troublesome question of the status of Italians in Tunisia; even more important, he promised staff talks and military cooperation. An agreement was signed at the end of June which seemed to relieve France of the threat of Italian hostility should war break out with

Germany. Indeed, there was even the possibility of Italian troops serving on the French frontier.

Here was a prize that Laval was naturally unwilling to lose. At the beginning of June he became Prime Minister for the second time but retained the foreign ministry as well. His government depended heavily on the backing of the Radicals, who were in general supporters of the League. If Ethiopia sought further help in Geneva, Laval might find himself faced with a choice between alienating Italy or losing domestic support, were he blatantly to ignore France's obligations under the Covenant. The British government faced a similar dilemma. The electorate were assumed to be in the main supporters of collective security and pacifist by inclination. Such were the conclusions that could reasonably be drawn from the peace ballot held by the League of Nations Union towards the end of June, and it was noticeable that the first Defence White Paper in March had a mixed reception. The British government had no wish for a conflict with Italy over Ethiopia, yet was anxious not to encourage her ambitions too openly.

When Mussolini sought assurances of British benevolence at the end of January and again in May, he received no direct answer. Nor did Ethiopia feature in the main discussions at Stresa in April. It was only after the government changes in June, when Baldwin replaced MacDonald as Prime Minister and Hoare became Foreign Secretary in place of Simon, that Britain made a response to Mussolini's overtures. An attempt was made to buy him off by revising an earlier Ethiopian proposal that she should acquire the port of Zeila in British Somaliland in exchange for frontier adjustments. Now it was proposed that in return for Zeila Ethiopia should cede territory to Italy. Mussolini, however, rejected a compromise which would give his intended victim an outlet to the sea and deny him a showy military success. After three-power talks in Paris during August he again rejected a similar proposal. Thus Britain and France had still not escaped from their dilemma when the League Assembly met in September. Privately Hoare and Laval agreed that their governments would restrict themselves to economic sanctions against Italy and would continue to work for a compromise. Laval added the important qualification that a sanction on oil supplies must be avoided in case it provoked military retaliation from Italy. These qualifications were not apparent when Hoare addressed the Assembly on 11 September; on the contrary, he gave the impression of a stronger British commitment to firm action than was in fact the case. Although naval reinforcements were moved into the Mediterranean, there was a definite British intention to avoid provoking an Italian attack. What was the point of winning a local conflict at the cost of reducing Britain's capacity to deploy ships in the Far East?

After the Italian invasion of Ethiopia began in October, Britain and France supported only the imposition of partial sanctions and Britain refrained from closing the Suez canal to Italian shipping. It was assumed that the war would be a lengthy one; if so, pressure on the League to cut off oil supplies would probably increase and it would be in French and British interests to find a compromise before that awkward problem arose. As early as 17 October Mussolini seemed to be having second thoughts and hinted that he might settle for less than total conquest. It was this approach which led to the signing of the Hoare–Laval pact in Paris in December. That Ethiopia should be asked to cede territory and a zone of economic exploitation to Italy was in line with the earlier attempts at a settlement. These were not fully known in Britain and France, however, and when details of the plan appeared in the press of both countries there was a generally hostile reaction. The abandonment of collective action in the name of the League in favour of a cynical surrender of Ethiopian interests was too great a public reversal of policy to be easily defensible. Hoare was forced to resign, being replaced by Eden (previously Minister for League of Nations Affairs) and Laval fell from power in January 1936 to remain out of office for the rest of the decade.

The Stresa front was now clearly broken, although Italy did not formally denounce the agreements with Laval until the end of 1938. She had now no reason to make further attempts at a settlement. Fortunately for Mussolini's prestige he had not formally accepted the Hoare–Laval Plan by the time it leaked to the press, and he could now push on with military conquest. Resuming the offensive in February with the aid of mustard gas, the Italians scored considerable success. In May 1936 Ethiopia was formally annexed and the King of Italy was proclaimed emperor. The rapidity of the Italian conquest meant that the question of oil sanctions was never put to the test, although by the beginning of March the British government had reluctantly agreed on the need for their imposition. This alarmed the French; Flandin, Laval's successor as Foreign Minister, was just as unwilling to provoke Italy. The abandonment of sanctions by the League in July gave Britain and France some hope of improving their own strained relations and of restoring at least the semblance of friendship with Italy.

Mussolini, however, was not a forgiving man; he had been irritated by Franco-British support for the League, by what he regarded as French bad faith and by the inept handling of the Hoare–Laval Plan. As a result his attitude towards Germany began to change. In a conversation with the German ambassador in Rome on 7 January, Mussolini showed his pleasure at the benevolent neutrality which Hitler was displaying over the Ethiopian crisis. He made the significant concession that Italy would not object to Austria coming under Geman influence, provided that she retained a nominal independence.

Whether or not this was intended as an explicit signal of a complete change of front, Mussolini followed up in June by advising the Austrian Chancellor, Schuschnigg, to come to terms with Germany. Given such an obvious hint the Austrians had little choice; on 11 July they signed an agreement in which they promised to follow a foreign policy closer to that of Germany in return for a promise to maintain Austrian independence. Hitler could await a suitable opportunity to absorb Austria and there was now no obstacle to a general improvement in relations with Italy.

In June Mussolini again gave up the foreign ministry, this time to his son-in-law Ciano. The latter visited Berlin in October and, although no formal alliance was signed at this stage, Mussolini was able to proclaim at the beginning of November that there was now in existence a Rome–Berlin axis. The revisionist powers seemed to be drawing closer together when, at the end of the month, Germany and Japan signed the anti-Comintern pact. It was, however, to be nearly another year before Italy joined, and there were important differences of emphasis between Germany and Japan. The latter did not want to be drawn into specifically European problems and was primarily concerned with gaining support against the Soviet Union. There were divisions among the Japanese armed forces but on balance Russia seemed the main threat to Japanese influence in Manchukuo and North China. The anti-Comintern pact did not imply unanimous Japanese support for an anti-British policy. For their part the Germans were not as yet prepared to write off their interests in China.

Nevertheless the partial alignment of Germany, Italy and Japan was a setback for France and Britain. The latter in particular was more sharply confronted with the risk of simultaneous crises in Europe, the Mediterranean and the Far East. The end of the Ethiopian war might have removed one source of tension, but German reoccupation of the Rhineland and the outbreak of the Spanish Civil War made 1936 a year of continuing problems for France and Britain. Hitler had not originally planned to reoccupy the demilitarized zone for another year or so, but the Ethiopian crisis and the pending ratification of the Franco-Soviet treaty of May 1935 seemed to offer an excellent opportunity. Much to Soviet annoyance, Laval had delayed ratification, knowing that French opinion was sharply divided about the wisdom of collaboration with Russia. Germany, moreover, tried to play on these doubts by arguing that the treaty was a breach of Locarno. After Laval's fall the French Chamber of Deputies began discussions and in fact ratified the treaty on 27 February. By the middle of February Hitler had already decided to move, using ratification as a pretext and knowing that Mussolini was unlikely to interfere to uphold Locarno.

On 22 February Germany obtained confirmation of Italy's passive support and on 7 March German troops reoccupied the Rhineland. Shortly before they moved Hitler repeated his tactics of sending out confusing signals with proposals for non-aggression pacts and an air agreement. He even talked of rejoining the League. The French had no contingency plan to deal with the crisis and so were faced with a choice between inactivity or full-scale mobilization. Hesitant to act without support, they did nothing. The British government doubted whether public opinion would support military action and found the dominions opposed to the risk of war. A meeting of the League Council in London agreed that Germany was in breach of Versailles and Locarno but took no further action.

Once again Hitler had gambled successfully that Britain and France would not go beyond verbal complaint. He had also prevented any attempt to use remilitarization as a bargaining counter in negotiations for a general settlement, a possibility which the British had indeed considered. Although it would be some time before Germany's western frontier was effectively fortified, France would now find great difficulty in coming to the aid of Poland and Czechoslovakia even if she had the willpower to do so. Her inertia during the crisis was just as damaging in the eyes of her allies as the fact of remilitarization itself. Belgium reacted by announcing in October that she would revert to a policy of neutrality. It was not until April 1937 that Britain and France formally released her from the obligations of Locarno, but the damage was already done. The Maginot line had not been extended along the Belgian frontier, since France had assumed that in the event of a German attack she could move troops into Belgium with the latter's cooperation and consent. This could no longer be taken for granted.

Nor did France succeed in improving her position in eastern Europe. She agreed in September to make a loan to Poland for the purchase of military equipment but was subsequently unable to deliver the materials promised. An attempt to convert her existing treaties with the Little Entente into a full-scale alliance came to nothing, although talks dragged on from October 1936 until April 1937. It was significant that Czechoslovakia tried unsuccessfully in the second half of 1936 for some kind of agreement with Germany and that in March 1937 Yugoslavia signed a non-aggression pact with Italy. The Little Entente remained in existence but its members could no longer feel sure of French support in a crisis. It was therefore logical to attempt to improve relations with their powerful neighbours. This was easier for Yugoslavia, since Italy was happy to undermine French influence in the Balkans, whereas Hitler did not wish to tie his hands by an agreement with Czechoslovakia. Despite ratification of the treaty with Russia, France seemed unwilling to put any faith in it. Doubts of Soviet capacity and intentions were strong inside the

French armed forces. At Russian request, preliminary staff talks began in the autumn of 1936 but came to an inconclusive end in the spring of 1937. French policy seemed unable to attain momentum in any direction.

There was perhaps a crumb of comfort for the French in the British willingness to hold staff talks in April 1936 and even to promise to send two divisions to the Continent in the event of war. This was something of a departure from the previous British policy of avoiding the commitment of land forces in Europe. The staff talks, however, were not followed up by further meetings and the two countries went their separate ways over rearmament. A French programme was launched in September 1936 but was slow to produce results. Having increased defence spending in March 1936, the British government was forced to reconsider by the economic recession of 1937 and in December of that year plans for a sizeable Continental expeditionary force were dropped. It would be some three or four years before rearmament improved the Franco-British bargaining position. In the meantime they continued attempts to draw Germany back into a multilateral European arrangement. Hitler, however, had no intention of being ensnared in a replacement for Locarno; Mussolini and he rejected proposals made in August 1936 for a five power conference to produce a new agreement. Germany, too, faced problems as the result of rearmament. Confronted in 1936 by labour shortages, balance of payments difficulties and the danger of inflation, Hitler chose to press on with rearmament and with the attempt to make a Germany as self-sufficient as possible. The Four Year Plan, launched in October 1936 under Goering's direction, showed a disregard for the financial obstacles which worried Britain and France. In Hitler's view territorial expansion would solve the problem; economic difficulties only served to push him along a road which he wanted to take in any case.

The wish to gain time and avoid a premature confrontation with Germany had a considerable effect on French and British governmental attitudes to the military rising in Spain in July 1936. This was the beginning of a bitter civil war which embodied in miniature the ideological divisions of Europe and produced deep cleavages in French and British opinion. Acting independently of each other at first, Hitler and Mussolini both decided to help the rebels, thus enabling Franco to move his troops from Spanish Morocco to the mainland and then to maintain the momentum of his campaign. Mussolini built up a large army in Spain in the course of 1937, whereas Hitler concentrated on supplying planes and pilots. The Germans had a strong interest in obtaining supplies of iron ore; Mussolini for a time was tempted by the idea of establishing a naval base in the Balearic Islands. He could then threaten France's ability to move large numbers of troops from North Africa across the Mediterranean. For both Italy and Germany it would be valuable to have a friendly government on France's south-western border. Anticipating an early victory for Franco, they gave him diplomatic recognition in November 1936; the war, however, was to drag on much longer than they expected.

If Britain and Franch gave aid to the Spanish Republic there would be some risk of a European war. The British government was not especially sympathetic to the Republic, and with the Ethiopian war just ended did not want another confrontation with Italy. In France Leon Blum had formed a Popular Front government in June with Communist support. His personal sympathies lay with the Republic, but his government and the country were deeply divided: intervention might provoke Germany or lead to civil war in France itself. Blum was therefore only too willing to heed British warnings against aiding the Republic, although these reinforced rather than created his doubts. Having proclaimed a policy of non-intervention in August, after some fierce arguments in Cabinet, Blum tried to get international support for a general non-intervention agreement. In this the British government was prepared to help him, hoping to keep the conflict localized. The lack of French and British support had the effect of pushing the Spanish Republic into dependence on the Soviet Union, which began supplying aid in October 1936. Russian agents also helped to organize the groups of volunteers which became known as the International Brigades.

Germany, Italy and Russia were prepared to accept non-intervention as a convenient façade behind which they could pursue their respective policies. In September 1936 a non-intervention committee was set up in London, a formal agreement was signed in December, and in the end twenty-seven countries participated. Even if they had all been well-intentioned it would have been difficult to enforce both the agreement and the control scheme which was introduced in March 1937. Germany and Italy withdrew from the latter some three months later and in August Italian submarines began attacking shipping in the Mediterranean. In theory the origin of the attacks was unknown; in practice there was the danger of a serious Franco-Italian clash. Britain managed to head this off at the Nyon conference in September, when nine countries agreed on a system of anti-submarine patrols in the Mediterranean. Germany and Italy refused to attend because the Soviet Union would be present, but even before the conference British patrols had forced the Italians to call off their attacks. The Italians subsequently joined in the Nyon arrangements and there were no more serious incidents until January 1938.

A conflict in the Mediterranean was thus avoided but relations between France and Italy remained bad. Britain, however, continued to try for an agreement that would keep Italy detached from Germany. An exchange of notes in January 1937 – the so-called gentleman's agreement – promised that both countries would maintain the status quo in the Mediterranean. Mussolini had by now abandoned the hope of a naval base in the Balearics but he did not interpret the agreement to mean a withdrawal of Italian troops from Spain. Nevertheless, when Neville Chamberlain succeeded Baldwin as Prime Minister in May 1937 he actively pursued a more general agreement with Italy as well as continuing efforts for an overall settlement with Germany. Chamberlain, in other words, did not invent appeasement; Britain had been trying to meet German grievances in one way or another since 1933, but the new Prime Minister's methods were more forceful and consistent than those of Baldwin.

Mussolini was anxious to secure recognition of the annexation of Ethiopia; in return he could be induced to withdraw troops from Spain. It was over this potential agreement that Eden resigned as Foreign Secretary in February 1938, on the grounds that Britain would be making a bad bargain. During 1937 Mussolini had shown few signs of becoming detached from Hitler. On the contrary he had paid a formal visit to Germany in September; Italy had signed the anti-Comintern pact in November; in the following month she announced her withdrawal from the League. Yet it seemed unwise to abandon Italy entirely to German friendship. By maintaining links with her Britain might hope to limit or prevent further crises in the Mediterranean. Such reasoning led Chamberlain and Halifax, Eden's successor, to negotiate the Anglo-Italian agreement of April 1938, which came into force in November. Italy thus gained British recognition of the conquest of Ethiopia. Although 10,000 troops were withdrawn from Spain some 12,000 remained, and the Civil War continued to move in Franco's favour. The Soviet Union was by now running down her aid to the Republic. It could be argued, therefore, that British gains from the agreement were purely negative: Italy, if not a friend, was not an outright enemy and the fiction of non-intervention could be preserved.

The cautious British attitude over Spain and the Mediterranean was reinforced by a new crisis in the Far East. A clash between Japanese and Chinese troops near Peking in July 1937 rapidly turned into a full-scale war. Unlike the Manchurian crisis of 1931, this incident had not been planned in advance by the Japanese military. They soon committed themselves, however, to an attempt at establishing outright control over China. In the course of 1937 and 1938 Japanese forces occupied the main cities, seaports and communication centres. Chiang Kai-Shek's government was forced back to Chungking in the south-west, but refused to admit defeat. The Japanese were unable therefore to terminate the 'China incident', as they called it, by obtaining Chinese submission to their dominance. Nevertheless, the Japanese were in a strong enough position to issue a statement on 3 November 1938 in which they proclaimed the aim of establishing a new order in East Asia. Other powers would be expected to accept Japan's policy and to adapt their behaviour accordingly.

Japan's claim to exclusive control over China was a direct challenge to European and American interests. Britain and France were unwilling to take a strong line that might involve them in a quarrel with Japan unless they could get support from the United States, but Roosevelt was unwilling to make joint representations or undertake joint action. This became clear in December 1937, when the American gunboat *Panay* was sunk by Japanese bombers and the British gunboat *Ladybird* was damaged by artillery fire. The Japanese government apologized and agreed to pay compensation but similar incidents could happen again, and the American reluctance to form a common front with Britain meant that it would be difficult to bring effective diplomatic pressure to bear on Tokyo. This was confirmed by the fate of China's appeal to the League. The latter body merely passed the problem over to the signatories of the nine power Washington treaty of 1922 and thus effectively washed its hands of the question. The nine, augmented by some other states including the Soviet Union, met in Brussels in November 1937 but failed to agree on any positive course of action. Japan herself did not attend and ignored such criticisms of her policy as were made at the conference.

There were, of course, good reasons for Roosevelt's caution. As defaulters on their war debts, Britain and France were unpopular in the United States. The system of imperial preference established by the Ottawa conference in 1932 was regarded with suspicion in Washington as a barrier to American exports. In Congress there was a good deal of support for the belief that Anglo-French intrigues had been responsible for the United States' entry into the war in 1917. As a result various neutrality acts were passed from 1935 onwards which prevented the sale of American arms to belligerents in wartime, and at the beginning of 1937 Congress also passed an act banning arms exports to either side in the Spanish Civil War. Thus the President's hands were formally tied and it would be politically unwise for him to defend openly British and French interests in the Far East. His attempts to rouse American opinion to the dangers of the international situation had only a limited effect and tended to strengthen Anglo-French doubts about American reliability. On 5 October 1937 Roosevelt made the famous speech in which he spoke of the possibility of imposing a quarantine on the dictators. It turned out that in practice he had no specific policies in mind. At the beginning of 1938 he attempted to launch an international conference to discuss disarmament and economic problems but Chamberlain rejected the proposal, fearing it would complicate his own attempts to get agreements with Germany and Italy. Roosevelt was having some difficulty in living down his cavalier behaviour during the world economic conference of 1933. One significant development did take place, however, when in January 1938 he sent a naval officer to London for secret talks with the Admiralty about possible cooperation against Japan. News of the contacts leaked to Congress, and as a result Roosevelt did not immediately follow them up.

As far as confronting Germany was concerned, Britain and France were still very much dependent on their own resources. During 1937 Hitler carried out no coup comparable to the reoccupation of the Rhineland but there were some significant developments in his assessment of the European situation. He seemed to have given up the hope of British friendship or neutrality. In a speech to senior officers on 5 November he described France and Britain as hate-inspired antagonists and argued that Germany would have to achieve her aims, by force if necessary, before the period 1943 to 1945 when the military balance would begin to shift against her. He then went on to speculate about various possibilities which might arise in the near future for an attack on Czechoslovakia. The situation in the Mediterranean might lead to a war between France and Italy, which would in turn allow Germany to attack Czechoslovakia with impunity. The significance of this speech has been much debated; Hitler may have been talking largely for effect. Yet in December 1937 German military planning was amended to give priority to a surprise attack on Czechoslovakia. Hitler thus appeared more confident about the possibility of sudden moves in eastern Europe. His domestic position was strengthened at the beginning of February 1938 by a purge of senior army officers as a result of which Hitler himself took the post of War Minister. At the same time he appointed Ribbentrop Foreign Minister and thus removed the small degree of independence which the professional diplomats had managed to retain.

Chamberlain had still not given up hope of a general agreement with Germany. Halifax made a semi-official visit in November 1937 and returned to London with the belief that it would be possible to come to terms over colonies and over eastern Europe. The British tended to overestimate Hitler's interest in colonies; more important was the difference of emphasis on eastern Europe. Halifax was prepared to concede German influence but not an exclusive predominance that would shut out British trade. He also expected Germany to observe certain rules of international behaviour, and in particular to avoid the use of force. Unfortunately, the impression conveyed to Hitler was that Britain would concede him a free hand and would not fight over eastern Europe. He failed to grasp that Britain would not indefinitely go on making concessions.

In contrast to his bellicose talk about attacking Czechoslovakia, Hitler still seemed content to let events take their course in Austria. The local Nazis were likely to obtain greater influence over the government. If they could secure a request for union with Germany by legal means, Britain and France were unlikely to do more than register a protest. The Austrian Nazis were impatient, however, and not much concerned to use constitutional procedures. In January 1938 the Austrian government uncovered evidence of a Nazi plot to provoke German intervention. This led Chancellor Schuschnigg to seek an interview with Hitler in the hope of maintaining Austrian independence by offering concessions to the Nazis. When the two men met on 12 February Schuschnigg was bullied into signing an agreement that gave the vital post of Minister of the Interior to the Nazi Seyss-Inquart.

When the French government discovered what had happened at the interview it showed some alarm but found itself once again without supporters. Relations with Italy were bad and Mussolini was now unlikely to protect Austria as he had done in 1934. Britain had no treaty obligation to Austria and had just put some new proposals to Germany about colonial questions. She was not anxious, therefore, to make an issue of Austria. Schuschnigg could expect little international support if he tried to resist German pressure. Even so, he decided to put up a fight and on 9 March announced a plebiscite for the 13th on the subject of Austrian independence. On Hitler's instructions the Austrian Nazis forced Schuschnigg to call off the plebiscite and to resign. Seyss-Inquart requested German intervention in terms prearranged by Goering, and German troops crossed the frontier on 12 March. Next day Austria was formally annexed. Britain and France did no more than protest; France was in any case paralysed by the lack of a government. The Chautemps ministry fell on the 10th and Blum did not form his second ministry until the 13th. Hitler had hesitated at first to intervene openly and the invasion itself was ill-coordinated, but another gamble had given him one more of his objectives with no resistance from Britain and France. Not only had Germany acquired Austria's manpower and economic resources but she had also outflanked the main Czech defences on the frontier of Bohemia. His improvised but easy success encouraged Hitler to put pressure on Prague.

From its creation the Czechoslovak Republic had contained a minority of some 3 million Germans, concentrated mainly in the Sudetenland. The Germans had some genuine complaints about educational and linguistic discrimination, yet from 1926 onwards German politicians participated in coalition governments in Prague. Support for union with Germany was limited until Hitler's rise to power created a more intransigent mood. In the elections of 1935 Konrad Henlein's Sudeten German party gained two-thirds of the

German-speaking vote. Henlein claimed to be independent of Berlin although in fact he received subsidies and advice from Nazi organizations. Ostensibly his party sought only autonomy within the existing Czech state but by the end of 1937 Henlein was committed to union with Germany, however ambiguous his public utterances might be.

Riots in the Sudetenland in October 1937 were easily suppressed but they showed how internal disturbances might offer Hitler a pretext for intervention. Britain had no formal commitment to help Czechoslovakia comparable to the French treaty of 1924. If France came to Czechoslovakia's aid then the Soviet Union would be obliged to do so as well under the terms of the Russian-Czech treaty of May 1935. If the Soviet Union were to intervene effectively she would need rights of passage over Polish and Rumanian territory. By late 1937 the extent of the purges in the Red Army had increased Franco-British doubts about Soviet military effectiveness. At the end of November Chautemps and his foreign minister Delbos visited London for talks. Chamberlain made clear British opposition to any commitment in eastern Europe; Delbos reaffirmed France's obligation to Czechoslovakia, although in muted tones. Neither government saw the Czechs as blameless: the Sudeten Germans were assumed to have genuine cause for complaint (which was true) and Henlein was seen as a reasonably moderate figure (which he was not). If German grievances could be dealt with Hitler would be deprived of an excuse for intervention. Even before the disappearance of Austria it was therefore doubtful how far Britain and France would be prepared to go on Czechoslovakia's behalf. Delbos tried to give a public indication of support by visiting Poland, Rumania, Yugoslavia and Czechoslovakia in December 1937. It was noticeable that he omitted the Soviet Union from his tour.

The takeover of Austria increased unrest among the Sudeten Germans. German Social Democratic members of the Czech government withdrew early in April. Henlein received instructions from Hitler at the end of March to ask for more than the Czechs could be expected to concede. He formulated a series of demands on 24 April which amounted to a call for full autonomy. Meanwhile France acquired yet another government, but this one was to survive until early 1940. On 10 April Daladier became Prime Minister for the third time and made Bonnet his Foreign Minister. Daladier gave an impression of firmness which concealed inner indecision; Bonnet had an unfortunate gift for creating mistrust and spreading an atmosphere of pessimism. Neither man sought an open confrontation with Germany over Czechoslovakia, yet neither wished to publicly renege on France's obligations. When they visited London at the end of April 1938 they agreed with Chamberlain on the need for Czechoslovakia to make concessions. Bonnet was ambiguous and half-hearted, however, in his approaches to the Czech government, preferring to let Britain make the running.

A crisis blew up suddenly in May, when reports of German troop movements led the Czechs to call up some reservists. It is not entirely clear whether Hitler was in fact planning a surprise attack but, faced with Czech resolution and cautious Anglo-French warnings, he denied that any troop movements were taking place. The crisis fizzled out but it had some important consequences. Annoyed by his humiliation, Hitler decided to have his revenge and confirmed at the end of May that he would destroy Czechoslovakia by military force. Britain and France were alarmed by what they regarded as Czech rashness in helping to precipitate a crisis. On 22 May Halifax warned the French that Britain was not obliged to intervene if they went to the aid of Czechoslovakia. The French for their part were careful not to follow up a Soviet proposal for military talks made shortly before the May crisis. On 20 July Bonnet at last gave the Czechs a clear warning that France would not fight over the Sudetenland.

With negotiations between the Czech government and the Sudeten Germans in a stalemate, Britain and France continued to press Prague to make concessions. In early September, therefore, President Benes virtually gave Henlein all that he had demanded in April, much to the latter's disgust. He found an excuse to break off discussions on the 8th. On the previous day *The Times* had suggested that some German-speaking districts might be ceded to Germany. It was not the first paper to do so but its reputation as a semi-official organ gave respectability to the principle of cession as distinct from autonomy. Violent speeches by Goering and Hitler at the Nuremberg party rally produced rioting in the Sudetenland on the 13th. On that same day Chamberlain proposed a personal meeting with Hitler. At their first encounter the British Prime Minister accepted in principle that certain German-speaking areas would have to be handed over. Daladier and Bonnet came to London again on the 18th and on the following day a joint plan was presented to the Czechs, whereby they would hand over districts in which at least half the population was German-speaking. After some initial resistance the Czechs agreed, although Prime Minister Hodza resigned in protest.

It might seem that Hitler had gained a bloodless victory and could accept what Britain and France were offering him. Perhaps he wanted to extract more concessions, perhaps he did not want to be deprived of a military success, or, as he said afterwards, perhaps he hoped to occupy the whole of Czechoslovakia. When Chamberlain visited him again on 22 and 23 September, Hitler increased his demands: he now wanted even larger areas handed over by 1 October, and introduced the question of Polish and Hungarian claims. These new proposals produced some resistance in both the British and French cabinets. In the last week of September there seemed to be a real possibility of war until Hitler retreated. There was a clear lack of enthusiasm among the population of Berlin and Mussolini was unwilling to be drawn into war over Czechoslovakia. On the 28th Hitler accepted Mussolini's proposal for a four power conference. Britain had in fact put the idea to Rome and Mussolini was only too glad to play the role of mediator in a crisis.

The Munich conference of 29 and 30 September merely registered what had already been decided: Germany was to occupy the Sudetenland, although there was some windowdressing in the form of an international commission which in fact never functioned. The four powers were supposed to guarantee what was left of Czechoslovakia but the terms of the guarantee were never clearly worked out. The Poles seized Teschen and at the beginning of November Czechoslovakia was forced to cede southern Slovakia to Hungary under the first Vienna award. Beneš had by then resigned the presidency in disgust. The Czechs were not represented at Munich but were summoned at the end of the conference to hear its decisions. The European powers had reallocated the territory of a lesser state to suit their own interests, thus bringing a shadowy revival of the traditional concert of the powers. Mussolini could congratulate himself on posing as the arbiter of Europe and thus concealing Italy's weakness. Chamberlain regarded the declaration on Anglo-German friendship which Hitler signed at Munich as perhaps even more important than the Czech settlement. The French were anxious to obtain a similar agreement and for that reason invited Ribbentrop to Paris in December. Bonnet did not concede anything in return but like Halifax he failed to make explicit French reservations over German predominance in eastern Europe.

The apparent gains of Italy, Britain and France were to be proved illusory. Germany had further strengthened her own position and again revealed a lack of resolve on the part of France and Britain. This was duly noted in the Soviet Union, who had professed herself willing to help Czechoslovakia provided she obtained formal consent for her troops to pass through Poland and Rumania. Had this consent been requested it is doubtful if the two countries would have agreed, but Russian planes could easily have overflown Rumanian airspace. Britain and France, however, did not seek direct Russian intervention and the Soviet Union could only conclude that at best they were unwilling to fight Germany, at worst they were encouraging Hitler to turn east against her. Moreover, there were serious clashes between Russian and Japanese troops on the Manchurian border in July and August. This reminder of a possible attack in the Far East makes it uncertain how far Russia would have committed herself on behalf of Czechoslovakia. Nevertheless it is still possible to debate whether Britain and France would have done better to fight in Sep-

tember 1938 instead of a year later. At the time both countries per-
ceived themselves as militarily inferior to Germany and in both
opinion was divided. Later the Munich settlement was to be bitterly
denounced but the contemporary reaction was in general one of relief
that war had been averted. Roosevelt, too, initially approved of the
settlement despite his dislike of Anglo-French weakness. It was still
possible to hope that Hitler's aims were limited and that a period of
stability, however brief, would follow. Such hope was vain. For the
moment Hitler was prepared to tolerate a weakened Czechoslovakia,
which in November granted autonomy to the Slovaks and Ruthenes.
It would be easy enough to stir up trouble among these two minorities at a suitable moment. On 17 December Hitler gave orders to
the German army to be prepared for an occupation of Czechoslovakia, which he assumed would be unopposed.

This directive was not public knowledge, but the very uncertainty
of Hitler's intentions soon dissipated the euphoria of Munich. Systematic attacks on German Jews in November were a reminder of
the racial side of National Socialism. 1939 opened in a nervous
atmosphere. Even if Hitler could be believed when he claimed that
he did not want to absorb non-Germans, there were still German
minorities to be rescued in Danzig, the Polish corridor and the Lith-
uanian port of Memel. Germany had not wasted much time in
approaching Poland after Munich. In October 1938 Ribbentrop suggested to the Polish ambassador, Lipski, that it was time for a general
settlement. Danzig would return to Germany, who would also gain
extra-territorial rights for transport across the corridor. The Poles
rejected this offer, but Hitler tried again in January 1939, inviting
Beck to Germany and hinting that Poland would find compensation
in a further partition of Czechoslovakia. Beck was unresponsive and
remained so when Ribbentrop visited Warsaw later in the month.
Even so, Hitler seems to have thought he might win the Poles over
and use them against the Soviet Union. It would be easy enough to
put pressure on them by raising tension inside Danzig and a combination of reward and punishment might obtain the city for
Germany without a fight.

The early months of 1939 were an uncertain period for Britain and
France. Britain continued her attempts to keep Italy detached from
Germany, but a visit to Rome in January by Chamberlain and Halifax produced little. French relations with Italy remained bad and the
French had some fears that Britain might urge them to make concessions in the Mediterranean. They had no intention of yielding to Italian propaganda demands for Nice, Corsica and Tunis. Apart from
that, the Anglo-French strategic position was clearly weakened by
Franco's success in the Spanish Civil War. Yielding to the inevitable,
Britain and France recognized his government at the end of February,
a month before the fall of Madrid ended the conflict. Spain's adhesion

to the anti-Comintern pact in April raised the worrying question of how closely she would collaborate with the Axis powers. On the other hand, Britain took the initiative in February in proposing staff talks to the French and revived plans for a Continental expeditionary force. Under some pressure from France and also from the United States, Britain introduced a limited measure of conscription in April despite some reluctance to take such a step in peacetime. There was a move towards closer and more sustained military cooperation with France and in the background Roosevelt was cautiously trying to help. He renewed the secret naval contacts with London and in April agreed to move the American fleet from the Atlantic to the Pacific in an effort to restrain Japan. His efforts to get Congress to increase defence spending and to modify the neutrality legislation were not, however, immediately successful.

The uneasy European calm was decisively broken on 15 March by the destruction of Czechoslovakia. Unrest in Slovakia and Ruthenia led President Hacha to make an ill-fated visit to Hitler in a search for help. Instead Hitler bullied him into accepting the partition of his country. German troops occupied Bohemia and Moravia, which were formed into a protectorate; Hungary was given Ruthenia; Slovakia was allowed to retain a nominal independence. As if this were not enough Germany within a few days forced Lithuania to return Memel. Angry at being upstaged by Hitler, Mussolini decided to press on with his own plans for seizing Albania. The country was occupied and annexed in April and King Zog, whom Mussolini had sponsored in the 1920s, was driven into exile. The partition of Czechoslovakia was the most significant of these sudden developments. Germany had gained considerable economic resources and had weakened Poland's strategic position. Even more important was the fact that for the first time Hitler had annexed non-German territory. It was now clear that his ambitions were not limited to uniting German minorities with the fatherland. What was to stop him from dominating eastern and south-east Europe? There was alarm in London at an alleged German attempt to establish control over Rumania's economy. This proved to be a false alarm but the Germans were certainly anxious to ensure regular supplies of Rumanian oil and wheat. Moreover, there was the possibility that Hungary, her appetite whetted by the seizure of Ruthenia, would try to fulfil her revisionist ambitions by occupying Transylvania. Relations between Hungary and Rumania continued to be tense for a month or so after the coup of 15 March.

It was against this background of rumour and crisis that Britain and France had to face the failure of appeasement and the need to restore their credibility. The problem was to organize effective resistance to further German expansion and to demonstrate firmness of purpose. The Franco-British answer, arrived at after some hesitation, was to give a guarantee to Poland at the end of March, pending the negotiation of a formal Anglo-Polish treaty. Similar guarantees were given to Rumania and Greece in April and to Turkey in May. France was thus seeking to revive her moribund influence in eastern Europe but for Britain it was a considerable departure from previous policy. The pressure of events, however, made some action necessary, even though it would be difficult if war broke out to give direct assistance to Poland. The immediate aim of Britain and France was to deter Germany rather than to produce a cohesive alliance system.

The Axis powers were not unduly impressed by this sign of resolution: they thought that Britain and France would retreat as they had done before when confronted by the risk of outright conflict. Hitler made his attitude clear in a speech on 28 April. He denounced both the German-Polish non-aggression pact of 1934 and the Anglo-German naval treaty of 1935, and indicated publicly his intention to regain Danzig and the Corridor. He could now begin another war of nerves against the Poles and the western powers. Mussolini might have been expected to show some concern, given his reaction to the occupation of Czechoslovakia. Instead he took the opportunity of a visit by Ribbentrop to Italy in early May to propose the signing of a formal alliance. Germany had been trying to arrange a tripartite alliance but Japan had been making difficulties. The pact of Steel with Italy, signed on 22 May, was therefore something of a second best for Germany but it involved Italy in a dangerously open-ended commitment. Even Mussolini had second thoughts about his impulsive gesture and sent the Germans a qualifying memorandum at the end of May, in which he stated the assumption that there would be no war for three years. On the 23rd, however, Hitler had instructed his generals to plan for a localized war against Poland. He had abandoned the hopes of January that it might be possible to reach a peaceful agreement with Poland but he still assumed that in the last resort Britain and France would not fight.

The Anglo-French guarantees made the attitude of the Soviet Union of critical importance. Having been left on the sidelines at Munich, the Russians were careful to keep their options open until they saw which side had the best bargain to offer. On 17 April Litvinov proposed to Britain and France a tripartite political agreement to be accompanied by a military agreement. At about the same time the Russians were dropping hints in Berlin that relations could be improved. Hitler was at first dubious, despite Ribbentrop's support for an agreement, and it was not until the end of May that the Germans began to show serious interest. The British were unenthusiastic about the Soviet proposals; the French showed rather more interest. Both knew that Beck was unwilling to accept Russian help and that neither Poland nor Rumania was likely to allow the entry of Soviet troops. Beck in fact remained unyielding on this point.

Doubts and a weak bargaining position combined to delay the Anglo-French response to Litvinov's opening offer. They were still hesitating when on 4 May he was replaced by Molotov, an indication that support for an agreement with Britain and France was under threat in Moscow. Certainly Molotov proved a hard bargainer as the British and French ambassadors continued talks on a political agreement. These dragged on until the end of July, when the Russians abruptly proposed their adjournment and the start of talks on a military agreement. By then Britain and France had made various concessions. They had accepted the principle of a three power alliance and had agreed that in a secret protocol certain named states would be given guarantees of protection whether they wanted them or not. On the other hand there was still disagreement over the Russian concept of indirect aggression. Molotov argued that internal developments or external pressures upon a state stopping short of military attack might make it necessary for the three allies to intervene. Britain and France feared that this would give the Soviet Union too much scope for interfering in her neighbours's affairs.

Meanwhile the Russians had remained cautious in the face of increasing German interest in an agreement. By the beginning of August Ribbentrop was talking to the Soviet chargé in Berlin of a possible understanding over Poland. German approaches may have induced the Russians to press on with military talks and find out what Britain and France had to offer. Here the western powers made the tactical error of sending somewhat low-powered delegations by a slow boat. As a result the talks did not begin until 12 August. Two days later the Russians raised the essential question of whether their troops would be able to enter Polish and Rumanian territory. They received no answer. Although the military talks lingered on until the 2lst they had lost their point. On the German side Ribbentrop was pressing by the 18th for an invitation to Moscow. The attack on Poland was set for the 26th and could not be postponed beyond the beginning of September because of the autumn rains. It took a personal appeal from Hitler on the 21st before Stalin agreed to receive Ribbentrop on the 23rd. On that day the two men signed a non-aggression pact accompanied by a secret protocol delimiting German and Soviet spheres of influence in eastern Europe. It is difficult to be sure at what point Stalin wrote off the possibility of agreement with the western powers. Germany was not only a direct threat to Russia in a way that Britain and France were not, but she could also offer a sharing of spoils which they could not match. During the summer there had been heavy fighting with Japanese troops on the Mongolian border. A pact with Germany seemed the best way to avoid trouble and buy time.

To Hitler's surprise Britain and France did not now abandon Poland. Indeed, on 25 August Britain and Poland concluded a formal treaty, and on the same day Mussolini warned Hitler that Italy could not contemplate war without massive aid. The Japanese were clearly annoyed by the German–Soviet pact. Hitler hesitated in the face of these developments and postponed the attack on Poland. The last days of August were taken up by a German diplomatic offensive designed to weaken Anglo-French resolve. Mussolini indicated that he was prepared to mediate again as at Munich and preside over the transfer of Danzig to Germany. Britain and France were not completely impervious to these approaches, but they were not going to repeat Munich. They went as far as persuading Beck to enter into direct negotiations with Germany. This, however, he only agreed to in principle; he was not prepared to meet a German ultimatum that a negotiator with full powers must arrive in Berlin by midnight on the 30th. Hitler in any case had recovered from his earlier indecision and German troops invaded Poland on 1 September. The British and French declarations of war were delayed until 3 September and were made separately. The French Cabinet was divided and Bonnet was unwilling to abandon the idea of an Italian-sponsored peace conference until the British made clear that pressure in the House of Commons would force them to go ahead. Thus Hitler had bought off Russia and isolated Poland but he had not frightened Britain and France into another retreat.

CHAPTER SEVEN

The League of Nations and collective security

The League of Nations ended in failure. It was, however, the first attempt to operate an international organization designed to promote the peaceful settlement of disputes and to prevent the arbitrary use of force. As such its performance and problems are of considerable interest. The drafters of the Covenant and those who represented their states at Geneva in the early 1920s were entering new territory and it is not surprising that unforeseen difficulties appeared in the search for international peace and security. The idea of such a body was not new, but the outbreak of war in 1914 stimulated considerable public interest, especially in Britain and the United States, in the creation of an institution which could prevent the recurrence of similar episodes. 1915 saw the appearance of the League of Nations Society in Britain and the League to Enforce Peace in the United States. Thus the term League made an early appearance and soon became generally accepted.

However important the activities of these and other groups in creating a climate of opinion, what mattered was the commitment of governments. As early as May 1916, in a speech to the League to Enforce Peace, President Wilson spoke of America's willingness to join 'a universal association of nations' after the war. He made the important proviso that the peace settlement must be based on certain principles; even so it was significant that Wilson was prepared to go so far at a time when America was still neutral, and when none of the belligerents had made a similar promise. Indeed, it was only as a result of Wilson's inquiry about war aims in December 1916 that the Allies in their reply of 10 January 1917 publicly gave support to the creation of a League of Nations, one purpose of which should be to ensure that international agreements were observed. Further public endorsement was given by General Smuts (then in the War Cabinet) when he addressed a meeting organized by the League of Nations Society in May 1917.

Thus far American and Allied statements consisted largely of generalities. What were to be the precise functions of such a body and what was to be its structure? There were important differences of emphasis in American and British thinking about these problems, as was shown in the respective statements of Wilson and Lloyd George in January 1918. In his fourteenth point the American President called for 'mutual guarantees of political independence and territorial integrity' by the new body. Lloyd George in his address to a trade union audience in London called for 'the creation of some international organization to limit the burden of armaments and diminish the probability of war'. This was much less far-reaching in its implications than Wilson's phraseology. At this stage Wilson had not worked out a detailed scheme and indeed did not do so until August 1918. Despite his strong commitment to the creation of a League he avoided public discussion in case the question became prejudged before the peace settlement. For that reason he persuaded the British government not to publish the report of the Phillimore Committee, which met between January and March 1918. The essence of its report was that members of the proposed organization would agree not to go to war without first submitting their disputes either to a conference of member states or to some form of arbitration. Nor would they go to war with any state which accepted the resulting recommendations or award. Any state breaking these rules would automatically find itself at war with all the other members and could then be subjected to economic or military sanctions. These proposals did not necessitate the creation of new permanent institutions; the Phillimore Committee was in the main seeking to regularize the European concert of powers. Conferences of ambassadors or ministers could meet on an *ad hoc* basis and it would be for member states to decide what sanctions they would impose.

Nevertheless, the Phillimore proposals were an important element in the scheme which the British had worked out by January 1919. To the idea of peaceful settlement of disputes was now added regular meetings of the major powers aided by a secretariat. More general meetings of all members would take place every four years or so. The lesser states, in other words, would have only a small role to play. There were considerable divisions within the British government and the War Cabinet over the scope of the new body and varying degrees of enthusiasm. Lord Robert Cecil and General Smuts showed much more support for the League than some of their colleagues, who argued that there was something to be said for maintaining the institutions of wartime cooperation such as the Supreme Council rather than launching a new body. Smuts went further than official British policy in a pamphlet published in December 1918. He was prepared to allow temporary seats for the lesser states on the proposed council of the major powers and he also took up the idea of mandates over territories and colonies detached from the central powers. Wilson's approach was quite different. He came to Europe to replace traditional great power diplomacy, not to make it work more effectively. In addition to his emphasis on a general guarantee of independence and integrity he was also a strong supporter of a system of compulsory arbitration with compulsory enforcement of decisions. This had been a noticeable element in prewar American thinking about the resolution of international disputes and was therefore by no means peculiar to Wilson.

Despite these significant variations in their underlying assumptions, the British and American delegations at Paris succeeded in agreeing on a joint draft during talks held in January and early February 1919, and this became the basis for discussion in the League of Nations commission which met from February to April. Wilson himself chaired the meetings of the commission, which followed the rule that amendments must receive unanimous support. As a result no alternative scheme was able to challenge effectively the Anglo-American proposals. The French failed in an attempt to have the League supplied with military forces under the supervision of an international general staff. Clemenceau was sceptical of the League's value, but when the French proposals were defeated he was not prepared to offer total opposition to the joint draft. The Italians were also unsuccessful; their scheme would have given the League control over the international distribution of food and raw materials. The Japanese failed to obtain the inclusion of a statement on racial equality, since neither the United States nor Australia was prepared to face the risk of losing their immigration controls. Thus three of the major allies were unable to bring about significant changes in the Anglo-American draft. The neutral states, to their annoyance, had virtually no influence on the discussions. The final version of the League Covenant was therefore very much an Anglo-American product.

As a result, it contained a number of compromises between the views of the two delegations. Britain retreated over the admission of smaller states to the League Council. It was agreed that the Assembly would initially choose four of its members to sit on the Council alongside the permanent members. The important questions of how long the temporary members would serve and whether they would be eligible for re-election were for the time being left unanswered. The British also had to modify their proposal that transgressor states should automatically find themselves at war with all other members, since Wilson argued that this infringed the constitutional right of the United States Congress to declare war. Article 16 therefore said that a state resorting to war in disregard of its obligations under the Covenant would be 'deemed' to have committed an act of war against all other members. They would automatically impose economic sanctions upon it but the Council would only recommend what military action should be taken.

On the other hand Wilson compromised over his proposal for a guarantee of the political independence and territorial integrity of all members. The British argued that this would be too rigid and might prevent reasonable changes, so the formula adopted in article 10 said that states would 'respect and preserve' the independence and integrity of their fellow members, and article 19 permitted the Assembly to recommend reconsideration of certain treaties. It was not, however, compelled to do so and in practice this attempt to allow for revision proved ineffective. Wilson was also persuaded not to write into the Covenant proposals for compulsory arbitration. He agreed instead to the creation of an entirely separate institution – the Permanent Court of International Justice. His most serious defeat came over the question of mandates for the former German colonies and Turkish territories in the Middle East. Wilson originally intended the League to take direct responsibility for these areas, but Britain, France, South Africa and Australia were all determined to obtain the spoils of victory. It was therefore agreed that mandates would be allocated to individual states. They were to be supervised by a mandates commission and this did at least establish the principle that the holders had a public responsibility for their actions. In practice, however, the role of the commission was limited. It received annual reports but had no powers of on-the-spot investigation; nor was it allowed to receive oral as distinct from written evidence. Critics of the system could argue that mandates were simply a form of disguised annexation.

In addition to these Anglo-American compromises two other points should be noted. It was agreed that the League would base itself in Geneva. There had been some consideration of other sites – Brussels, for example – but it was generally felt that if the League was to have universal appeal its headquarters should be on neutral territory. There was also general agreement that decisions of the Council and the Assembly should be unanimous unless the Covenant specifically provided otherwise. This, it is true, gave a right to veto to any state which wished to block particular proposals, but it was unlikely that states would willingly submit to an adverse majority vote when their vital interest were at stake. Article 15, which dealt with the peaceful settlement of disputes, specifically prevented parties to a dispute from voting on recommendations of the Council or the Assembly, thus removing one obvious danger of the unanimity rule. This provision was not, however, written into article 11, which allowed the League to consider threats to peace, and this was to prove of considerable significance in the early stages of the Manchurian crisis.

The term 'collective security' later came into use as a convenient shorthand for the principles underlying the League Covenant. States agreed to attempt to settle their disputes peacefully and not to resort to war until the procedures laid down in the Covenant were exhausted. (It was still possible in certain circumstances for states to declare war – the so-called 'gap' in the Covenant.) Any state which broke the rules would not only be immediately subjected to economic sanctions but would also face an overwhelming preponderance of military power. States would presumably hesitate to put themselves in such a position. Collective security, however, involved certain assumptions which were not clearly articulated in the discussions of 1919. All member states must share an equal willingness to take action irrespective of their own involvement, or lack of it, in a particular dispute. Moreover, it was assumed that transgressors would be immediately and clearly identifiable. There would be little doubt about the rights and wrongs of the matter at issue. Transgressors would lack friends and allies and would therefore be especially susceptible to economic pressure. The efficacy of economic sanctions alone seems to have been rather taken for granted. In practice these various assumptions were to prove ill-founded, but this did not become clear until the 1930s.

Wilson insisted that the Covenant must be an integral part of the peace settlement, in order to show that the treaties represented certain principles of international behaviour. If the treaties were drawn up first it might prove difficult to get agreement on the Covenant later; the enthusiasm of the victors was likely to wane the longer the creation of the League was delayed. Whatever reservations the other members of the League of Nations commission may have had, they were not prepared to oppose in principle either the creation of the new body or its link with the peace settlement. The Covenant was certainly discussed in some haste in an excited atmosphere, but it is not certain that lengthier and later discussion would have produced a better document. Up to a point there was something to be said for Wilson's argument; where he went wrong was in assuming that the United States would be less likely to reject the Covenant and the treaty with Germany if they were presented as a package. His opposition to the reservations put forward by Henry Cabot Lodge has been criticized but they were so broad as to render American membership meaningless. The United States would have been excused from any obligation to maintain the integrity of other states, to apply sanctions or to promote disarmament.

Nevertheless the Senate's failure in March 1920 to accept the Covenant as it stood was a severe blow to the new organization. (The Council had held its first meeting in January.) Non-membership of one of the League's original sponsors was a serious blow to morale and undermined its claims to universality. Even more serious was the extent to which the United States tried to limit the League's influence in Latin America and the Far East. The Washington conference showed how far she was prepared to go in promoting a major political settlement and a disarmament agreement outside the League. In the later 1920s the United States was to become more cooperative, though still keeping the League at arm's length. By then, however, the damage had been done. States began to have second thoughts about their obligations under the Covenant. In theory at least, they might be called upon to impose economic sanctions upon the United States or take military action against her, since there was provision for the application of article 16 to non-members. In view of her long frontier with the United States Canada was particularly alarmed at this prospect, but she was not the only state unwilling to consider conflict with Washington. In 1921 an Assembly resolution declared that sanctions should not be applied automatically and completely but only by stages and after discussion and consultation. Another Assembly resolution in 1923 urged that individual states should decide what military action to take when called upon by the Council. Neither of the resolutions became formal amendments of the Covenant but they were significant indications that states were beginning to reserve their position even in the early years of the League.

The League had the added problem of asserting its authority against the conference of ambassadors. The latter body was specifically concerned with the implementation of the peace treaties and in the period before Locarno this gave it considerable scope to deal with a variety of matters. Apart from its general concern with international peace and security the League too had certain specific tasks laid upon it by the peace treaties, such as the protection of minorities. Some clash of jurisdiction was therefore inevitable. The ambassadors tried to keep matters relevant to the peace treaties in their own hands unless they became awkward, whereas the League Council claimed the right to discuss any issue, whatever the ambassadors might be doing about it.

There were some cases in which neither body was able to exert much influence. Neither was able to reverse the Polish seizure of Vilna from Lithuania in 1920 or to improve relations between the two countries. Indeed, in 1923 the ambassadors formally awarded Vilna to Poland under article 87 of the Versailles treaty, which gave the Allies power to determine those Polish frontiers not laid down in the treaty itself. Lithuania, supported by the Soviet Union, refused to recognize this decision. Given Soviet distrust of the League and Poland's bad relations with her neighbours it was difficult for any outside body to exert much influence over Poland's eastern frontiers. Nor were the ambassadors and the League much more successful over the question of the former East Prussian port of Memel, which was placed under Allied administration in 1920 pending its transfer to Lithuania. The latter became impatient and seized the port at the beginning of 1923. The ambassadors' conference was prepared to accept the takeover but tried to get an agreement on the status of the German population and on Polish rights to use the port. On the latter point in particular the Lithuanians proved obstinate and in September 1923 the ambassadors passed the issue over to the League. The Council set up a three-man commission which was successful in producing a convention that Lithuania was willing to accept. The Poles did not actively oppose the convention but remained dissatisfied, and between Berlin and Lithuania there was continuing friction over the position of the Germans, who formed a majority in the city itself. Nevertheless, the League could claim to have played a more constructive role over Memel than the ambassadors. It could also claim a qualified success in the case of Upper Silesia. Here a plebiscite was held in March 1921 which gave an overall majority to Germany but gave no guidance on how a viable frontier could be drawn. This time it was the Supreme War Council that was divided; Britain tended to favour the German argument that the area was an economic unity which could not be divided whereas France openly supported Polish claims to obtain the lion's share. Unable to agree, the Supreme Council passed the issue to the League in 1921. The frontier line which the League Council recommended in October 1921 was not ideal but was to be accompanied by an agreement between Germany and Poland which would allow free movement across the frontier and effectively maintain Upper Silesia as an economic unit. Somewhat unwillingly the two countries signed such an agreement in May 1922. It worked with less friction than might have been expected.

In the case of Albania the League could claim a success over the ambassadors but also had to admit to a defeat. Albania had become independent as a result of the Balkan wars of 1912 and 1913 but its frontiers were still not completely defined when more general war broke out in 1914. Albania was admitted to the League in 1920 but with Yugoslav, Greek and Italian troops on her territory there was a danger that she might disappear altogether. It required pressure from the League Council in 1921 to secure the evacuation of foreign troops and to induce the conference of ambassadors to press on with the delimitation of Albania's boundaries. This success was largely the result of Britain's wish to use pressure from the League to maintain Albanian independence while keeping the frontier question in the hands of the ambassadors. The work of delimitation duly proceeded until in August 1923 a group of Italian officers were murdered on Greek territory. Mussolini demanded compensation and occupied the island of Corfu. At best this was an over-reaction; at worst a permanent member of the League Council had committed what could be regarded as an act of war. A confused situation now developed. The conference of ambassadors interested itself in the crisis since the dead officers had been acting as its agents. Greece took the issue before the League but did not dispute the right of the ambassadors to consider it as well. Italy argued before the League Council that the ambassadors had prior claims to handle the question and therefore the League had no competence. She received some help from France, who was anxious to retain Italian support for the occupation of the Ruhr. Britain was unhappy at Mussolini's action but wanted to avoid a direct clash between the League and the ambassadors. The upshot was that the ambassadors effectively took over the dispute, although the League Council did discuss it and make recommendations. In that sense, therefore, the League suffered a defeat. On the other hand, Mussolini in the end accepted the decisions of the ambassadors, received an indemnity and withdrew from Corfu. Facing general international criticism and with only the qualified support of France, he retreated from his threats to leave the League. In this case, it could be argued, the existence of the ambassadors' conference shielded the League from a direct confrontation with Italy.

Where it was in direct competition with the ambassadors the League's record was uneven. It was more successful, in the early years in matters where there was no direct challenge to its competence. In the period before Locarno it did enough in the way of settling disputes and promoting cooperation to make itself an established part of Europe's diplomatic machinery. Where the permanent members had no direct interest in a question or did not seek to take a strong line it was possible for the League to mediate successfully. This can be seen in the case of the very first dispute to come before it in 1920, over the Aaland Islands in the Baltic. Prior to the revolution of 1917 these had formed part of the Grand Duchy of Finland. After she gained independence Finland continued to regard them as hers, although their population was largely Swedish, and rejected claims that they should therefore be united with Sweden. Both countries agreed to accept mediation by the Council which set up a committee of enquiry. This recommended in 1921 that the islands should remain under Finnish sovereignty but with certain safeguards for the autonomy of the inhabitants. Despite her disappointment Sweden accepted the decision; the League was much helped by the reasonableness of both parties to the dispute.

Its greatest success appeared at the time to be the rapid settlement of the Greek–Bulgarian fighting in October 1925. A minor incident on the frontier led to a Greek invasion of Bulgaria. The latter appealed to the League. Briand as President of the Council sent telegrams to both sides calling for an end to the fighting and an emergency meeting of the Council was held in Paris. This passed a resolution reinforcing Briand's telegrams and threatening action in the case of non-compliance. The fighting soon stopped and the Greeks withdrew. Thus the Council had acted with speed and efficiency, but it was helped by the fact that none of its members had much to gain by promoting either the Greek or Bulgarian cause. The

Locarno agreements had just been signed and as a result the atmosphere between Britain, France and Italy was good. Greece in particular was isolated and if she did not withdraw her troops would be vulnerable to economic or military pressure. This was one case where the basic requirements of collective security were fulfilled. There was a clear-cut situation and a clear preponderance of power could be used against Greece.

Certain obligations were laid on the League in the peace treaties. It was to be responsible for the government of the Saar for fifteen years, after which a plebiscite would be held to determine the future of the territory. This experiment in international government was indeed an innovation. The intention was that the Saar commission would act as a buffer between the inhabitants and the French, who were in military occupation of the area and in receipt of its coal. It was therefore unfortunate that the first chairman of the commission was a Frenchman, Victor Rault, who was accused of both partiality and ruthlessness. Matters came to a head when the French occupation of the Ruhr provoked a miners' strike in the Saar. The League Council held public hearings with the members of the commission and this assertion of its authority did a good deal to ease tension. Rault was replaced and although the Saarlanders were not converted into friends of the commission, matters on the whole ran more smoothly after 1923.

The position in Danzig was a more difficult one. Predominantly German in population, it was detached from East Prussia and turned into a free city. Poland was to have rights in the port and to control the city's external relations, although it would retain autonomy in internal affairs. The League would appoint a High Commissioner to act as middleman between Poland and the city authorities. From the first this was a difficult task in view of the mutual antipathy of Poles and Germans. Unlike the Saar experiment there was no time limit laid down for this uneasy situation. Not surprisingly, Weimar Germany took a strong interest in Danzig and after its entry into the League was able to exert much more influence, in particular on the choice of High Commissioner. Nevertheless, the League's role in Danzig prevented a difficult situation from becoming worse. The protection of minorities in general was a source of constant friction. Minorities had a right to petition the League under various treaties but this was open to abuse and much resented by the governments concerned. It was certainly a further irritant in German–Polish relations.

In the Covenant itself one of the most important commitments was that laid down in article 8. The Council was to formulate plans for the reduction of armaments 'to the lowest point consistent with national safety'. Here progress was slow. To some extent this was outside the League's control: the Allies were not prepared to allow the League to proceed until satisfied that Germany had been effectively disarmed, which meant that little could be done before Locarno. In addition, attempts to supplement the Covenant by arrangements for security linked to disarmament – such as the draft treaty and the Geneva protocol – used up much time and energy and tended to confuse the issue. When the preparatory commission did begin its work at the end of 1925 it soon ran into the difficulties to be expected in considering the technical problems of disarmament. Hopes of a general conference before the end of the 1920s proved over-optimistic.

It was agreed at Locarno that Germany would be admitted to the League and obtain a permanent seat on the Council. This produced claims from other states for permanent seats, in particular from Brazil, Poland and Spain. In turn these requests brought to a head the question of temporary members. The number had been increased from four to six in 1922 but this in itself did not solve the essential problem. How long were temporary members to serve and were they eligible for immediate re-election? If so, now that a seat on that body had become a matter of some prestige, certain states might become virtually permanent members and limit the opportunity for others to serve on the Council. As a result, special sessions of the Council and Assembly early in 1926 ended in deadlock and Germany was not admitted until the September of that year. The compromise which was then reached entailed an increase in the temporary seats to nine. All temporary members would serve for three years and up to three of them could be re-elected if the Assembly so voted by a two-thirds majority. Article 4 of the Covenant was amended to make clear that the Assembly had the general power to make rules regarding the election of non-permanent members. In effect, this created a new class of semi-permanent members although the immediate aim was to satisfy the claims of Brazil, Poland and Spain. Poland accepted the arrangement and benefited from it considerably; already a member of the Council since 1923 she was to remain on it until 1938. The other two countries, however, announced their withdrawal from the League, although Spain changed her mind and returned in 1928. She served on the Council from then until 1937. From one point of view, therefore, the 1926 compromise was a success but, as was pointed out at the time, it did make the Council a rather unwieldy body. Two more temporary seats were to be added during the 1930s but only one new permanent seat was created – for the Soviet Union when she joined in 1934. The departure of Germany, Italy and Japan during the 1930s left the temporary members very much in the majority.

Germany's entry made the League more representative and

increased the value of Geneva as a meeting-place. Foreign Ministers would meet there and settle business under cover of attending formal sessions of the Council or the Assembly. There were some complaints from the smaller states that important decisions tended more and more to be made in private. It was not surprising however, that corridor and hotel-room diplomacy should play a large part in the League's activities; indeed, it was a sign of the institution's growing reputation that governments should want to use it for informal contacts. That the Locarno powers should seek to arrange matters among themselves reflected the fact that they were a partial concert of the European powers. Japan had little interest in European matters and in the absence of the United States and the Soviet Union the Locarno powers were able to enjoy a brief period of cooperation and predominance. On the other hand, it was not surprising that the smaller states resented this situation. The League had given them a regular opportunity to speak on equal terms with the great and to participate in decision-making. They did not like to be reminded too obviously that in the last resort the League depended on the goodwill and support of the major powers.

This unpalatable truth becomes clear when one examines the evolution of the secretariat. To build up an international civil service from scratch was a considerable achievement on the part of the first Secretary – General Sir Eric Drummond. He himself established a reputation as a reliable negotiator and adviser behind the scenes. It was not his style to make major public speeches or to intervene openly in disputes. This meant that his advice was more readily accepted by governments and by their representatives at Geneva. It is doubtful if dramatic statements and gestures would have increased his influence, and in any case he regarded the League's potential as limited, especially in the absence of the United States. It could adjust disputes, it could try to mediate between states, but it could not coerce them. By his cautious private diplomacy Drummond achieved a good deal. Yet he perhaps was too willing to be all things to all men, and to retreat in the face of pressure from the permanent members. Admittedly he faced a difficult problem in recruiting for the secretariat. The major powers wanted their share of senior posts and when a vacancy occurred it was generally assumed that it should be filled by a national from the same state as the previous holder. This limited the possibilities for promotion on merit. There was the further problem of how far League officials could be expected to ignore the interests of their own country and suppress national loyalties. Some made an attempt to do so, others blatantly put the interests of their own government before loyalty to the League. Germany and Italy made it quite clear that they saw their appointees as essentially representatives of Berlin or Rome. In the early years the secretariat drew heavily on British and French personnel, though a number of Americans also joined as individuals. By the end of the 1920s both Germany and Italy were pressing for a larger share of the senior posts and were supporting proposals to limit the power of the Secretary-General by forcing him to consult a committee of his senior colleagues. Drummond resisted these proposals but it was clear that appointments to the secretariat were likely to become more overtly political.

Until 1931, therefore, the League's record was one of qualified success. For an entirely new institution this was perhaps as much as could be expected, but the loyalty of member states had not yet been fully tested and there was a dangerous gap between public optimism about the League's potential and the caution, not to say cynicism, of governments. This was particularly so in Britain, where the League of Nations Union (a successor to the earlier League of Nations Society) had since 1918 been an effective propagandist for the achievements of Geneva. It helped also, however, to foster the assumption that the League was an entity capable of independent action. It was only in the 1930s that the falsity of this belief and the problems inherent in a system of collective security were to be clearly revealed.

Nevertheless, the League continued to have some success with minor disputes during the 1930s. It helped to solve a territorial dispute between Colombia and Peru over the district of Leticia. The latter had in fact ceded the area to Colombia, which thus gained access to the Amazon river. Local resistance in 1932 to the Colombian takeover led the Peruvian government to change its mind and to send troops into the area. The League in 1933 got both countries to agree that it should administer the area for a year while they negotiated a settlement. In May 1934 Peru finally conceded that Leticia belonged to Colombia. The three-man commission that governed the territory was assisted by Colombian troops, but these were technically an international force under the control of the League. This was the first occasion on which the League used anything similar to the peacekeeping forces later to be set up by the United Nations.

The only truly international force which acted in the name of the League was assembled to supervise the Saar plebiscite in January 1935. It was generally expected that a large majority would vote for a return to Germany. Hitler had no wish, therefore, for disorders which might lead to the plebiscite being postponed or declared void. The French for their part did not wish to intervene unilaterally in the event of trouble; French troops had been withdrawn from the Saar in 1927 and their return might provoke a sharp German reaction. Laval therefore suggested a joint Anglo-French force but the British government was not enthusiastic. They developed instead the idea of an international force from which French and German troops would be excluded. The League Council approved the idea in December 1934 and Hitler for once was prepared to subdue his opposition to the League. A force with contingents from Britain, Italy, the Netherlands and Sweden kept order during the plebiscite, which was conducted by staff supplied by the League. As expected there was a large majority for reunion with Germany and all passed off peacefully. Without the international force there might have been a Franco-German crisis at a time when Hitler was not prepared for one. A year or so later he would be in a much less accommodating mood towards the League.

It was interesting that Britain was prepared to take to the League a dispute between Persia and the Anglo-Persian Oil Company (1932–33) in which the British government had a majority holding. Britain wanted to offset the bad effect that the Manchurian crisis was having on the League's reputation and show herself in a reasonable light. It was the Persian government which at first hesitated, fearing that the Council would favour the British case, but it then came to see the advantages of gaining favourable publicity in Geneva. Britain, however, narrowly got in first in putting the matter on the Council's agenda. With the help of Council mediation the Anglo-Persian Oil Company negotiated a new agreement with the Persian government, which withdrew its earlier threats to cancel the concession completely. Thus Britain avoided possible accusations that here was another case of a great power browbeating a smaller one.

In the three examples just mentioned the states involved were prepared to use the machinery of the League because they saw it as in their interest to do so. This was not the case in the Manchurian and Ethiopian crises, which were to overshadow the League's other activities in the 1930s and undermine its reputation. To begin with, the situation in Manchuria was far from clear-cut. The control of the central Chinese government over the province was largely nominal and Japan had a special position dating back to 1906. Given Japan's good record (until then) as a member of the League and Chiang Kai-Shek's hostility to European interests in China, the League Council was not initially predisposed to see China as an innocent victim of Japanese aggression. First news of the Mukden incident in September 1931 did not make clear the full extent of Japanese military action, so the Council not unreasonably waited for clarification. This was to play into the hands of the Japanese army; the further they extended control over Manchuria the harder it would be for the League to restore the original situation. This illustrated another difficulty inherent in collective security – remedial action is more difficult to apply than preventive action. Moreover, the government in Tokyo was not in control of the army in Manchuria and it was not therefore in a position to make concessions in Geneva. The best strategy for Japan therefore seemed to be one of prolonging discussions in the Council as long as possible.

China brought the dispute before the Council under article 11, which gave members a general right to raise any matter that seemed likely to be a threat to peace. Article 11 was more flexible than article 15 in that it did not commit the Council to a particular procedure and did not necessarily imply the imposition of economic or military sanctions. Thus it was often used simply to secure Council discussion without any commitment to specific action. Article 11 did not, however, prevent parties to a dispute from voting and Japan was therefore able to veto the resolution of 24 October 1931 which called on Japanese forces to withdraw to the railway zone. This gave the Council an excuse for further inaction. In view of the Council's lack of enthusiasm for economic sanctions or military action, it is not clear that much would have been gained if Japan had been prohibited from voting. She would have been technically in the wrong in not complying with the resolution, but this would only have brought into the open somewhat earlier the unwillingness of the permanent members of the Council to take action. Italy and Germany had little direct interest in the question; Britain and France were unwilling to provoke Japan at a time of economic and financial crisis. It would have fallen upon them to take the lead in any proposed action. There was in fact no preponderance of power against Japan. The United States was not prepared to put her navy at the League's disposal, nor was the Soviet Union willing to employ her army to liberate Manchuria. The significance of the League's lack of universality was thus clearly revealed. If the major powers would not take the initiative the lesser states would remain cautious, as China discovered when she took the question before the Assembly under article 15 in March 1932. She received a good deal of sympathy but little else. The establishment of the Lytton commission was perhaps the best that the League could hope to achieve. At least it would show that the Council was not washing its hands of the matter, and a clearer picture of the situation in Manchuria would emerge. The committee's report did not appear until October 1932 and by then Japan had little reason to seek a compromise. Her withdrawal from the League made clear her dislike of the criticisms contained in the Lytton report and seriously weakened the League's ability to influence developments in the Far East.

The Manchurian crisis had revealed the ineffectiveness of the League if the permanent members of the Council were unwilling to act. Moreover, it was one of the permanent members which had defied its colleagues and then set a precedent by withdrawing when faced with criticism. Germany was soon to become the second permanent member to leave. The failure of the disarmament conference added to the sense of doubt – the League had failed to produce any general agreement after so many years of effort. Yet these were defeats rather than a complete rout. It was precisely the need to show that the League could resist aggression that led most of its members to support the imposition of sanctions on Italy when she invaded Ethiopia.

Here the situation was in one way much simpler than in the Manchurian case. The build-up of Italian forces in East Africa during 1935 left little doubt of Mussolini's intentions but the position was also more complicated than in 1931 in so far as Britain and France were actively seeking Italian help against Germany. The Covenant had not allowed for such a conflict of interest or for the simultaneous existence of more than one threat to peace. Nevertheless, the League did for the first time attempt to apply article 16. In early October 1935 both Council and Assembly agreed that Italy's invasion of Ethiopia was in breach of the Covenant. Of the fifty-four members of the Assembly, fifty agreed that sanctions must be applied; the four dissenters were Italy herself and Austria, Hungary and Albania. These three had close links with Italy and were anxious not to offend her. The fifty constituted themselves into a coordinating committee and subsequently set up a sub-committee of eighteen. Various proposals made by the sub-committee came into force on 18 November: the export to Italy of arms, rubber, iron-ore and various other metals was forbidden; she was to receive no loans or credits and most imports from Italy were prohibited. Certain important commodities were not included in the export ban – oil, iron and steel, coal and coke. In part this was the result of Franco-British unwillingness to offend Italy. It would also be necessary to secure the cooperation of the United States if sanctions on these key commodities were to be effective.

In practice, therefore, the subcommittee of eighteen did not apply the automatic and complete sanctions envisaged in article 16 but proceeded instead in the spirit of the Assembly resolution of 1921. It is doubtful if a strict interpretation of article 16 could have been enforced in practice. Not all member states agreed to all the proposals – some made reservations, as was the case with Switzerland. Of states outside the League, Germany, Japan and Brazil gave no support to sanctions and the United States rested on its own neutrality legislation which meant in practice that it prohibited the supply of arms and loans to both Italy and Ethiopia. Roosevelt found little support in Congress for any attempt to apply an oil embargo. So sanctions came into effect in a piecemeal fashion and there were large gaps from the very beginning. It was early 1936 before they began to have an effect on the Italian economy. Nevertheless, Italian exports dropped sharply during 1936 and there was a noticeable decline in her gold reserves. The latter development was the result of her need to pay for imports, which she was still able to obtain in some quantity from non-member States. In January the sub-committee of eighteen set up a group of experts to consider the possibility of an oil sanction. It reported in February that an oil embargo would become effective in three to four months but with an important proviso: the embargo would need to be universally enforced. If it were applied only by the group of fifty, the United States would need to cooperate in limiting her oil supplies to Italy.

Whether an effective oil embargo could have been imposed must remain open to doubt in view of the loopholes in the sanctions that were in fact applied. Damage was certainly done to Italy's economy but not enough to divert Mussolini from the conquest of Ethiopia. Italy's reserves of gold and oil had not yet been exhausted when the war came to an end. The ability of sanctions to induce a state to change its policies remained unproven. In the long run, of course, Italy would have faced increasing difficulty, especially if sanctions had been extended to oil, iron and steel, coal and coke. But effective enforcement might well have required some form of naval blockade – e.g. to prevent oil tankers from reaching Italian ports. Britain and France were clearly unwilling to undertake action of this kind. The experience of the non-intervention committee during the Spanish Civil War suggests how difficult it would have been to maintain a joint blockade, especially in the face of opposition from the Italian navy. These considerations raised a further question – how effective could sanctions be if not supported by military force?

In July 1936, when the League formally abandoned sanctions, it. was clear that they had failed to save Ethiopia. As in the case of Manchuria, it would now require a large-scale military effort to dislodge Italy and nobody was prepared to undertake this. British troops were to liberate Ethiopia in 1941 but that was under conditions of full belligerency as part of a large-scale war, not something which members of the League were prepared to contemplate in 1936. The ending of sanctions marked also the collapse of the League's influence on international affairs. It played little part in either the Spanish Civil War or the Sino-Japanese war. The machinery of non-intervention was set up outside the League, and although both Council and Assembly passed resolutions calling for the withdrawal of foreign troops from Spain, these had no practical effect and the Republican government thus found membership of the Council in 1936 and 1937 of little value. When fighting began between China and Japan in the summer of 1937 the League was quick to pass the problem over to the signatories of the nine-power pact. This led only to the abortive Brussels conference. During 1938 and 1939 China continued to press the League for assistance. In September 1938 the

Council did invite Japan as a non-member to accept the obligations of membership for the purpose of considering the dispute. This procedure was laid down in article 17, which also said that if a non-member refused such a request then the provisions of article 16 should apply. Japan declined the invitation and after some discussion the Council decided that it was for individual members to apply article 16. Needless to say, none of them did. As over Manchuria, the Chinese government received much sympathy but little practical support.

In the events of 1938 and 1939 leading up to the Second World War the League played virtually no part. In Danzig the High Commisioner found himself increasingly ignored and ineffective. By this time the League's loss of prestige had also produced a drop in membership. The withdrawal of Germany, Italy and Japan encouraged nine other states to leave. As a result of German and Italian conquests, Austria, Albania, Ethiopia and Czechoslovakia disappeared from membership. The fall in membership in turn produced a drop in revenue, so that by September 1939 the League was in serious financial difficulty.

The secretariat could hardly be expected to flourish in the gloomy atmosphere of the 1930s and its fortunes were not improved by Drummond's decision in 1932 to retire. By then he was feeling the pressures of his task and wanted to return to the British diplomatic service. When he was appointed in 1919 it had been agreed that his successor should be a Frenchman. Since 1923 Joseph Avenol had been his deputy and took over as Secretary-General in the summer of 1933. Drummond had his doubts about Avenol's capacity and the Germans protested at a Frenchman being appointed to this important post. Drummond's doubts were justified, and the Germans need not have worried. Avenol's appointment gave them the opportunity to secure an agreement that not more than two of the senior posts in the Secretariat should be held by the nationals of one country. There was now a much more blatant sharing out of senior posts on a political basis, and time limits were now usually imposed on contracts. Drummond could have served indefinitely but Avenol was limited to ten years with a possible three-year renewal. Members of the secretariat would now have to think more carefully before taking actions that offended their own government in case they found it difficult to obtain suitable employment when their term with the League expired.

As Secretary-General Avenol was a disaster. Devious, lazy and a poor administrator, he had no loyalty to the League as an institution. In this view he could do only what the powers told him to do, and he argued that the League should restrict itself largely to non-political activities. He considerably reduced the press and publicity work of the League and went to some trouble to weed out officials who disagreed with his views. A more positive Secretary-General would have found it difficult to swim against the tide in the 1930s; Avenol was content to be carried along by it. One of the few active steps he took was to encourage the expulsion of the Soviet Union in December 1939 for her attack on Finland. This was a product of his anti-Communism rather than the expression of any principle. It was ironic that the League should carry out its first expulsion when it was already enfeebled and without much influence. The Finns gained little in practical terms from the League's last fling. Avenol welcomed the German successes of 1940 and proposed winding up the League in favour of some new European body under German auspices. He was frustrated in this aim by the opposition of his own permanent officials and by the newly established Vichy government, which ordered him to resign. The Irishman Sean Lester, who had served for a time as High Commissioner in Danzig, succeeded in keeping a skeleton organization in being in Geneva during the war, with some encouragement from Britain. When the League was formally wound up in 1946 he was retrospectively converted from acting to full Sectary-General. He deserves credit for keeping the League alive until it was clear what would replace it.

It is true that the League achieved a good deal in the economic and social fields. It sponsored loans for Austria and Hungary in the early 1920s which enabled both countries to reconstruct their economies. Much was done to help refugees, improve health standards, control the traffic in drugs and so on. The secretariat proved a most useful coordinator and supervisor of these various activities. The International Labour Organization which functioned as an independent institution, although in association with the League, had considerable success in improving working conditions. There is no doubt that in its many non-political activities the League demonstrated what an international organization could achieve. Nevertheless, in its primary political aim of reducing or eliminating inter-state conflicts it had clearly failed despite a promising start. Would an improved version emerge from the Second World War?

CHAPTER EIGHT
The Second World War, 1939–45: the emergence of America and Russia

The Polish campaign quickly demonstrated German capacity to wage lightning war. The fighting was virtually over by 17 September, when Soviet troops crossed Poland's eastern border to claim Russia's share of the spoils. Britain and France remained inactive; having assumed a lengthy war in which Germany would be steadily worn down by economic blockade, they lacked the means to attempt a rapid counter-blow. Ribbentrop and Stalin signed a treaty on 28 September which somewhat modified their earlier agreement which had envisaged the survival of a rump Polish state: it was now decided that the country should be completely partitioned. Stalin gave up some territory in Poland in exchange for control over Lithuania. The three Baltic states were forced to grant bases to the Soviet Union and to allow the stationing of Russian troops on their soil, but for the time being they retained a nominal independence; the Soviet Union even returned Vilna to Lithuania. The areas taken from Poland, however, were absorbed directly into Russia. Thus Stalin reversed the results of the treaty of Riga of 1920 and in so doing created a buffer zone against a possible German attack. A ceasefire was signed with the Japanese on 15 September, freeing the Soviet Union from military pressure on her Far Eastern frontier.

With Poland's fate settled, Hitler ordered his general to prepare for an offensive in the west, originally setting a target date of 12 November. For one reason or another the offensive was postponed. It is not clear how seriously Hitler expected Britain and France to treat his peace offer, made in a speech of 6 October. It was scarcely surprising that they rejected proposals which would have left Germany in possession of her Polish conquests. Thereafter the Western Front settled down to the inaction of the 'Phoney War.' Instead of striking directly at Germany, Britain and France showed much more interest in attempting to cut off her supplies of iron-ore from northern Sweden. This was expected to deal a serious blow to the German war effort. Much of the iron-ore came out through the Norwegian port of Narvik, so one possibility was to plant mines in Norwegian coastal waters. An expedition could even be sent to occupy the iron-ore mines themselves. Neither Norway nor Sweden had given any sign of tolerating such infringements on their neutrality when the situation was altered by Russia's attack on Finland at the end of November.

In October the Russians had asked the Finns for a naval base and for frontier changes intended to improve the defence of Leningrad. Overestimating the degree of support they could expect from other states, the Finns refused to give way. Initially the Soviet military performance was inept and the Finns more than held their own. They gained a good deal of sympathy in Britain, France and the United States; the expulsion of Russia from the League in December was of little practical help to Finland but was indicative of the general mood. More important was the attention that the British and French governments now devoted to combining an occupation of the Swedish iron-ore mines with sending troops to Finland. Daladier was particularly anxious to be seen to be helping Finland but doubts and disagreements between the two allies meant that nothing had been done by the time the Russians renewed the offensive more successfully in February 1940. On 12 March Finland signed a peace treaty which conceded a naval base at Hangö and yielded some 16,000 square miles of territory.

The immediate result of the Finnish defeat was the fall of Daladier and his replacement by Reynaud. The obvious British and French sympathy for Finland made Stalin even more suspicious of their motives. They appeared more willing to risk a conflict with Russia than to fight actively against Germany. The poor showing of the Red Army led to a dangerous under-estimation of its capacity by both Germany and the western powers. They largely ignored its much better performance against the Japanese. For the moment, however, the Russians appeared to have further strengthened their European frontiers. They were soon to be unpleasantly surprised by the speed with which Germany altered the military balance in Europe.

At the end of March Britain and France at last agreed on the mining of Norwegian waters, an act which was carried out on 8 April. The following day German forces invaded Denmark and Norway; Hitler had begun to consider such a campaign as early as the previous December and he issued a directive for the invasion on 1 March. The Allies were unable to halt the German advance; their failures led to the fall of Chamberlain on 10 May. Churchill became head of a coalition government just as Germany launched her much-postponed offensive in the west. Norway did not surrender until 9 June, but by then her fate was overshadowed by the extent of German successes. The Netherlands and Belgium had surrendered; the bulk of the British expeditionary force had been evacuated through Dunkirk at the cost of losing most of its equipment; the French were clearly on the brink of defeat. Mussolini, who had spent the winter in uneasy neutrality, joined the war on 10 June, anxious to obtain a share in the fruits of victory. Reynaud resigned on 16 June in favour of Marshal Pétain, the hero of Verdun. The latter asked for an armistice on the following day and one was signed on 22nd. Thus the Germans had atoned for their near-miss of 1914. They were to occupy most of France, leaving the south and south-east as an unoccupied zone. Here Pétain's government establish itself in the spa town of Vichy and during July proceeded to suspend the constitutional laws and vote full powers to the Marshal himself. But the real power in the new regime was Laval, who now emerged from the political darkness which had surrounded him since the Ethiopian crisis. The Third Republic, which had survived the challenge of the First World War and a series of domestic crises, now came to an ignominious end.

It seemed doubtful whether Britain could survive much longer than her former ally. The Soviet Union, Japan and the United States, all as yet outside the main conflict, had to decide how to react to the new situation in Europe. Stalin chose to consolidate his position before Hitler acquired a completely free hand in Europe. The three Baltic republics were now absorbed into the Soviet Union. Rumania was forced to give up Bessarabia and Northern Bukovina, although the latter had not been included in the agreements on spheres of influence with Germany. Japan was also encouraged to exploit Hitler's successes, having followed a cautious policy in the wake of the Nazi-Soviet pact and her own defeat at the hands of the Russians. During the summer of 1939 Japan had blockaded the British concession at Tientsin but after protracted negotiations had made an agreement on 12 June 1940 which gave some hope of improvement in Anglo-Japanese relations. But the opportunity of exploiting British weakness and French defeat was too good to miss – in July Britain had to agree to the closure of the Burma Road for three months; the Japanese much resented the existence of this supply route to Chiang Kai-Shek. In September Japanese troops established themselves in northern French Indo-China. The local Vichy administration was in no position to resist. There was clearly a general threat to the European empires in South-east Asia.

Since September 1939 the United States had faced difficulties both in Europe and in the Far East. She wanted to restrain Japan but was by no means committed to fight in defence of European colonies and there were divisions within the Roosevelt administration over the best way of restraining Japan short of war. Roosevelt moved cautiously towards a policy of partial economic sanctions. At the beginning of 1940 he ended the commercial treaty of 1911, and in the course of the year introduced embargoes on the export of certain products to Japan, including scrap iron. As far as the Anglo-French war with Germany was concerned his sympathies were much more obvious. In November 1939 Congress was induced to modify the neutrality legislation so that belligerents could buy arms in the United States provided they could pay for and transport them. Up to a point this could be expected to benefit Britain and France so long as they had ready cash available. In December 1939 a 'moral embargo' was imposed to dissuade American businessmen from selling goods of military value to the Soviet Union in case they were passed on to Germany. Certainly, during 1940 Russia was a valuable source of raw materials for Germany and an important gap in the Allied blockade. The 'moral embargo' was ended at the beginning of 1941 but by then most of the products concerned were covered by export licences.

Churchill had begun his personal correspondence with Roosevelt even before becoming Prime Minister. His appeals for help in the summer of 1940 raised the question of whether it was worthwhile supporting a potential loser. Against the advice of some of his advisers, Roosevelt decided to take the risk; in September 1940 it was agreed that the United States would supply Britain with fifty over-age destroyers in exchange for naval bases in Newfoundland and the Caribbean. It was clear by then that Britain was running out of the capacity to pay for purchases in the United States. Roosevelt for his part had to be cautious; the international situation had helped to impel him to run for a third term, against constitutional convention. Until his re-election in November he had to proceed carefully. At the beginning of 1941 the first of the lend-lease Acts, under which Britain and other countries could be loaned goods and equipment for which they would not be required to pay until after the war, was introduced in Congress, becoming law in March. In this way Roosevelt hoped to avoid the arguments that had arisen over war debts in the interwar period.

In March 1941 Britain was still fighting. She had not been subdued by aerial bombardment and there had been no attempt at an invasion. In Continental Europe, however, Germany seemed supreme. By the second Vienna award of 30 August 1940 she had forced Rumania to cede territory to both Hungary and Bulgaria, forestalling any unilateral attempt at revenge by these minor revisionists. In October German troops moved into the rump of Rumania and Hitler guaranteed its independence, or, putting it more bluntly, declared the country to be a German satellite. The tripartite pact of 27 September 1940 renewed the formal links between Germany, Italy and Japan which had been damaged by the Nazi–Soviet pact. The three signatories agreed to help each other if one of them was attacked by a country 'at present not involved in the European war or in the Sino-Japanese conflict'. Although aimed mainly at the United States this was also a warning to the Soviet Union to be on her best behaviour. The tripartite pact was later to be signed by Hungary, Rumania, Slovakia, Bulgaria and Yugoslavia.

To Hitler himself the United States did not appear to be a major problem. As early as July 1940 his attention was turning to his long-cherished plans for an attack on Russia. At the end of the month he told his generals that he had taken a definite decision, although the campaign would have to wait until the summer of 1941. On the other hand he was prepared to permit an attempt at a political agreement with the Soviet Union which might divert her away from eastern Europe and bring her into closer association with the tripartite pact. Accordingly, at Ribbentrop's invitation, Molotov arrived in Berlin for talks in November 1940. The Soviet Union had good reason to be cautious in the light of the Vienna award and the tripartite pact, but Molotov made clear that the Soviet Union was unwilling to abandon her interests in eastern Europe and the Baltic. He refused to be tempted by Ribbentrop's suggestion that Russia should expand towards the Indian Ocean. The visit produced no agreement and confirmed Hitler in his decision to attack the Soviet Union. The latter subsequently showed further interest in an association with the tripartite powers but Hitler and Ribbentrop did not pursue what they now regarded as a diplomatic dead-end.

During 1940 Germany found it difficult to convert military success into an effective European coalition. This was in part the result of the ambiguous status of Vichy France, which had been granted an armistice but not a peace treaty, and was a client of Germany but not a formal ally. From Germany's point of view this had the advantage of keeping the resources of the French colonial empire out of British hands. Britain attacked and destroyed much of the French fleet at Oran in July, fearing that it might be handed over to Germany. This ensured Vichy hostility to Britain, but Pétain did not go beyond breaking off diplomatic relations. This uneasy situation meant that Britain gave only qualified support to General de Gaulle, who had escaped to England in June and proclaimed himself leader of a Free French movement. To the British he was useful, but initially he attracted only limited support within France and in the empire as a whole. It would have been foolish to drive Vichy into total collaboration with Germany by a policy of outright support for the Free French. Roosevelt and his Secretary of State Hull held a similar view, strengthened by strong personal antipathy for de Gaulle.

Hitler's problem was somewhat different. He showed little interest in an alliance with Vichy, but wanted to keep her as an amenable client. This meant that he could not satisfy Mussolini's ambitions in the Mediterranean. Italy therefore gained little from her last-minute intervention against France. A further difficulty for Hitler appeared when he met Franco in October. The latter asked for large areas of French North Africa and for considerable military aid as his price for joining the war. He may have deliberately pitched his bid high as a good reason for staying neutral; it was certainly not sensible for Germany to risk the alienation of Vichy for the sake of uncertain Spanish cooperation. In any case, Hitler's diplomatic and military style was not suited to the management of a coalition. He preferred to deal with his allies and clients separately and was unwilling to treat them as equals. This was most apparent in the case of Italy. The distrust noticeable in German–Italian relations, and the unwillingness of either country to keep the other fully informed of its plans which had been evident in 1938 and 1939, continued after Mussolini's entry into the war. No joint command was set up and Italy found herself increasingly dependent on Germany for supplies and direct military support. For Germany the Italians became more and more of a military liability. To some extent the relationship was similar to that between Germany and Austria-Hungary in the First World War. Little could be done to save Italy's East African empire, which fell to the British in the spring of 1941. The Italian defeat in Libya at the end of 1940, however, led to the despatch of German troops under Rommel in February 1941 and the beginning of a fluctuating struggle with the British Eighth Army.

Even before these developments Mussolini had run into serious difficulties in the Balkans. Anxious to secure a military triumph of his own, he declared war on Greece in October 1940 and Italian forces in Albania launched a short-lived offensive. By the end of the year Greek troops had pushed them back and themselves established a foothold in Albania: the Italian attack prompted Britain to supply aid to Greece and then to begin a build-up of forces in early 1941. British bombers based in northern Greece would be a threat to the Rumanian oilfields, so here too Hitler would have to rescue Mussolini from the results of his military incompetence. At first Hitler intended only an attack from Bulgaria but developments in Yugoslavia changed his mind. The Yugoslav government signed the tripartite pact on 25 March in the hope of avoiding direct military occupation. This prompted a coup two days later by a group of officers who overthrew the Regent, Prince Paul, and proclaimed Yugoslavia's neutrality. Enraged by this defiance Hitler ordered her occupation in the coming offensive. German troops attacked on 6 April and by the end of the month Yugoslavia and Greece had both been overrun and the British forced off the mainland. Worse was to follow in May, when the Germans gained control of Crete. Greece was jointly occupied by Germany and Italy while Yugoslavia was partitioned. Bulgaria and Italy both gained some of the territories they had coveted in the First World War, a separate Croatian state was established, and the rump of Yugoslavia was left under a suitably pro-German government.

This further successful demonstration of lightning war confirmed German dominance in the Balkans and was a further warning to Stalin of the need to strengthen Russia's diplomatic position. He had in fact tried to do so by making a non-aggression pact with Yugoslavia. Its signature, just a day before the German attack, was ill-timed and made Soviet diplomacy look clumsy. Stalin was now in an isolated position. In his desire not to provoke Germany he had kept his distance from Britain and relations with the United States were not good. It was difficult to see where else he could look for assistance. Some consolation was obtained by the signing of a five-year neutrality pact with Japan on 13 April. The unpredictable Matsuoka, who had become Japanese Foreign Minister in July 1940, visited Europe in search of a diplomatic coup that would improve his own position, and the pact was the result. This was not entirely a personal whim, since Japan had raised the question of a pact in 1940 but Russia had asked too high a price in economic concessions. In April 1941 Stalin had much better reason to remove one possible danger.

Nevertheless, the Soviet Union was in a vulnerable position when Germany attacked on 22 June, aided by contingents from Hungary, Rumania, Slovakia and Finland. Mussolini was not informed until the attack had started, but subsequently Italian troops participated. Franco sent a division as a token of support. Germany could claim to be leading at least the semblance of an anti-Bolshevik crusade. It is doubtful if the Yugoslav and Greek campaigns in themselves delayed the attack from mid-May, which was a target date for readiness, not necessarily for the offensive. In any event Stalin was taken by surprise; apparently he had expected Hitler to make demands upon Russia before resorting to war, a situation which would have allowed him to play for time. He had therefore ignored or discounted various warnings of the coming offensive. Churchill announced his support for the Soviet Union: any enemy of Hitler was Britain's friend. Roosevelt secured the extension of lend-lease to Russia in October. But until the Russians checked the German advance before Moscow in December and launched a counter-offensive Britain and America were faced with the question of whether the Soviet Union could hold out, and the Russians themselves had to face the danger that Japan might take the opportunity to attack, notwithstanding the neutrality pact.

Hitler had not told the Japanese of his plans and they were just as surprised as anyone else. Matsuoka did indeed support the idea of an offensive against Russia but he was already out of favour and was dismissed in July. Apart from that, the Japanese Cabinet had decided by the end of June to move against South-east Asia. With large numbers of troops tied up in China, Japan could not launch a Siberian offensive as well. Would the United States resist a move against the European colonies in South-east Asia? After some unofficial contacts the Japanese opened formal negotiations when Admiral Nomura arrived in Washington as ambassador in March 1941; Hull conducted the talks on the American side. It soon became clear that China was the real difficulty since the Japanese continued to ask for a free hand there, which the United States would not concede.

The situation took a turn for the worse in July, when the Japanese occupied the whole of French Indo-China, a move which clearly indicated an intention to invade South-east Asia. The American response was to impose a total embargo on trade with Japan. The latter now saw herself as faced with the choice between achieving a satisfactory political settlement or having to fight the United States. To wait until her oil supplies ran out would be a humiliation. It was decided in Tokyo early in September that Japan would fight if no agreement was reached by the end of November. In that month Japan offered to withdraw troops from southern Indo-China in return for a lifting of the embargo on oil supplies. Hull considered an agreement on these lines for three months only. But China, the Netherlands and Britain objected to what they saw as a dangerous retreat. This was the nearest that America and Japan came to a settlement before the attack on Pearl Harbor in December. Even a three-month agreement would not have solved the underlying problem of China.

The British and the Dutch were told little of the course of the Hull-Nomura talks. Neither could be sure what the United States would do if Japan attacked their colonies. It was not until early December that Roosevelt gave a definite promise of help if British and Dutch possessions were attacked. During 1941 he was much more forthcoming over developments in Europe. In secret staff talks early in the year Britain and America had agreed on 'Europe first' if the United States became involved in hostilities. This meant that she would concentrate on defeating Germany before Japan and would not divert all her resources to the Pacific. The assumption was that the United States would somehow find herself at war with all the tripartite powers, yet in the course of the year it was by no means clear that this would come about. Hitler showed little reaction as the United States became involved in convoy work in the Atlantic. In August Churchill and Roosevelt had their first wartime meeting off Newfoundland and agreed on a series of general principles which were enunciated in the Atlantic Charter. Roosevelt was anxious to show the American public that he was supporting a just cause; in this he was following in Wilson's footsteps. The Atlantic Charter was less ambitious and less specific than the Fourteen Points, and it was a joint

The Second World War, 1939–1945

effort, not a unilateral declaration. Nevertheless, Churchill had reservations about accepting the principle of free trade if this meant undermining imperial preference or of agreeing to self-determination if this meant the break-up of the British Empire. In public, however, these disagreements were to an extent concealed. Britain and America could at least claim to stand for certain principles of international conduct.

This had little effect on German policy. It took the Japanese attack on Pearl Harbor to push Hitler and Mussolini into declaring war on the United States, apparently without much consideration of the consequences. The war was now truly global, only the Soviet Union and Japan maintaining their neutrality pact because neither wished to fight on an extra front. Thus a coalition had been created which in the long run could mobilize economic resources superior to those of the tripartite powers. In the short term, however, the latter continued to prosper. The Japanese occupied South-east Asia with remarkable ease, in the process undermining European prestige. It was the battle of Midway in June 1942 which brought her first real defeat. Nevertheless, Japan could hope to maintain a defensive perimeter against American attacks. In Europe the tide did not begin to turn until the autumn. The British at last gained the upper hand over Rommel at El Alamein in October; in the following month British and American forces invaded French North Africa, and the Russians cut off the German forces in Stalingrad. Moreover, it was only at the beginning of 1942 that the German economy was fully mobilized for the war effort. As a result, production of armaments continued to rise until the summer of 1944, despite the Anglo-American bombing campaigns.

In the first half of 1942, therefore, German power in Europe stood for a brief moment at its zenith. The partial achievement of Hitler's aims revealed clearly the instability and the cruelty of the new order. Germany had to move forward from one conquest to the next; there could be no status quo, no point at which Germany could regard herself as a satisfied power. Up to a point the Japanese had a much clearer idea of what they wanted. It was noticeable that during 1942 there was little attempt to coordinate strategy with Germany, even allowing for geographical difficulties. Increasingly the two powers went their own way to separate defeats. The brutal treatment of the Slavs in Poland and Czechoslovakia and then in the areas captured from Russia showed what the defeated could expect. It was at the Wannsee conference in January 1942 that the 'final solution' for the Jewish problem was formally launched. The shift from persecution to extermination was inherent in Nazi racialist ideology; it meant that Hitler's Germany could not claim to be the benevolent autocrat maintaining its own sphere of influence – an image to which Imperial

Germany had aspired in the First World War. There were, of course, collaborators with the Germans; without some cooperation they could not have maintained as much control as they did over their conquests. But there were also resistance movements of varying degrees of effectiveness. In Yugoslavia and Greece they tied down large numbers of German and Italian troops in guarding towns and the main lines of communication. In both countries there was a significant division between Communist-led and non-Communist groups, and a similar pattern could be observed in Poland. Here was a possible source of conflict between the United States, Britain and the Soviet Union, forced by their enemies into an uncertain cooperation.

Twenty-six governments signed the United Nations declaration of 1 January 1942, in which they accepted the principles of the Atlantic Charter and promised not to make a separate peace with the tripartite powers. But the effective prosecution of the war against Germany would depend on the degree of cooperation achieved between 'the Big Three'. The United States and Britain never signed a formal alliance, but the personal relationship between Roosevelt and Churchill and the work of the Combined Chiefs of Staff (set up at the beginning of 1942) produced remarkably close collaboration, despite differences over strategy and postwar intentions. Britain tended to become more and more the junior partner, especially in the Far East. Relations with the Soviet Union were less close yet meetings between Roosevelt, Churchill and Stalin and their civilian and military advisors produced much more effective cooperation than that attained by the tripartite powers. The Allies were of course by no means united; Roosevelt saw his role as a mediating one between the rival European ambitions of his two colleagues.

British and Soviet troops occupied Iran in August 1941 to obtain the removal of German personnel and to protect an important supply line. Turkish neutrality prevented supplies to Russia from going through the Black Sea, and too much use of Vladivostock might provoke the Japanese. August also saw the first convoy from Britain to the north Russian ports, but the Arctic route was at best a dangerous one. Apart from these practical difficulties, Stalin soon made clear to Churchill his wish for a political agreement, something which he had failed to obtain from Britain in 1939. Eden, who had returned to the Foreign Office at the end of 1940, arrived in Moscow for discussions just as the Japanese attacked Pearl Harbor. American entry into the war gave added weight to her warnings that Britain should not strike any territorial bargain with Russia. Roosevelt did not want to have his hands tied at the peace settlement by specific agreements, secret or otherwise.

Eden, however, found that Stalin wanted confirmation of his territorial gains of 1939 and 1940. Nothing was signed in Moscow but the question of a treaty dragged on during the first half of 1942. Eden was prepared to concede recognition of the absorption of the Baltic states but wished to reserve his position on the Polish–Soviet frontier; the United States remained adamantly opposed to any territorial agreement. The American attitude and the need for military assistance induced Stalin to accept a British proposal for a treaty of alliance which made no mention of frontiers. Molotov signed this in London in May and travelled on to Washington to urge upon Roosevelt the need for an early Second Front in Europe. The political problem was thus replaced by a military one. Anxious to be reassuring, Roosevelt allowed a reference to a Second Front in 1942 in the communique on the visit which Molotov chose to interpret as a firm promise, although the British made their reservations clear to him.

In fact, the Americans were contemplating only a limited cross-Channel operation in 1942 with the main invasion to come in the following year. At first the British seemed to accept this plan, but Churchill began to argue strongly in the summer of 1942 against what he regarded as too risky an enterprise; if it failed the prospects for a full-scale invasion would be poor indeed. He persuaded Roosevelt to revert to an earlier idea, the invasion of French North Africa in order to improve the Allied position in the Mediterranean. Having obtained one success Churchill followed it with another; he travelled to Moscow in August, and in his first encounter with Stalin persuaded the latter to accept, somewhat grudgingly, the change in plans.

American and British forces landed in French North Africa on 8 November. German troops were moved into Tunisia and it was not until May 1943 that the Allies obtained complete control of the North African coast. Long before that some important results of the invasion became clear. German troops occupied the whole of France in November and such independence as Vichy had enjoyed now disappeared. The Americans had expected to be welcomed by the Vichy forces in North Africa; the British had taken over Syria in 1941 and Madagascar earlier in 1942, so that Vichy hostility would presumably be directed against them rather than the Americans. In practice French troops put up stiff resistance and the Americans were forced to make a ceasefire with the local Vichy authorities. This caused a good deal of criticism in Britain and the United States. The Americans were further embarrassed by the failure of General Giraud to attract support. They had seen him as a potential replacement for de Gaulle as leader of the non-Vichy French. Somewhat reluctantly the United States had to accept that de Gaulle could not be ignored. After much argument a French Committee of National Liberation was established in Algiers in June 1943 with de Gaulle and Giraud as joint presidents. By November de Gaulle had established himself as sole president but found the United States unwilling to concede full recognition to the committee. Britain and the Soviet Union were more forthcoming but as a result of the American attitude they too stopped short of full recognition. France had still to re-establish her claim to be regarded as a power of significance.

Roosevelt and Churchill had other problems besides de Gaulle to occupy their minds when they met at Casablanca in January 1943. Roosevelt produced the doctrine of unconditional surrender which was intended both to reassure public opinion that there would be no repetition of the North African compromise and also to avert controversy about peace terms before the war was won. As a slogan it perhaps had some value; in practice it did not prevent a good deal of argument over individual armistic arrangements. The most significant military decision at Casablanca was the agreement that Sicily should be invaded. With troops and shipping available in the Mediterranean it seemed sensible to keep up the momentum of advance. This, however, made a cross-Channel invasion in 1943 extremely unlikely, even if Roosevelt and Churchill were at first unwilling to admit this to themselves or to Stalin, who kept trying to extract from them a detailed account of their plans.

At this point a new complication appeared in Russia's relations with her allies. The Soviet Union had established diplomatic relations at the end of July 1941 with the Polish government in exile, based in London. Both sides remained suspicious of the other; the London Poles were unwilling to accept the loss of the eastern territories to Russia as final. In April 1943 the Germans announced the discovery of a mass grave at Katyn containing the bodies of some 4,000 Polish officers. When the London Poles asked the International Red Cross to investigate the Soviet Union broke off relations on the grounds that the Poles were cooperating with German propaganda against Russia. Whether or not Stalin had previously intended to break with the London Poles he now had the option of setting up a rival government based on Polish Communist exiles in Moscow. For the time being he did not do so, but the difficulty of reaching a general agreement on the Soviet/Polish frontier was greatly increased.

At the beginning of June Stalin was informed that the cross-Channel invasion had been put off until the summer of 1944: once Sicily was occupied Britain and America would invade the mainland of Italy in the hope of forcing her out of the war. This was intended to be a limited operation, since troops would be transferred to Britain for the cross-Channel invasion. Stalin ignored this qualification and accused his allies of bad faith in once again postponing a Second Front. To further emphasize his displeasure he recalled his ambassadors from Washington and London. Thus relations between Russia and her allies reached a low point in the summer of 1943 just as the war was shifting further in their favour. The surrender of the German forces at Stalingrad in January had been a severe blow; the defeat of their offensive at Kursk in July confirmed that the initiative was now passing to the Russians. By then Britain and America had clearly won the battle of the Atlantic against German submarines. As in 1917, the threat to Britain's supply routes had been serious but the U-boats once again failed to achieve a decisive breakthrough. Yet there were rumours of Russian and German contacts for peace moves in Stockholm which are said to have failed because the Germans wanted to maintain an independent Ukraine. Did Stalin seriously contemplate a separate peace, distrusting his allies and believing that the Soviet Union had done enough to ensure her survival?

If so, he soon changed his mind. American and British forces invaded Sicily on 10 July. The Fascist Grand Council overthrew Mussolini on the 25th and Marshal Badoglio became prime minister. It was likely that the new government would soon try to make peace and approaches were made to the British embassy in Madrid during August. Stalin now began to show an active interest in a meeting with Roosevelt and Churchill, preceded by a meeting of foreign ministers. After some hesitation Italy signed an armistice on 3 September on the same day that Allied troops invaded the mainland. When the armistice was made public on the 8th, the Germans quickly occupied Rome and disarmed Italian forces in northern Italy. The stubborn defensive campaign which the Germans proceeded to fight limited the military value for the Allies of Italy's surrender. Nevertheless, Germany had lost her junior partner and now had the liability of propping up Mussolini in the north. His control over the so-called 'republic' of Salo existed only on paper, for he was now almost totally dependent on German support. Badoglio signed a full-scale surrender with the Allies at the end of September and in October declared war on Germany.

Because of these developments the foreign ministers' conference in Moscow in October took place in a friendly atmosphere. The participants all gained something, or thought that they did. Hull secured agreement to a four power declaration after some Russian objections to the inclusion of China. The four signatories promised to cooperate in maintaining postwar security and to establish a general international organization. This was the first public commitment to create a successor to the League. Eden obtained the creation of a European Advisory Commission to be based in London and to deal with problems arising from the surrender of enemy states. This body never became as influential as the British hoped, partly because Roosevelt was unwilling to give it much scope. Molotov was able to keep Russia's hands free in eastern Europe and the Balkans, assisted by Hull's unwillingness to become involved in the problems of these areas. The American Secretary of State was pleased by Stalin's promise that the Soviet Union would join in the war against Japan after the defeat of Germany. This suggested that the war in the Pacific might be much shortened.

Thus the stage was set for the first meeting of Roosevelt, Churchill and Stalin at Teheran at the end of November. The extent to which British influence was now declining became clear when Churchill found himself isolated in the discussions over strategy. His pleas that a fixed date for the cross-Channel invasion should not be allowed to inhibit operations in the Mediterranean fell on deaf ears. Stalin supported Roosevelt in arguing that the invasion of France must take precedence. Roosevelt made a point of emphasizing his independence by seeing Stalin alone. The latter showed general support for the proposed new international organization but also made clear his concern for effective control over Germany after her defeat. Various political issues were discussed at Teheran but not examined in detail. There appeared to be general agreement that Germany should be split up into separate states but no precise scheme was worked out. Similarly there was agreement in principle that Poland would lose territory to the Soviet Union but would be compensated at Germany's expense. Stalin expressed himself willing to accept the Curzon line of 1920 as the basis for Russia's frontier with Poland. This would give him rather less than the line agreed with Germany in 1939, but in compensation he asked for the port of Königsberg in East Prussia. Neither Churchill nor Roosevelt opposed the general outline of these proposals; the latter did not wish to take a public stand on Polish questions in what would be an election year. Little was said about the more delicate question of a future Polish government.

The Teheran conference went well precisely because matters of controversy were largely avoided and matters of detail were left hazy. The arguments about strategy and the Second Front had in the main been settled and the problems of the postwar settlement could be postponed. During 1944 the situation began to change: the defeat of Germany became increasingly certain and the potential victors had to consider more closely what use should be made of their success. The invasion of France at last came in June 1944. Roosevelt still had reservations about de Gaulle but by October he brought himself to agree with Churchill in recognizing the French Committee of National Liberation as a provisional government. De Gaulle could now formally claim to speak for French interests even if he could not obtain a place in the major Allied conferences. In eastern Europe Germany's clients one by one fell out of the war in the face of the Soviet advance. In September both Finland and Rumania signed armistices. In that same month the Soviet Union declared war on Bulgaria (who had not joined in the attack on Russia) and soon forced her to submit. This intervention shortcircuited a Bulgarian attempt to negotiate surrender terms with Britain; an armistice was signed in October in Moscow. In all three countries the Russians dominated the Allied Control Commissions set up to enforce the armistice agreements, and they tended to restrict the freedom of movement of their Allied colleagues. (This was less true in the case of the Finnish Commission.)

During May and June 1944 the Russians had some contacts with the London Poles but Stalin seems to have decided that little could be expected from them. In July the Soviet Union recognized a Polish Committee of National Liberation as the temporary administration of Poland; this body established itself in Lublin. Stalin was now supporting an overtly Communist group. The inaction of the Red Army during the Warsaw rising of August and September meant the elimination of the main non-Communist resistance forces. Had the resistance been successful in seizing the city it would have given the London Poles a strong bargaining position. It seemed as if the Soviet Union was moving, by obvious and ruthless methods, towards the establishment of a sphere of influence in which there would be little scope for outside powers.

This did not necessarily mean that the Soviet Union intended to break off cooperation with her allies completely – her aims might be limited to securing her predominance in eastern Europe. The dissolution of the Comintern in May 1943 was widely interpreted in Britain and America as showing that the Soviet Union was now concentrating on the pursuit of national interests and was less concerned with ideological subversion. If so, it should be possible to bargain with her. This Churchill tried to do when he visited Moscow in October 1944 and made the famous percentages agreement with Stalin. To some extent this simply confirmed the existing situation; Russia was clearly predominant in Rumania and Bulgaria, Britain in Greece. Indeed, in December British troops intervened to prevent the Communist resistance seizing power in Athens. Hungary had still to be liberated and in Yugoslavia both Britain and Russia were finding Tito too independent to be easily dominated. Before the talks began Roosevelt made clear that the United States was not a party to them; the American Ambassador was present at some of the meetings as an observer only. Although Roosevelt was not told the details of the percentages agreement, he had at least a general idea of what was said. His attitude was ambiguous; he did not approve of the attempt to demarcate spheres of influence yet he did not openly oppose it. During 1944 his policy towards eastern Europe was largely passive. It was, of course, an election year, in which Roosevelt won an unprecedented fourth term. His own health was failing. Hull had to resign in November because of illness and his successor Stettinius was an administrator rather than an initiator of new policies.

During 1944 the United States was largely concerned with creating the machinery for postwar international cooperation. In July the Bretton Woods conference met to consider monetary and financial problems and produced agreements for the creation of an international monetary fund and an international bank for reconstruction and development. Stable exchange rates and systematic reconstruction would of course benefit American exports as well as the international economy at large. Thus the United States was trying to develop a system of economic security to match the political security that would be provided by the United Nations Organization. The United States, Britain and the Soviet Union discussed this successor to the League at Dumbarton Oaks in August and September. After the Russians left, the Chinese joined in for a short period at the beginning of October. The general structure agreed upon was similar to that of the League, but the Security Council was to remain in permanent session and was to have armed forces at its disposal. The main point of disagreement which had to be left over concerned voting in the Security Council: it was agreed that the power of veto should be restricted to the permanent members, but the Soviet Union wanted the veto to be applicable to topics for discussion and not only to proposals for action. On the whole the United States and Britain agreed that it would be wrong to prevent the airing of problems before the Security Council. The Soviet Union was not opposed to the creation of the new organization but she was clearly anxious to protect her own position within it and to keep as much control as possible in the hands of the permanent members.

While the United States concentrated on international cooperation the Soviet Union was pursuing more immediate and specific interests in eastern Europe. The two states were not by any means on a collision course but the United States would at some point have to define her position in Europe. Roosevelt, however, liked to keep his options open as long as possible. It would be wrong to conclude that he had implicit faith in Soviet goodwill: he agreed with Churchill in September 1944 that America and Britain would keep to themselves the knowledge derived from their programme to make an atomic bomb, and that their nuclear collaboration would continue after the war. This long-term caution did not remove the need to deal with immediate problems. The London Poles continued to reject territorial concessions to Stalin while at the end of December the Soviet Union recognized the Lublin Poles as a provisional government. Who should rule Poland was now an open and obvious source of dissent among the Allies. They also needed to clarify their policies for the treatment of Germany, and Stalin had made it clear that he would expect a reward for joining in the war against Japan.

Such was the position when the three Allies met at Yalta in the Crimea in February 1945. Agreement was reached on voting in the

Security Council, with the Russians accepting a restricted use of the veto, and it was decided to hold a conference in San Francisco in April for detailed drafting of a charter. The occupation zones for Germany which had been worked out in the European Advisory Commission were accepted, with the important alteration that France was to have a zone and a seat on the Control Council. Since she was also invited to become sponsor of the San Francisco conference, France had thus regained some formal standing as a power, even though absent from Yalta. Britain was particularly anxious for France to obtain an occupation zone, because it was not certain how long American troops would remain in Europe: Roosevelt spoke at Yalta of a period of two years; Britain did not wish to be left virtually alone with the Soviet Union in policing Germany. The zones were not intended to become permanent boundaries, but little was said about dismemberment of Germany. After the conference the Soviet Union was to come out in favour of keeping Germany united: in March she informed her allies that dismemberment was no longer essential. Stalin was prepared to attempt to maintain four-power control over a united Germany.

The two topics that caused most argument were reparations and the reconstruction of the Polish government. All three powers were agreed that reparations would be taken in kind, not in money, but the Russians wanted a fixed figure whereas the British did not. In the event, Roosevelt agreed to take the proposed Soviet figure of $20,000 million as a basis for discussion, but details were left over. There was also an unresolved dispute whether reparations should be a first charge on the German economy or whether they should only be extracted after a certain minimum level of activity had been attained. As for Poland's frontiers, it was agreed that the boundary with Russia would more or less follow the Curzon line and territory would be taken from Germany in compensation. Details were to be settled at the peace conference.

Between the Soviet Union and Britain there was a clear division of opinion over the Polish government. In the Russian view the Lublin Poles should form the basis of any new government, whereas Britain wanted a fresh start. Roosevelt seems to have seen himself as mediating between the two viewpoints and this led to some confusion in the American position. Not surprisingly, the upshot was a rather ambiguous compromise that the Lublin government should be 'reorganized on a broader democratic basis'. Roosevelt and Churchill were to some extent reassured by the promise that the new government would hold early elections. Perhaps concerned by the extent of Soviet influence in eastern Europe, Roosevelt induced his two colleagues to sign a declaration on liberated Europe whereby they promised to consult each other when necessary to help liberated states from representative governments and carry out free elections. This was a modified version of his original proposal; the Russians removed a phrase suggesting an automatic commitment for the three powers to act together in the affairs of liberated states. In practice the Russians were able to defend their policies on the basis of individual armistice and Control Commission agreements.

Whatever his doubts about Soviet policy in Europe, Roosevelt was prepared to sign a secret agreement with Stalin on the Far East. At a suitable moment the United States would induce Chiang Kai-Shek to make concessions which would in effect restore to Russia the position she had held in Manchuria before the war with Japan in 1904 and would confirm the independence of Outer Mongolia (a Soviet client since the early 1920s). Roosevelt seems to have had few doubts about departing from his own principles. Soviet help against Japan was still regarded as important and Stalin's good offices could be used to prevent the resumption of civil war in China between Chiang Kai-Shek and the Communists. That Britain was not involved in the negotiation of this agreement was a further indication of her junior status.

Yalta made clear that what mattered for the future of Europe was the degree of harmony that could be maintained among the three Allies. The final collapse of the Axis was almost an anticlimax; Mussolini was shot by Italian partisans on 28 April; two days later Hitler committed suicide; the war in Europe formally came to an end on 9 May. By then relations among the Allies had begun to turn sour. At the beginning of March the Russians forced the King of Rumania to appoint a new government. The United States and Britain protested and refused to recognize the new government, but Roosevelt was not prepared to make an issue of what could be regarded as a breach of the declaration on liberated Europe; nor had America and Britain as yet recognized the Bulgarian government established the previous September. The Russians, for their part, accused their allies of acting in bad faith when trying to secure the surrender of German forces in Italy through contacts in Switzerland. On 3 April Stalin alleged to Roosevelt that this was part of a plan to allow the Germans to concentrate their troops against the Russians while American and British forces could move forward unopposed. Although the allegation angered Roosevelt he again chose to avoid a confrontation.

There was also by early April a deadlock over Poland. Not only did the Russians stick to their argument that the Yalta formula involved merely the addition of a few people to the Lublin government but also they claimed that the latter had a right of veto over potential candidates. Stalin also emphasized the importance to Russia of a friendly government in Poland. There was a contradiction in American policy which Roosevelt either failed or refused to see: freely elected governments in eastern Europe were unlikely to be particularly friendly to the Soviet Union. His death on 12 April left the problem to Truman, inexperienced and unbriefed in foreign policy. The new President took over when the pace of events was increasing and, as he soon discovered, at a time when the United States was likely to test an atomic bomb within three or four months.

It is not clear how far this influenced his decisions about the problems that faced him in his first months in office. Precisely because of his inexperience Truman was anxious to appear decisive and he was essentially less sympathetic to the Soviet Union than Roosevelt. Nevertheless he retreated from early attempts to take a firmer line. The abrupt cancellation of lend-lease in early May annoyed the Russians and had to be reversed. After initially taking a hard line on Poland, Truman in early June accepted a settlement which gave Stalin what he wanted. There were a few additions to the Lublin Poles and in July America and Britain recognized the new government. Churchill was unhappy but had little choice save to accept. Indeed, it was noticeable that Truman was just as careful as Roosevelt not to align himself with British policy. He did not accept Churchill's proposal that Anglo-American forces in Germany should refuse to withdraw to the agreed occupation zones as a means of extracting concessions from the Russians. He also wavered somewhat in his support of Churchill's firm line against Tito's attempts to secure the port of Trieste for Yugoslavia. Nor did Truman abandon the Yalta agreement on the Far East, despite some second thoughts in the State Department. Sino-Soviet negotiations began in June and produced a treaty in August which again gave Stalin what he wanted. In June the Russians persuaded Czechoslovakia – without much difficulty – to cede sub-Carpathian Ruthenia, thus ensuring direct access to Hungary should the need arise. Thus Stalin had obtained the position of dominance in eastern Europe to which Imperial Russia had aspired in vain in the First World War.

Yet when the 'Big Three' met at Potsdam in July the atmosphere was not one of outright confrontation. The conference marked a transition between war and peace and brought with it a change of faces. Truman arrived for his only meeting with Stalin accompanied by Byrnes, who had taken over as Secretary of State at the beginning of the month. During the conference Churchill and Eden were replaced by Attlee and Bevin as a result of the British general election. Once again a number of issues were not dealt with. The Allies were in no hurry to create a German government and peace treaties were to be drawn up by a council of foreign ministers. America and Britain still refused to recognize the governments of Rumania and Bulgaria. They also objected to the fact that the Poles had been allowed to occupy German territory up to the line of the rivers Oder and Western Neisse in anticipation of a definitive settlement. Byrnes, however, offered to accept this if Russia would agree to the American proposals on reparations. This the Russians did, although they thus abandoned their earlier attempt to establish a fixed figure. Each power would take reparations from its own zone; in addition the Soviet Union would receive an unspecified quantity of equipment from the other three zones in return for the supply of foodstuffs from her zone. This was a somewhat uncertain basis for an attempt to treat Germany as an economic unit.

During the conference Truman received news of the successful atomic test in New Mexico. Although he told Stalin little the latter immediately ordered a speeding-up of the planned attack on Manchuria. In April the Soviet Union had warned Japan that the neutrality pact would not be renewed but Japan had continued to hope for Soviet good offices in mediating with the United States. Neither Truman nor Stalin showed interest in exploring a negotiated peace. The dropping of two atomic bombs and Russian intervention combined to bring the Pacific war to a quick end in August, leaving the United States with a dominant role in the occupation of Japan. In Europe the position was more uncertain. In Germany America and Russia confronted each other, no longer quite allies, not yet open enemies. It was still uncertain how far the United States would commit herself to the defence and rehabilitation of western Europe. Britain, France and Italy could no longer claim the status of great powers; Germany had been clearly defeated. Thus four countries which during the twentieth century had claimed the right to direct the European system found themselves, like their lesser companions, dependent on the future development of American-Soviet relations.

Foreign ministers (or the equivalent office-holder) of the powers 1914–1945

Austria-Hungary

Berchtold	Feb. 1912–Jan. 1915
Burian	Jan. 1915–Dec. 1916
Czernin	Dec. 1916–Apr. 1918
Burian	Apr.–Oct. 1918
Andrassy	Oct.–Nov. 1918

Germany

Jagow	Jan. 1913–Nov. 1916
Zimmermann	Nov. 1916–Aug. 1917
Kuhlmann	Aug. 1917–July 1918
Hintze	July–Oct. 1918
Solf	Oct.–Dec. 1918
Brockdorf Rantzau	Dec. 1918–June 1919
Müller	June 1919–Apr. 1920
Koster	Apr.–June 1920
Simons	June 1920–May 1921
Rosen	May–Oct. 1921
Wirth	Oct. 1921–Jan. 1922
Rathenau	Jan.–June 1922
Wirth	June–Nov. 1922
Rosenberg	Nov. 1922–Aug. 1923
Stresemann	Aug. 1923–Oct. 1929
Curtius	Oct. 1929–Oct. 1931
Brüning	Oct. 1931–June 1932
von Neurath	June 1932–Feb. 1938
Ribbentrop	Feb. 1938–May 1945

Russia

Sazonoff	Dec. 1910–July 1916
Sturmer	July 1916–Nov. 1916
Trepoff	Nov.–Dec. 1916

Pokrowsky	Dec. 1916–Mar. 1917
Miliukoff	Mar.–May 1917
Tereshchenko	May–Nov. 1917
Trotsky	Nov. 1917–Mar. 1918
Chicherin	Mar. 1918–July 1930
Litvinov	July 1930–May 1939
Molotov	May 1939–Mar. 1949

Italy

San Guiliano	Mar. 1910–Oct. 1914
Salandra	Oct.–Nov. 1914
Sonnino	Nov. 1914–June 1919
Tittoni	June–Nov. 1919
Scialoza	Nov. 1919–June 1920
Sforza	June 1920–July 1921
Della Torretta	July 1921–Feb. 1922
Schanzer	Feb.–Oct. 1922
Mussolini	Oct. 1922–Sept. 1929
Grandi	Sept. 1929–July 1932
Mussolini	July 1932–June 1936
Ciano	June 1936–Feb. 1943
Mussolini	Feb.–July 1943

Great Britain

Grey	Dec. 1905–Dec. 1916
Balfour	Dec. 1916–Oct. 1919
Curzon	Oct. 1919–Jan. 1924
MacDonald	Jan.–Nov. 1924
Austen Chamberlain	Nov. 1924–June 1929
Henderson	June 1929–Aug. 1931
Reading	Aug.–Nov. 1931
Simon	Nov. 1931–June 1935
Hoare	June–Dec. 1935
Eden	Dec. 1935–Feb. 1938
Halifax	Feb. 1938–Dec. 1940
Eden	Dec. 1940–July 1945

France

Doumergue	Aug. 1914
Delcassé	Aug. 1914–Oct. 1915
Briand	Oct. 1915–Mar. 1917
Ribot	Mar.–Oct. 1917
Barthou	Oct.–Nov. 1917
Pichon	Nov. 1917–Jan. 1920
Millerand	Jan.–Sept. 1920
Leygues	Sept. 1920–Jan. 1921

Briand	Jan. 1921–Jan. 1922
Poincaré	Jan. 1922–June 1924
Du Prey	June 1924
Herriot	June 1924–Apr. 1925
Briand	Apr. 1925–July 1926
Herriot	July 1926
Briand	July 1926–Jan. 1932
Laval	Jan.–Feb. 1932
Tardieu	Feb.–June 1932
Herriot	June–Dec. 1932
Paul-Boncour	Dec. 1932–Jan. 1934
Daladier	Jan.–Feb. 1934
Barthou	Feb.–Oct. 1934
Laval	Oct. 1934–Jan. 1936
Flandin	Jan.–June 1936
Delbos	June 1936–Mar. 1938
Paul-Boncour	Mar.–Apr. 1938
Bonnet	Apr. 1938–Sept. 1939
Daladier	Sept. 1939–Mar. 1940
Reynaud	Mar.–May 1940
Daladier	May–June 1940
Reynaud	June 1940
Baudoin	June–Oct. 1940
Laval	Oct.–Dec. 1940
Flandin	Dec. 1940–Feb. 1941
Darlan	Feb. 1941–Apr. 1942
Laval	Apr. 1942–Aug. 1944

(Bidault was the first Foreign Minister of the French provisional government recognised by the Allies in October 1944. He served from September 1944 to December 1946.)

United States of America

Bryan	Mar. 1913–June 1915
Lansing	June 1915–Feb. 1920
Colby	Feb. 1920–Mar. 1921
Hughes	Mar. 1921–Mar. 1925
Kellogg	Mar. 1925–Mar. 1929
Stimson	Mar. 1929–Mar. 1933
Hull	Mar. 1933–Nov. 1944
Stettinius	Nov. 1944–July 1945
Byrnes	July 1945–Jan. 1947

Japan

Kato	Apr. 1914–Aug. 1915
Ishii	Aug. 1915–Oct. 1916
Motono	Oct. 1916–Apr. 1918

Goto	Apr.–Sept. 1918
Ushida	Sept. 1918–Sept. 1923
Yamamoto	Sept. 1923
Ijuin	Sept. 1923–Jan. 1924
Matsui	Jan.–June 1924
Shidehara	June 1924–Apr. 1927
Tanaka	Apr. 1927–July 1929
Shidehara	July 1929–Dec. 1931
Inukai	Dec. 1931
Yoshizawa	Dec. 1931–May 1932
Saito	May–June 1932
Ushida	June 1932–Sept. 1933
Hirota	Sept. 1933–Apr. 1936
Arita	Apr. 1936–Mar. 1937
Sato	Mar.–June 1937
Hirota	June 1937–May 1938
Ugake	May–Sept. 1938
Konoye	Sept–Oct. 1938
Arita	Oct. 1938–Aug. 1939
Abe	Aug.–Sept. 1939
Nomura	Sept. 1939–Jan 1940
Arita	Jan.–July 1940
Matsuoka	July 1940–July 1941
Toyoda	July–Oct. 1941
Togo	Oct. 1941–Sept. 1942
Tani	Sept. 1942–Apr. 1943
Shigemitsu	Apr. 1943–Apr. 1945
Togo	Apr. 1945
Shigemitsu	Apr.–Aug. 1945

Chronology

Jan.	31	Germany announces unrestricted submarine warfare
Mar.	15	Abdication of Nicholas II of Russia
Apr.	6	USA declares war on Germany
July	19	Reichstag peace motion
	20	Declaration of Corfu on creating a South Slav state
Aug.	15	Pope's peace note published
Nov.	7	Bolsheviks seize power in Russia
	29	First meeting of Supreme War Council

1918

Jan.	5	Lloyd George states Allied peace aims
	8	Wilson's Fourteen Points
Mar.	3	Treaty of Brest-Litovsk
May	7	Treaty of Bucharest
Sept.	29	Bulgaria signs armistice
Oct.	4/5	Austrian and German peace notes to Wilson
	30	Turkey signs armistice
Nov.	3	Austria-Hungary signs armistice with Italy
	9	William II abdicates in Germany
	11	Germany signs armistice
	12	Emperor Charles abdicates in Austria

1919

Jan.	18	Opening of Paris peace conference
Mar.	4	Comintern established
June	28	Signature of peace treaty with Germany
July	31	Constitution of German Republic approved in Weimar
Sept.	10	Signature of treaty of St Germain with Austria
	12	D'Annunzio seizes Fiume
Nov.	19	US Senate fails to ratify the peace treaty with Germany
	27	Signature of treaty of Neuilly with Bulgaria

1920

Jan.	10	Peace treaty with Germany comes into force
	16	First meeting of League Council
Mar.	19	US Senate rejects the peace treaty with Germany
June	4	Signature of treaty of Trianon with Hungary
Aug.	10	Signature of treaty of Sèvres with Turkey
Oct.	9	Poland seizes Vilna
Nov.	12	Rapallo agreement between Italy and Yugoslavia

1921

Mar.	18	Treaty of Riga between Poland and Russia
	20	Plebiscite in Upper Silesia
Nov.	12	Washington conference begins (ends 6 Feb. 1922)

1922

Apr.	10	Opening of Genoa economic conference (ends 19 May)
	16	Treaty of Rapallo between Germany and Russia
Oct.	1	Balfour note on war debts
	4	Agreement on loan for Austria
	30	Mussolini becomes prime minister in Italy

1923

Jan.	1	USSR formally established
	10	Lithuania seizes Memel
	11	France and Belgium begin to occupy the Ruhr
June	19	Britain signs agreement on war debts with USA
July	24	Treaty of Lausanne signed with Turkish Nationalists
Aug.	31	Italy occupies Corfu
Sept.	26	Germany abandons passive resistance in the Ruhr

1924

Jan.	25	Franco-Czech alliance signed
Feb.	1	Britain recognizes USSR
July	16	Opening of London conference (ends 16 August) which approves the Dawes Plan.
Oct.	25	Publication of Zinoviev letter
	28	France recognizes USSR

1925

Apr.	3	Britain returns to the Gold Standard
	25	Hindenburg elected president of Germany
Oct.	22	Beginning of Greek-Bulgarian incident
Dec.	1	Locarno treaties signed in London

1926

Jan.	31	First zone of the Rhineland evacuated
Apr.	24	Treaty of Berlin between Germany and Russia
Sept.	10	Germany enters the League
	17	Briand and Stresemann meet at Thoiry
Nov.	27	Treaty of Tirana between Italy and Albania

1927

Jan.	31	End of Allied Control Commission for Germany
May	2	World Economic Conference at Geneva (ends 23 May)
May	27	Britain breaks off diplomatic relations with USSR
June	20	Geneva Naval Conference (ends 4 August)

1928

Aug.	2	Friendship treaty between Italy and Ethiopia
	27	Kellogg-Briand pact signed in Paris
Sept.	1	Albania proclaimed a kingdom under Zog

1929

Aug.	6	Beginning of Hague conference (ends 31 August) which adopts the Young Plan
Oct.	3	Britain reopens relations with USSR
	29	Wall Street crash
Nov.	30	Second Rhineland zone evacuated

1930

Jan.	3	Beginning of second Hague conference on reparations (ends 20 January)
Apr.	22	London naval treaty
June	30	Evacuation of the Rhineland completed
Sept.	14	Nazis win 107 seats in the Reichstag

1931

Mar.	21	Proposal for an Austro-German customs union
May	11	Failure of Credit-Anstalt
June	20	Hoover proposes moratorium
Sept.	18	Mukden incident. Beginning of Japanese conquest of Manchuria
	21	Britain abandons the Gold Standard

1932

Feb.	2	Disarmament conference opens in Geneva
June	16	Lausanne conference on reparations opens (ends 9 July)
July	21	Ottawa conference begins (ends 20 August) Produces system of imperial preference
	31	Nazis win 230 seats in Reichstag

1933

Jan.	30	Hitler becomes Chancellor of Germany

Feb.	24	League adopts Lytton Report
Mar.	24	Enabling Act gives Hitler wide powers
	27	Japan announces that she will leave the League
June	7	Four power pact initialled in Rome
	12	Opening of World Economic Conference in London (ends 27 July)
Oct.	14	Germany leaves the disarmament conference and the League
Nov.	16	USA recognizes USSR

1934

Jan.	26	German–Polish non-aggression pact signed
Mar.	17	Rome protocols signed by Italy, Austria and Hungary
June	11	Effective end of the disarmament conference
	14/15	Hitler and Mussolini meet in Venice
	30	Purge of Hitler's opponents in Germany
July	25	Murder of Dollfuss in Vienna
Aug.	2	Hindenburg dies. Hitler combines the offices of president and chancellor
Sept.	18	Russia joins the League
Oct.	9	Assassination of King Alexander I of Yugoslavia and Barthou
Dec.	29	Japan denounces Washington naval treaty of 1922

1935

Jan.	13	Plebiscite in the Saar. (Returned to Germany 1 March)
Mar.	16	Germany reintroduces conscription
	23	USSR sells her interest in Chinese Eastern Railway to Japan
Apr.	11/14	Stresa conference
May	2	Signature of Franco–Russian treaty
	16	Signature of Czech–Russian treaty
June	18	Anglo-German naval agreement
Oct.	3	Italy invades Ethiopia
	11	League Assembly decides to impose sanctions on Italy
Dec.	9	Hoare–Laval Plan published in French press. Opening of London naval conference

1936

Jan.	15	Japan withdraws from London naval conference
Mar.	7	Germany re-occupies the Rhineland
May	9	Italy annexes Ethiopia

June	4	Popular Front government formed in France
July	4	League Assembly recommends end to sanctions
	17	Beginning of the Spanish Civil War
	20	Montreux Convention gives Turkey effective control over the Straits
Oct.	14	Belgium announces return to neutrality
Nov.	1	Mussolini proclaims existence of Rome–Berlin Axis
	25	Germany and Japan sign Anti-Comintern Pact

1937

Jan.	2	Britain and France agree to maintain status quo in Mediterranean
July	7	Beginning of Sino-Japanese war
Sept.	10/14	Nyon conference
Nov.	3/24	Brussels conference on Sino-Japanese war
	6	Italy joins Anti-Comintern pact
Dec.	11	Italy leaves the League

1938

Mar.	13	Austria united with Germany
May	20	Rumours of German troop movements against Czechoslovakia
Sept.	15	Chamberlain flies to meet Hitler at Berchtesgaden
	22	Chamberlain and Hitler meet again at Godesburg
	29/30	Munich conference
Dec.	6	Franco-German declaration of friendship

1939

Jan.	5	Beck visits Hitler
	11/14	Chamberlain and Halifax in Rome
Mar.	16	Germany announces protectorate over Bohemia and Moravia
	22	Lithuania agrees to cede Memel to Germany
	28	End of the Spanish Civil War
	31	Anglo-French guarantee to Poland
Apr.	7	Italy invades Albania
	13	Anglo-French guarantees to Greece and Rumania
	17	The USSR proposes alliance to Britain and France
May	22	Pact of Steel signed
June	14	Beginning of Japanese blockade of Tientsin
July	26	America denounces 1911 trade treaty with Japan

Aug.	12	Britain and France begin military talks with Russia in Moscow
	23	Signature of Nazi-Soviet pact
	25	Anglo-Polish treaty signed
Sept.	1	Germany invades Poland. Italy announces her neutrality
	3	Britain and France declare war on Germany
	17	USSR invades Poland
Nov.	30	USSR invades Finland
Dec.	14	USSR expelled from the League

1940

Mar.	12	Finland signs peace treaty with USSR
Apr.	9	German troops invade Denmark and Norway
May	10	Beginning of German offensive in the west
June	10	Italy enters the war
	22	France signs armistice with Germany
Aug.	30	Japan occupies northern Indo-China
Sept.	27	Tripartite pact signed in Berlin
Oct.	28	Italy invades Greece
Nov.	12/14	Molotov visits Berlin

1941

Apr.	6	Germany invades Yugoslavia and Greece
	13	Russo-Japanese neutrality pact signed in Moscow
June	22	Germany invades USSR
July	21	Vichy France agrees to let Japan occupy the whole of Indo-China
	26	America freezes Japanese assets
Aug.	14	Publication of Atlantic Charter
	25	British and Soviet troops occupy Iran
Dec.	5	Eden arrives in Moscow
	7	Japanese attack on Pearl Harbor
	11	Germany and Italy declare war on the United States

1942

Jan.	1	Declaration of the United Nations
May	26	Anglo-Soviet treaty signed
Aug.	12/15	Churchill's first visit to Moscow
Nov.	8	Allies land in French North Africa
	11	German troops enter the unoccupied zone of France

1943

| Jan. | 14/23 | Churchill and Roosevelt meet at Casablanca |

	31	Germans surrender at Stalingrad
Apr.	26	USSR breaks off diplomatic relations with the Polish government in exile in London
May	12	German surrender in Tunisia
	22	Comintern dissolved
June	3	French Committee of National Liberation set up in Algiers
July	25	Fall of Mussolini
Sept.	3	Italy signs armistice. Allies troops land on the mainland
Oct.	19/30	Foreign ministers conference in Moscow
Nov.	28	Teheran conference (ends 1 December)

1944

June	6	Allied landings in Normandy
July	1	Bretton Woods monetary conference opens (ends 22 July)
Aug.	1	Warsaw rising begins (finally crushed 2 October)
	13	Rumania signs armistice
	21	Dumbarton Oaks conference on UNO opens (ends 7 October)
Sept.	19	Finland signs armistice
Oct.	9/18	Churchill's second visit to Moscow
	23	Allies recognize Committee of National Liberation as provisional government of France
	28	Bulgaria signs armistice
Dec.	31	USSR recognizes Lublin group as provisional government of Poland

1945

Jan.	20	Hungary signs armistice
Feb.	4/11	Yalta conference
Apr.	12	Death of Roosevelt
	25	San Francisco conference on UN Charter opens (ends 26 June)
	28	Death of Mussolini
	30	Death of Hitler
May	9	Official end of the war in Europe
June	29	Czechoslovakia cedes sub-Carpathian Ruthenia to USSR
July	17	Potsdam conference opens (ends 2 August)
Aug.	6	First atomic bomb dropped on Hiroshima
	8	USSR declares war on Japan
	9	Second atomic bomb dropped on Nagasaki
	14	USSR signs treaty with China
	15	Official end of the war in the Far East
Sept.	2	Japan signs formal capitulation

Maps

Map 1.   The settlement of central and eastern Europe 1917–22
From J. M. Roberts, *Europe 1880–1945* (Longman 1967) p. 317

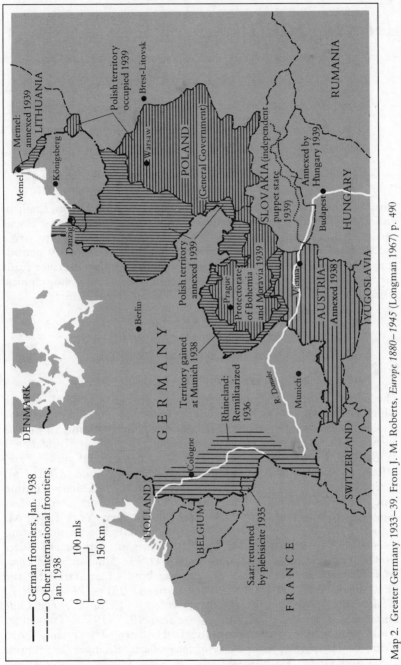

Map 2. Greater Germany 1933–39. From J. M. Roberts, *Europe 1880–1945* (Longman 1967) p. 490

Key:
- German frontiers, Jan. 1938
- Other international frontiers, Jan. 1938

Scale:
- 0 ——— 100 mls
- 0 ——— 150 km

Labels: DENMARK; LITHUANIA; Memel: annexed 1939; Königsberg; Memel; Danzig; Polish territory occupied 1939; Brest-Litovsk; Warsaw; POLAND (General Government); RUMANIA; Berlin; GERMANY; Polish territory annexed 1939; Prague; Protectorate of Bohemia and Moravia 1939; SLOVAKIA (independent puppet state 1939); Annexed by Hungary 1939; Budapest; HUNGARY; Vienna; AUSTRIA Annexed 1938; YUGOSLAVIA; Territory gained at Munich 1938; Rhineland: Remilitarized 1936; R. Danube; Munich; Cologne; HOLLAND; BELGIUM; Saar: returned by plebiscite 1935; FRANCE; SWITZERLAND

Maps

161

Bibliography

This bibliography consists mainly of secondary works in English, although reference is also made to important collections of documents. A few articles are cited, but it would be impossible to cover the mass of more specialized material available in scholarly periodicals in what is intended to be an introductory guide to further reading. Most of the books mentioned have more detailed bibliographies. The place of publication is London unless otherwise stated.

GENERAL

The period 1914 to 1945 is covered in a number of general surveys which either range over the twentieth century as a whole or concentrate on the interwar period. C. L. Mowat edited volume xii of *The New Cambridge Modern History: the Shifting Balance of World Forces 1898–1945* (Cambridge, England 1968). Other general surveys are: J. Roberts, *Europe 1880–1945* (1967); J. Joll, *Europe Since 1870* (1976); J. A. S. Grenville, *A World History of the Twentieth Century* Volume One: *European Dominance 1900–1945* (1980); E. N. Anderson, *Modern Europe in World Perspective: 1914 to the Present* (New York 1958); M. Gilbert, *The European Powers 1900–1945* (1965). For an interesting discussion of nationalism see H. Seton-Watson, *Nations and States* (1982). For economic developments see D. H. Aldcroft, *The European Economy 1914–1970* (1978). Among books that start after the First World War are: R. A. C. Parker, *Europe 1919–1945* (1969); E. Wiskemann, *Europe of the Dictators* (1966); A. Polonsky, *The Little Dictators: the History of Eastern Europe since 1918* (1975). Two older books still well worth reading are: E. H. Carr, *The Twenty Years Crisis: an Introduction to the Study of International Relations* (last reprint 1981) and G. M. Gathorne-Hardy, *A Short History of International*

Affairs (4th edn 1968). There is a good deal of valuable material in the *Surveys of International Affairs* produced by the Royal Institute of International Affairs in London (Chatham House). A volume on the period 1920–23 (pub. 1925) was then followed by annual surveys down to 1938 (pub. 1953). A separate series then covered the period 1939–46 (1952–58). A companion series of *Documents on International Affairs* covered the period from 1928 (pub. 1929) to 1938 (pub. 1942/43). Two volumes for the Second World War appeared in 1951 and 1954. On the conduct of diplomacy and the working of foreign ministries there is *The Times Survey of Foreign Ministries of the World* (1982) edited by Zara Steiner. G. A. Craig and F. Gilbert, *The Diplomats* (2 vols, New York 1963) is still useful, although overtaken in places by more recent research. J. A. S. Grenville, *The Major International Treaties 1914–1973* (1974) is an invaluable work of reference.

Published series of diplomatic documents vary in their coverage of this period. The most comprehensive so far are *Documents on British Foreign Policy 1919–1939* (1946–) and *Foreign Relations of the United States* (Washington 1922–69). *Documenti Diplomatici Italiani 1861–1943* (Rome 1952–) still have some gaps in the interwar period. *Documents Diplomatiques Français* (Paris 1963–) cover only 1932–39. In the case of Germany, the English version, *Documents on German Foreign Policy 1918–1945* (1948–64), in practice covers only 1933 to 1941. For the rest of the period it is necessary to consult the German edition, *Akten Zur Deutschen Auswärtigen Politik* (Göttingen 1968–). Series B covers 1925–33 and Series E covers 1942–45. We still await volumes for 1919–24. For the Soviet Union see J. Degras (ed.), *Soviet Documents on Foreign Policy 1917–1941* (3 vols 1951–53). Publication of documents is something in which smaller states can compete successfully with the great powers. *Documents Diplomatiques Belges 1920–1940* (five vols, Brussels 1964–66) are now complete but two still continuing series are *Buitenlandse Politiek van Nederland* (S'Gravenhage 1976– with English summaries) and *Documents Diplomatiques Suisses 1848–1945* (Berne 1979– in French and German). In both series some volumes have appeared for the 1920s and the Dutch documents also include some material on World War Two.

Overall surveys of the foreign policies of the powers in this period to some extent reflect the availability of source material. Britain and the United States are the best served. For British Foreign Policy there are: F. S. Northedge, *The Troubled Giant: Britain Among the Great Power* (1966); W. N. Medlicott, *British Foreign Policy since Versailles 1919–63* (1968); E. Monroe, *Britain's Moment in the Middle East 1914–1971* (1981); P. Kennedy, *The Realities behind Diplomacy: Background Influences on British External Policy* (1981); D. N. Dilks (ed.) *Retreat from Power: Studies in Britain's Foreign Policy of the Twentieth Century* (2 vols, 1981). Background on defence policy will be found in M. Howard, *The Continental Commitment: the Dilemma of British Defence Policy in the era of two World Wars* (1974) and B. Bond, *British Military Policy between the two World Wars* (Oxford 1980). On the United States one can consult F. R. Dulles, *America's Rise to World Power 1898–1945* (New York 1955); J. B. Duroselle, *From Wilson to Roosevelt* (1919); A. A. Offner, *The Origins of the Second World War: American Foreign Policy and World Politics 1917–1941* (New York 1975); S. Adler, *Uncertain Giant: American Foreign Policy 1921–1941* (New York 1965). There is much useful material in volumes 10 to 14 of *The American Secretaries of State and their Diplomacy* (New York 1963–65) edited by R. H. Ferrell and S. F. Bemis. A most useful bibliographical guide is G. K. Haines and J. S. Walker (eds), *American Foreign Relations: A Historiographical Review* (1981).

For France there is J. Neré, *The Foreign Policy of France 1914–1945* (1975) which is strongest on the 1930s. N. Waites edited a useful collection of essay in *Troubled Neighbours: Franco-British Relations in the Twentieth Century* (1971). For Italy see C. J. Lowe and F. Marzari, *Italian Foreign Policy 1870–1940* (1975). On the Soviet Union there is A. B. Ulam, *Expansion and Co-existence: Soviet Foreign Policy 1917–73* (New York 1974). For Japan there are two general surveys; I. Nish, *Japanese Foreign Policy 1860–1942* (1977) and R. Storry, *Japan and the Decline of the West in Asia 1894–1943* (1979). In the case of Germany there is a good general introduction; J. Hiden, *Germany 1919–1939* (1977) which gives guidance on secondary works in German. One should consult also G. A. Craig, *From Bismarck to Adenauer: Aspects of German Statecraft* (New York 1965) and the same author's *Germany 1866–1945* (Oxford 1978).

THE DIPLOMACY OF THE FIRST WORLD WAR

A general introduction is provided by Z. A. B. Zeman, *A Diplomatic History of the First World War* (1971). There is a useful collection of essays in B. Hunt and A. Preston (eds), *War Aims and Strategic Policy in the Great War* (1977), which disagrees with some received opinion. W. W. Gottlieb, *Studies in Secret Diplomacy during the First World War* (1964) remains a standard work on its subject. A. J. Mayer, *Political Origins of the New Diplomacy* (New York 1970) deals with the growing impact of Wilson and Lenin.

For a long time there was very little on French war aims. Two recent studies which fill the gap are; D. Stevenson, *French War Aims Against Germany 1914–1919* (Oxford 1982), and C. Andrew and A. S. Kanya-Forstner, *France Overseas: The Great War and the Climax of French Imperial Expansion* (1981). Two earlier books are; J. Nevakivi, *Britain, France and the Arab Middle East 1914–20* (1969), and J. C. King, *Generals and Politicians: Conflict between France's High Command, Parliament and Government* (1971). By contrast Britain has been better served. F. H. Hinsley (ed.) *British Foreign Policy under Sir Edward Grey* (Cambridge, England 1977) includes his wartime policies. V. H. Rothwell, *British War Aims and Peace Diplomacy 1914–1918* (Oxford 1971) gives a general survey which can be supplemented by: P. Guinn, *British Strategy and Politics* (Oxford 1965); K. J. Calder, *Britain and the Origins of the New Europe 1914–1918* (1976); W. Fest, *Peace or Partition: the Hapsburg Monarchy and British Policy 1914–1918* (1978). On British policy in the Middle East see: E. Kedourie, *England and the Middle East: the destruction of the Ottoman Empire* (Brighton 1977); B. C. Busch, *Britain, India and the Arabs 1914–1921* (1971); and I. Friedman, *The Question of Palestine 1914–1918* (1973).

For the foreign policy of Tsarist Russia one can use C. J. Smith, *The Russian Struggle for Power 1914–1917* (New York 1969) and *Russian Diplomacy and Eastern Europe* (New York 1963) edited by A. Dallin and others. On Bolshevik policy down to the end of the war there is an excellent study in R. K. Debo, *Revolution and Survival: the Foreign Policy of Soviet Russia 1917–1918* (Toronto 1979). Allied reactions can be followed in M. Kettle, *The Allies and the Russian Collapse: March 1917–March 1918* (1981). Other books on intervention in Russia will be mentioned in the next section. J. W. Wheeler-Bennett, *Brest-Litovsk; the Forgotten Peace* (1963) is still useful.

Work on German policy has been dominated by the argument over Fritz Fischer, *Germany's Aims in the First World War* (1967). It would be a pity, however, to miss an earlier book; H. W. Gatzke, *Germany's Drive to the West: a study of Germany's Western War Aims during the First World War* (Baltimore 1963). The views of Gerhard Ritter, one of Fischer's main opponents, can be found in volumes 3 and 4 of *The Sword and the Sceptre: the Problem of Militarism in Germany* (Coral Gables, Florida, 1972 and 1973). Other books to note are: L. L. Farrar, *The Short-War Illusion: German Policy, Strategy and Domestic Affairs, August–December 1914* (Oxford 1973) and the same author's *Divide and Conquer: German Efforts to Conclude a Separate Peace 1914–1918* (New York 1978). M. Kitchen, *The Silent Dictatorship: the Politics of the German High Command under Hindenburg and Ludendorff 1916–1918* (1976) has material on war aims and on relations with Austria-Hungary. Those seeking some introductory guidance through these troubled waters will find G. D. Feldman, *German Imperialism 1914–1918* (1972) a useful collection of documents with commentary. The impact of Fischer's approach is summed up in J. A. Moses, *The Politics of Illusion: the Fischer Controversy in German Historiography* (1972). Relations with Austria-Hungary are covered in F. Weber, *Eagles on the Cresent: Germany, Austria and the Diplomacy of the Turkish Alliance* (1970) and G. Silberstein, *The Troubled Alli-*

ance: German-Austrian Relations 1914–1916 (Lexington, Kentucky 1970). On Austria-Hungary itself there is A. May, *The Passing of the Hapsburg Monarchy* (2 vols, Philadelphia 1966); L. Valiani, *The End of Austria-Hungary* (1973) and a collection of papers edited by R. A. Kann, B. K. Kiraly and P. S. Fichtner, *The Hapsburg Empire in World War One* (Boulder, Colorado 1977) which has some interesting information on military aspects. Italy appears in a number of the books mentioned above but there is no overall survey in English of her wartime diplomacy.

For the United States there are: E. R. May, *The World War and American Isolation 1914–1917* (Cambridge, Mass. 1959); D. M. Smith *The Great Departure: the United States and World War One 1914–1920* (New York 1965); P. Devlin, *Too Proud to Fight: Woodrow Wilson's Neutrality* (1974); D. F. Trask, *The United States in the Supreme War Council: American War Aims and Inter-Allied Strategy 1917–1918* (Middletown, Connecticut 1961). On Wilson's diplomacy there is a good introduction in A. Link, *Woodrow Wilson; Revolution, War and Peace* (Arlington Heights, Illinois 1979). This is a completely revised edition of his earlier *Wilson the Diplomatist* (Baltimore 1957). Also valuable is J. J. Huthmacher and W. I. Susman (eds), *Wilson's Diplomacy: an International Symposium* (Cambridge, Mass. 1973). The last two books should also be consulted for Wilson's policies at Versailles.

1919–1933

A general survey of this period will be found in S. Marks, *The Illusion of Peace: International Relations in Europe 1918–1933* (1976) and economic background in D. H. Aldcroft, *From Versailles to Wall Street; the International Economy 1919–1929* (1971). G. Schulz, *Revolutions and Peace Treaties 1917–20* (1972) gives a short introduction to the Paris peace conference and its immediate results; A. J. Mayer, *Politics and Diplomacy of Peacemaking* (1968) is very detailed and emphasizes the influence of the Russian situation on activities in Paris. The same theme is treated in J. M. Thompson, *Russia, Bolschevism and the Versailles Peace* (Princeton 1966). Among other books on the peace settlement are: H. Elcock, *Portrait of a Decision; the Council of Four and the Treaty of Versailles* (1972); F. S. Marston, *The Peace Conference of 1919: Organisation and Procedure* (reprinted 1981); E. Mantoux, *The Carthaginian Peace* (1978); P. C. Helmreich, *From Paris to Sevres: the Partition of the Ottoman Empire at the Peace Conference of 1919–20* (1974). H. W. V. Temperley, *A History of the Peace Conference of Paris* (6 vols, reprinted 1969) was compiled in the early 1920s but is still a valuable source of information.

For the study of individual countries at the peace conference and immediately after Britain and the United States are well supplied. C. J. Lowe and M. L. Dockrill, *The Mirage of Power: British Foreign Policy 1920–1922* (3 vols 1972); M. L. Dockrill and J. D. Gould, *Peace without Promise: Britain and the Peace Conferences 1919–1923* (1981); J. Darwin, *Britain, Egypt and the Middle East: Imperial Policy in the Aftermath of War 1918–1922* (1981); K. O. Morgan, *Consensus and Disunity: the Lloyd George Coalition Government 1918–1922* (Oxford 1979); H. I. Nelson, *Land and Power, British and Allied Policy on Germany's Frontiers 1916–1919* (1971); all these are useful on British policy. For the United States see: L. E. Gelphand, *The Inquiry; American Preparations for Peace 1917–1919* (New Haven 1963); A. Walworth, *America's Moment: 1918. American Diplomacy at the end of World War One* (New York 1977); N. Levin, *Woodrow Wilson and World Politics* (1968), and the same author's *Woodrow Wilson and the Paris Peace Conference* (1972); I. Floto, *Colonel House in Paris* (Guildford 1980); S. P. Tillman, *Anglo-American Relations at the Paris Peace Conference of 1919* (Princeton 1961); K. L. Nelson, *Victors Divided: America and the Allies in Germany 1918–1923* (1975). On other countries see: J. C. King, *Foch versus Clemenceau; France and German Dismemberment 1918–1919* (Cambridge, Mass. 1960); R. Albrecht-Carrie, *Italy at the Paris Peace Conference* (New York 1966); N. Petsalis Diomedes, *Greece at the Paris Peace Conference* (Thessaloniki 1978); I. Lederer, *Yugoslavia at the Paris Peace Conference* (New Haven 1963); K. Lundgren Nielsen, *The Polish Problem at the Paris Peace Conference* (Odense 1979); S. Marks, *Innocent Abroad: Belgium at the Paris Peace Conference of 1919* (1981).

Contemporary developments in Germany and central Europe are covered in R. M. Watt, *The Kings Depart: the Tragedy of Germany: Versailles and the German Revolution* (1969); and in F. L. Carsten, *Revolution in Central Europe 1918–1919* (Berkeley, California 1972). On intervention in Russia see: G. F. Kennan, *The Decision to Intervene* (Princeton 1968); J. Bradley, *Allied Intervention in Russia 1917–1920* (New York 1968); R Ullman, *Anglo-Soviet Relations 1917–1921* (3 vols 1961–72); P. Wandycz, *Soviet-Polish Relations 1917–1921* (Cambridge, Mass. 1969).

The complicated and contentious question of reparations has produced various studies in recent years. For the background to British policy one can consult R. E. Bunselmeyer, *The Cost of the War 1914–1919: British Economic War Aims and the Origins of Reparation* (Hampden, Connecticut 1975). American historians have tended to take a more sympathetic view of the French case, as can be seen in: M. Trachtenberg, *Reparation in World Politics: France and European Economic Diplomacy 1914–1924* (Guildford 1978); W. A. McDougall, *France's Rhineland Diplomacy 1914–1924* (Guildford 1978); S. A. Schuker, *The End of French Predominance in Europe: the Financial Crisis of 1924 and the Adoption of the Dawes Plan* (Chapel Hill, North Carolina 1976). Two studies of German policy are: D. Felix, *Walter Rathenau and the Weimar Republic: the Politics of Reparations* (Baltimore 1971); H. Rupieper, *The Cuno Government and Reparations, 1922–1923* (1979).

On the Washington conference and its implications one can use: T. H. Buckley, *The United States and the Washington Conference 1921–22* (Knoxville, Tennessee 1970); R. Dingman, *Power in the Pacific: the Origins of Naval Disarmament 1914–1922* (1976); I. Nish, *Alliance in Decline: A Study in Anglo-Japanese relations 1908–1923* (1972); M. G. Fry, *Illusions of Security: North Atlantic Diplomacy 1918–1922* (Toronto 1972); and A. Iriye, *After Imperialism: the Search for a new Order in the Far East 1921–1931* (Cambridge, Mass. 1965).

For some of the political and strategic considerations that led Britain and France towards Locarno see: A. Orde, *Britain and International Security 1920–1926* (1978) and P. Wandycz, *France and her Eastern Allies 1919–25* (Minneapolis 1962). A. Cassels, *Mussolini's Early Diplomacy* (Princeton 1970) is indispensible. C. Maier, *Recasting Bourgeois Europe* (Princeton 1975) is interesting on the relationship between domestic politics, economic factors and foreign policy in the early and middle 1920s. On Locarno itself two valuable articles must be mentioned: G. Grun, 'Locarno, idea and reality', *International Affairs* (1955) vol. 31, pp. 477–85; and J. B. Duroselle, 'The spirit of Locarno: Illusions of pactomania', *Foreign Affairs* (1971/72) vol. 50, pp. 752–64. The standard secondary work is J. Jacobson, *Locarno Diplomacy: Germany and the West 1925–1929* (Princeton 1972). Stresemann's foreign policy has undergone a good deal of reassessment. The view given in H. C. Breton, *Stresemann and the Revision of Versailles* (Stanford 1969) would now be regarded as too benign and should be compared with H. A. Turner, *Stresemann and the Politics of the Weimar Republic* (1979) or with H. Gatzke, *Stresemann and the Rearmament of Germany* (Baltimore 1965). There is a useful short discussion in R. Grathwol, 'Gustav Stresemann: Reflections on his foreign policy', *Journal of Modern History* (1973) vol. 65, pp. 52–70. On specific aspects of Weimar diplomacy the following can be mentioned: H. Von Riekhoff, *German-Polish Relations 1918–1933* (1971); C. Kimmich, *The Free City: Danzig and German Foreign Policy 1919–1934* (1968); K. Rosenbaum, *Community of Fate: German-Soviet Diplomatic Relations 1922–1928* (Syracuse, New York 1965); H. L. Dyck *Weimar Germany and Soviet Russia* (1966); S. Suval, *The Anschluss Question in the Weimar Era* (1974); F. G. Campbell, *Confrontation in Central Europe: Weimar Germany and Czechoslovakia* (1975). G. Post, *The Civil-Military Fabric of Weimar Foreign Policy* (Princeton 1973) is very interesting on the relations between diplomats and soldiers. For the dying phase of Weimar's external relations one can consult two books by E. W. Bennett; *Germany and the*

Diplomacy of the Financial Crisis (Cambridge, Mass. 1962); *German Rearmament and the west 1932–1933* (Princeton 1979). For the shift in underlying French attitudes see J. M. Hughes, *To the Maginot Line; the Politics of French Military Preparation in the 1920s* (Cambridge, Mass. 1971). The growing problem which Japan posed to the Soviet Union can be examined in G. A. Lensen, *The Damned Inheritance: The Soviet Union and the Manchurian Crises 1924–1935* (Tallahassee, Florida 1974).

Finally, three studies of American policy can be mentioned: L. E. Ellis, *Republican Foreign Policy 1921–1933* (New Brunswick 1968); M. P. Leffler, *The Elusive Quest: America's Pursuit of European Stability and French Security 1919–1933* (Chapel Hill, North Carolina 1979); R. H. Ferrell, *American Diplomacy in the Great Depression* (1957).

1933–1939

A. Adamthwaite, *The Making of the Second World War* (1979) is a collection of documents with a most useful long introductory essay. E. M. Robertson (ed.) *The Origins of the Second World War* (1971) is a valuable collection of articles. M. Baumont, *The Origins of the Second World War* (1978) can still be read with profit. The English translation, however, is an unrevised version of the original French edition of 1969, which has in some places been overtaken by more recent research. On strategic considerations see D. C. Watt, *Too Serious a Business: European Armed Forces and the Approach to the Second World War* (1975); also A. Preston (ed.), *General Staffs and Diplomacy before the Second World War* (1978). For the economic background one can consult C. P. Kindleberger, *The World in Depression 1929–1939* (1977).

For an introduction to German foreign policy see: K. Hildebrand, *The Foreign Policy of the Third Reich* (1973). A much more detailed account is to be found in G. L. Weinberg, *The Foreign Policy of Hitler's Germany;* Vol. One, *Diplomatic Revolution in Europe 1933–1936* (Chicago 1970); Vol. Two, *Starting World War Two 1937–1939* (Chicago 1981). A. Bullock, *Hitler: a Study in Tyranny* has not been revised since the 1962 edition, although reprinted several times. It should be compared with the shorter *Hitler* by N. Stone (1980). Also useful are E. M. Robertson, *Hitler's pre-war Policy and Military Plans* (1963) and N. Rich, *Hitler's War Aims* (2 vols, 1973 and 1974). W. Carr, *Arms, Autarky and Aggression: a Study in German Foreign Policy 1933–1939* (1972) deals with the economic aspects of Hitler's policy. These can be pursued in more detail in B. Carroll, *Design for Total war. Arms and Economics in the Third Reich* (The Hague

1968); B. H. Klein, *Germany's Economic Preparation for War* (1967). On relations with Austria down to 1938 there are two studies: J. Behl, *Austria, Germany and the Anschluss 1931–1938* (1963); R. Luza, *Austro-German Relations in the Anschluss Era* (Princeton 1975). J. T. Emmerson, *The Rhineland Crisis* (1977) is the standard work on the subject. J. P. Fox fills a gap with *Germany and the Far Eastern Crisis 1931–1938* (Oxford 1982). An interesting reassessment of developments in Eastern Europe can be found in D. E. Kaiser, *Economic Diplomacy and the Origins of the Second World War: Germany, Britain, France and Eastern Europe 1930–1939* (Guildford 1980). On Italy we have D. M. Smith, *Mussolini's Roman Empire* (1976); G. Baer, *The Coming of the Italo-Ethiopian War* (Oxford 1967); F. Hardie, *The Abyssinian Crisis* (1974); E. M. Robertson, *Mussolini as Empire Builder 1932–1936* (1972); E. Wiskemann, *The Rome-Berlin Axis* (1966); M. Toscano, *The Origins of the Pact of Steel* (Baltimore 1967). For France, G. Warner *Pierre Laval and the Eclipse of France* (1968); A. Adamthwaite, *France and the Coming of the Second World War 1936–1939* (1977) and J. B. Duroselle, *La Decadence 1932–1939* (Paris 1979) provide an excellent trio. For military policy they are well supported by R. J. Young, *In Command of France* (1978).

In the case of Britain there has been a good deal of emphasis on the problems of rearmament and the uncertain situation in the Far East. N. Gibbs, *Grand Strategy, Vol. One: Rearmament Policy* (1976) is part of the Official British History. U. Bialer, *The Shadow of the Bomber: the Fear of Air Attack and British Politics 1932–1939* (1980) deals well with an important theme. R. P. Shay, *British Rearmament in the Thirties* (1977) and G. C. Peden, *British Rearmament and the Treasury 1932–1939 (Edinburgh 1979)* are both illuminating. M. Cowling, *The Impact of Hitler: British Politics and British Policy 1933–1940* (1975) is a stimulating examination of the relationship between external and domestic factors. On the Far East see: P. Haggie, *Britannia at Bay: the Defence of the British Empire against Japan 1931–1941* (Oxford 1981); A. Trotter, *Britain and East Asia 1933–1937* (1975); B. A. Lee, *Britain and the Sino-Japanese War 1937–1939* (1973); A. Shai, *Origins of the War in the East* (1976).

The international repercussions of the Spanish Civil War can be traced in: J. Edwards, *Britain and the Spanish Civil War* (1979); J. Coverdale, *Italian Intervention in the Spanish Civil War* (Princeton 1975); G. T. Harper, *German Economic Policy in Spain* (The Hague 1967); R. P. Traina, *American Diplomacy and the Spanish Civil War* (Bloomington, Indiana 1968); D. T. Cattell, *Soviet Diplomacy and the Spanish Civil War* (Berkeley, California 1957). The prelude to the Second World War is covered in: C. Thorne, *The Approach of War 1938–1939* (1979); K. Middlemass, *The Diplomacy of Illusion: the British Government and Germany 1937–1939* (1972); K. Robbins, *Munich* (1968); R. Douglas, *In the Year of Munich* (1977); T. Taylor, *Munich:*

The Price of Peace (1979); a very detailed account: A. M. Cienciala, *Poland and the Western Powers 1938–1939* (1968); S. Aster, *1939: the Making of the Second World War* (1973); S. Newman, *March 1939: the British Guarantee to Poland* (1976). On Japanese policy there is a valuable collection of translations from Japanese scholars in J. W. Morley (ed.), *Deterrent Diplomacy: Japan, Germany and the USSR 1935–1941* (New York 1976). For a Soviet version see I. K. Koblyakov, *USSR: for Peace against Aggression 1933–1941* (Moscow 1976); there is also a *Soviet Collection of Documents; Soviet Peace Efforts on the Eve of World War Two* (Moscow 1973).

There has been a good deal of interest in American policy during this period. R. Dallek, *Franklin D. Roosevelt and American Foreign Policy 1932–1945* (New York 1979) is the most recent overall reassessment of Roosevelt's foreign policy. D. F. Drummond, *The Passing of American Neutrality 1937–1941* (Ann Arbor, Michigan 1955) needs to be read in the light of later studies such as: A. A. Offner, *American Appeasement: United States Foreign Policy and Germany 1933–1938* (Cambridge, Mass. 1969); R. Ovendale, *Appeasement and the English-Speaking World* (Cardiff 1975); C. A. Macdonald, *The United States, Britain and Appeasement 1936–1939* (1981); D. A. Reynolds, *The Creation of the Anglo-American Alliance 1937–1941* (1981). On American relations with Japan there is an excellent collection of essays in D. Borg and S. Okamoto, *Pearl Harbor as History: Japanese-American Relations 1931–1941* (1973).

THE LEAGUE OF NATIONS

A discussion of the difficulties involved in a collective security system will be found in I. L. Claude, *Swords into Ploughshares: the Problems and Progress of International Organization* (New York 1971). F. P. Walters, *The History of the League of Nations* (1952) is a semi-official history by a former member of the League secretariat. G. Scott, *The Rise and Fall of the League of Nations* is written largely from the British point of view. E. Bendiner, *A Time for Angels: the Tragicomic History of the League of Nations* (1975) is a popular account. Two contemporary accounts are well worth looking at: Viscount Cecil, *A Great Experiment* (1941) and R. Dell, *The Geneva Racket* (1941). The latter, by an American observer, is particularly critical of British policy. On the creation of the League there is G. W. Egerton. *Great Britain and the Creation of the League of Nations: Strategy, Politics and International Organization 1914–1919* (1979). For the early years there is a useful summary in B. Dexter, *The Years of Opportunity: the League of Nations 1920–26* (New York 1967). The only recent study of the Conference of Ambassadors is in German: J. Heideking, *Areopag der Diplomaten: Die*

Pariser Botschafterkonferenz der Alliierten Hauptmächte und die Probleme der Europaischen Politik 1920–1931 (Husum 1979). On American policy D. F. Fleming wrote two books: *The United States and the League of Nations 1918–1920* (1932); *The United States and World Organization 1920–1933* (New York 1938). A. Rovine, *The First Fifty Years: the Secretary-General in World Politics* (Leyden 1970) gives short accounts of the activities of Drummond, Lester and Avenol. R. Veatch, *Canada and the League of Nations* (Toronto 1975) is important because of Canada's reservations about the League. For German policy there is C. M. Kimmich, *Germany and the League of Nations* (Chicago 1976). On the Manchurian crisis the indispensable book is C. Thorne, *The Limits of Foreign Policy: the West, the League and the Far Eastern Crisis of 1931–1933* (1972). On the Ethiopian crisis there is G. Baer, *Test Case: Italy, Ethiopia and the League of Nations* (Stanford 1976). D. Birn *The League of Nations Union* (Oxford 1981) illustrates the impact of a pressure group on British policy. J. Barros so far has four books on the League to his credit: *The Corfu Incident of 1923: Mussolini and the League of Nations* (Princeton 1965); *The League of Nations and the Great Powers: the Greek-Bulgarian Incident of 1925* (Oxford 1970); *Office without Power: Secretary-General Sir Eric Drummond* (Oxford 1979); *Betrayal from Within: Joseph Avenol, Secretary-General of the League of Nations 1933–1940* (1969).

WORLD WAR TWO

Coverage of the diplomacy of the war is somewhat unsatisfactory. We lack a good overall summary in English of the diplomacy of the Axis powers and Japan. Hitler's strategy has attracted more interest than his wartime diplomacy. Allied diplomacy, on the other hand, was for a long time regarded largely as a prelude to the Cold War. It will therefore be necessary to mention some books which are primarily concerned with the military history of the war. Two useful introductory surveys are: P. Calvocoressi and G. Wint, *Total War: Causes and Courses of the Second World War* (1974); H. Michel, *The Second World War* (1975). A. Millward, *War, Economy and Society* (1977) is a very good examination of the economic background. Two books concentrate on the period before Pearl Harbor: H. Baldwin, *The Crucial Years 1939–1941* (1976) and J. Lukacs, *The Last European War* (1971). The latter is idiosyncratic but interesting.

On the 'Phoney War' and its abrupt end there are: R. Douglas, *The Advent of war 1939–1940* (1978); M. Jakobson, *The Diplomacy of the Winter war* (Cambridge, Mass. 1961); E. M. Gates, *End of the Affair: the Collapse of the Anglo-French Alliance 1939–1940* (1981); P. M. H. Bell, *A Certain Eventuality: Britain and the Fall of France*

(1974). For German strategy in the period before the attack on Russia see: B. A. Leach, *German Strategy against Russia 1939–1941* (1973); R. Cecil, *Hitler's Decision to Invade Russia* (1975); M. Van Creveld, *Hitler's Strategy 1940–1941; the Balkan Clue* (1973). A. Millward again scores with *The German Economy at War* (1964). On German relations with Italy one must certainly consult the two volumes by F. W. Deakin: *The Brutal Friendship: Mussolini, Hitler and the Fall of Italian Fascism* and *The Last Days of Mussolini* (both 1966). For Italy itself there is M. Knox, *Mussolini Unleashed 1939–1941: Politics and Strategy in Fascist Italy's Last War* (Cambridge, England 1982). Vichy France's role as a German client can be studied in: A. D. Hytier, *Two Years of French Foreign Policy: Vichy 1940–1942* (Westport, Connecticut 1974); R. O. Paxton, *Vichy France: Old Guard and New Order 1940–1944* (New York 1972); R. T. Thomas, *Britain and Vichy: The Dilemma of Anglo-French Relations 1940–1942* (1979). The liquidation of the Jews and the suppression of the Slavs are examined in L. Davidowics, *The War against the Jews* (1975) and A. Dallin, *German Rule in Russia 1941–1945* (revised edn 1981). For Allied knowledge of, and reaction to, the 'Final Solution' see: W. Laqueur, *The Terrible Secret* (1980); M. Gilbert, *Auschwitz and the Allies* (1981); B. Wasserstein, *Britain and the Jews of Europe* (1979).

A useful introduction to the resistance movements will be found in: M. R. D. Foot, *Resistance: an Analysis of European Resistance to Nazism 1940–1945* (1976). British dealings with the various resistance groups in Yugoslavia and Greece and with their governments in exile can be traced in: P. Auty and R. Clogg (eds), *British Policy towards the Wartime Resistance in Greece and Yugoslavia* (1975); E. Barker, *British Policy in South-East Europe in the Second World War* (1976); C. M. Woodhouse, *The Struggle for Greece 1941–1949* (1976); W. R. Roberts, *Tito, Mihailovich and the Allies 1941–1945* (New Brunswick 1973). British diplomacy is examined in broader perspective and in considerable detail in Sir. E. L. Woodward's contribution to the British Official History: *British Foreign Policy in the Second World War* (5 vols 1970–76). Other books concerned with British policy are: F. Barker, *Churchill and Eden at War* (1978); T. H. Anderson, *The United States, Great Britain and the Cold War 1944–1947* (1981); V. Rothwell, *Britain and the Cold War 1941–1947* (1982); F. Kersaudy, *Churchill and de Gaulle* (1981).

On relations between America, Russia and Britain H. L. Feis, *Churchill, Roosevelt, Stalin* (1966) is still useful. R. Beitzell, *The Uneasy Alliance* (New York 1972) goes only as far as the Teheran conference. J. W. Wheeler-Bennett and A. Nicholls, *The Semblance of Peace: the Political Settlement after the Second World War* (1972) has a good deal of material on wartime diplomacy. V. M. Mastny, *Russia's Road to the Cold War: Diplomacy, Warfare and the Politics of Communism 1941–1945* (Guildford 1979) is an excellent account of Soviet policy.

For a Russian perspective one can consult V. Issraeljan, *The Anti-Hitler Coalition* (Moscow 1971). Correspondence among the wartime leaders will be found in *Stalin's Correspondence with Churchill, Attlee, Roosevelt and Truman* (2 vols, Moscow 1976), and in *Roosevelt and Churchill: Their Secret Wartime Correspondence* (1975). The latter, edited by F. L. Loewenheim, H. D. Langley and M. Jonas, is only a selection.

The Polish question has not surprisingly received a good deal of attention. A. Polonsky, *The Great Powers and the Polish Question 1941–1945* (1976) is a collection of documents but with a long introductory essay. More documents will be found in the two volumes published by the General Sikorski Historical Institute, *Documents on Polish-Soviet Relations 1939–1945* (1961 and 1967). It is also worth looking at G. V. Kacewicz, *Great Britain, the Soviet Union and the Polish Government in Exile 1939–1945* (1979) and R. C. Lukas, *The Strange Allies: the United States and Poland 1941–1945* (Knoxville, Tennessee 1978). Among books which deal with American policy are: R. A. Divine, *The Reluctant Belligerent: American Entry into World War Two* (1965); G. Smith, *American Diplomacy during the Second World War* (1965); J. L. Gaddis, *The United States and the Origins of the Cold War 1941–1947* (1972); D. Yergin, *The Shattered Peace* (1980); G. C. Herring, *Aid to Russia 1941–1946* (1973). Dallek's book on Roosevelt mentioned in the previous section is also most useful for the war period. A critical view of American policy will be found in G. Kolko, *The Politics of War: the World and United States Foreign Policy 1943–1945* (1968).

Two important books on Anglo-American relations are: W. R. Louis, *Imperialism at Bay 1941–1945: the United States and the Decolonization of the British Empire* (1977); C. Thorne, *Allies of a kind: the United States, Britain and the War against Japan 1941–1945* (1978). For Japanese policy there is a further useful collection of translations in J. W. Morley (ed.), *The Fateful Choice: Japan's Advance in South-East Asia 1939–1941* (Guildford 1980). Soviet relations with Japan are covered in G. A. Lensen, *The Strange Neutrality* (Tallahassee, Florida 1972). Two other useful books on the Far East in this period are P. Lowe, *Great Britain and the Origins of the Pacific War 1937–1941* (1977), and A. Iriye, *Power and Culture: the Japanese-American War* (1981). For more detailed examination of Japanese policy one can consult two books by R. J. C. Butow; *Tojo and the Coming of the War* (Princeton 1961); *Japan's Decision to Surrender* (Stanford 1965). Nobutaka Ike, *Japan's Decision for War* (Stanford 1967) is a useful collection of documents and commentary.

Index

The following abbreviations are used in this index:
WW1 = World War One
WW2 = World War Two